I BELIEVE THAT WE WILL WIN

I BELIEVE THAT WE WILL WIN

THE PATH TO A US MEN'S WORLD CUP VICTORY

PHIL WEST

The Overlook Press
New York, NY

This edition first published in hardcover in the United States in 2018
The Overlook Press, Peter Mayer Publishers, Inc.

NEW YORK
141 Wooster Street
New York, NY 10012
www.overlookpress.com
For bulk and special sales, please contact sales@overlookny.com,
or write us at the above address.

Cataloging-in-Publication Data is available from the Library of Congress

Book design and typeformatting by Bernard Schleifer
Manufactured in the United States of America
FIRST EDITION
ISBN 978-1-4683-1519-6
2 4 6 8 10 9 7 5 3 1

To Emmeline, Lucas, and Noah,
my first and foremost hopes for the future

CONTENTS

INTRODUCTION

HOW AMERICAN SOCCER GOT ITS OWN DAY OF INFAMY

AMERICAN SOCCER FANS WOKE UP ON OCTOBER 10, 2017, FEELING CONFIDENT and expecting to clinch an eighth straight trip to a World Cup. They went to bed that night reeling from what will go down in the annals of American soccer as a Day of Infamy.

It hadn't been an easy qualifying campaign, as opening November 2016 losses to Mexico and Costa Rica left the Americans in very real danger of missing out on the global tournament for the first time since 1986. In the ten months that followed, the United States Men's National Team (USMNT) won and drew enough to stay in contention, though they reaped two unfortunate outcomes in September 2017—a 2–0 loss in New Jersey's Red Bull Arena to Costa Rica, followed by a 1–1 draw in Honduras. This left the US fourth in the six-team competition to determine which three teams would automatically advance to the 2018 FIFA World Cup to represent CONCACAF (Confederation of North, Central America and Caribbean Association Football), the federation of forty soccer-playing nations founded in 1961.[1] With only the Mexican team clinching a CONCACAF berth by September, the two international dates in October would determine who else would go on to the Russia-hosted World Cup and who would stay home.

In their penultimate qualifying match, against Panama in Orlando, the US won 4–0 and looked every part the cohesive team that could go deep into a World Cup, let alone qualify for one. The team then traveled to Trinidad & Tobago for the final qualifying match, playing before a mere 1,500 fans (including a small-but-spirited contingent of Americans) in the 10,000-seat Ato Boldon Stadium in Couva.

A win over Trinidad & Tobago, most everyone's expected outcome, would send the USMNT on to Russia. Even a draw would suffice—in part because the US had padded its goal differential with the Panama win and by overwhelming Honduras 6–0 earlier in the campaign. Even a *loss*, in almost every configuration, would have allowed the Americans a pathway to at least the November home-and-away playoff against Australia, the Asian Football Confederation's fifth-place team.

ESPN's SPI (Soccer Power Index), defined by the sports media giant as "an international and club rating system designed to be the best possible representation of a team's current overall skill level,"[2] gave the US a 93 percent chance of advancing to the World Cup going into the final days of qualifying, compared to 41 percent for Panama and 11 percent for Honduras. "USMNT is in great shape," ESPN's Paul Carr cheerfully observed on Twitter alongside an image showing the figures, "but still with a bit of work to do."[3]

The stray 7 percent chance of not qualifying was bound up in an unlikely but still possible scenario: Panama beating Costa Rica and Honduras beating Mexico, coupled with a US loss against Trinidad & Tobago. (Given the latter two teams' relative strengths, that outcome would be considered more a collapse than a loss.)

The first domino fell relatively early—and, unexpectedly, in Couva. In the seventeenth minute, USMNT defender Omar Gonzalez attempted to clear a cross—presumably over his team's goal line—but it looped sickeningly upward, in a parabola that arced over goalkeeper Tim Howard and behind him for an own goal. Twenty minutes later, Trinidadian rightback Alvin Jones sent a speculative shot from nearly thirty yards out, and it swerved and arced past Howard to double the lead.

Then, the rest of the awful equation began to lock into place.

Honduras came back from a 2–1 deficit in its game, outlasting Mexico 3–2. Honduras's goals came from Alberth Elis and Romell Quioto, who are key offensive players for the Houston Dynamo (of Major League Soccer (MLS), the United States' and Canada's top-tier soccer league), as well as from a bizarre own-goal sequence in which a Honduras shot caromed off the crossbar, hit Mexican goalkeeper Memo Ochoa's head, and bounced in.

The Panama/Costa Rica match provided even more drama. Panama's equalizing fifty-third-minute goal came on a corner kick in which veteran striker (and notorious agitator) Blas Pérez, formerly of MLS's FC Dallas, fell near the ball and nudged it with his shoulder (or, illegally, his arm) toward goal. Replays clearly showed that the ball never crossed the line, but the goal was controversially counted all the same.

These matches played out simultaneously; by the time Panama had equalized in its match, the US had just crawled halfway back from its un-expected 2–0 first half deficit with a forty-seventh-minute goal by Chris-tian Pulisic. A second US goal bringing the match to a tie would automatically send the team to the World Cup even if Panama scored five more times.

But if the US didn't score again, Panama could fulfill its own World Cup dreams with just a single goal. In the eighty-eighth minute, Panamanian defender and MLS player Román Torres scored, and in the ensuing moments, the sick, sinking realization of defeat descended like a fog over the American fans in Couva and across the US, as the end of regular time gave way to five futile and fruitless stoppage-time minutes.

Ten months after leading his Seattle Sounders FC to its first MLS Cup win, Torres had lifted Panama into its first World Cup appearance, taking the third and final automatic qualifier's spot. Honduras, by virtue of its win, secured fourth place and an intercontinental playoff date with Aus-tralia it would eventually end up losing. The US wouldn't even get that opportunity; it was definitively and shockingly locked out of the World Cup for at least the next five years.

In Couva, there were previously unfathomable scenes of American players silently imploding under the weight of the loss. There would be terse statements to come in post-game interviews, owning the failure, reg-istering the disappointment, but in the moments following the final whis-tle, there was just staggering, weighty disbelief and heartbreak. Pulisic cut the most striking figure of all, crouched on the field, one hand ex-tended in front of him for balance, the other hand cradling his downward-slumped head, his jersey pulled up over his face, held in place by his palm.

It best captured the shattered-dream quality of what American players and fans were experiencing.

For US fans who dared to hope their team could win the World Cup, that prospect seemed further away than ever.

In 2015, Americans triumphed on the largest stage world soccer had to offer that year—the FIFA Women's World Cup, held in neighboring Canada. For the United States Women's National Team (USWNT), it was a third World Cup victory, following wins in 1991 and 1999. Carli Lloyd, named the female FIFA World Player of the Year in both 2015 and 2016, capped off a hat trick performance in the final match with an audacious shot from over fifty yards out, near the midfield line, in which she caught the goalkeeper off her line. She was remarkable, but also part of a dominant team effort. While it's not a given that the USWNT will win any given Women's World Cup in the modern era, they are one of the favorites to win when it's hosted by France in 2019, and they'll be a favorite for the foreseeable future of Women's World Cups.

For the USMNT, success has been decidedly more elusive. For a nation accustomed to winning big on the world stage—witness any Olympics, starting with the massive contingent of Americans qualified in an array of events and favored in most of those—the World Cup doesn't quite fit the narrative. Perceptions of a talent and experience gap or a lack of luck are pervasive for those who don't follow all the subtle intricacies of world soccer. But the simple fact is that it's not easy, even for talented teams from nations whose top athletes disproportionately play soccer, to win a World Cup.

Surprisingly few men's national teams have won the World Cup since its inception. Host nation Uruguay won the inaugural edition of the tournament in 1930 and won a second in 1950, after a twelve-year gap in World Cup play due to World War II and its aftermath. Italy won the first of its three titles as the 1934 host and won again in 1938, but the third didn't come until 2006. Germany won three titles as West Germany, the last in 1990 just before reunification, and its fourth in 2014 as a unified Germany. Brazil started its record five victories in 1958, winning at least one a decade (save for the 1980s) up through 2002. England won in 1966 when it hosted, and its fans have been wallowing (or, in some cases, masochistically reveling) in a cycle of anticipation and dashed hope ever since.

Argentina won in 1978 as hosts, and in 1986 largely due to Diego Maradona's brilliance, but they have not yet been able to parlay Lionel Messi's brilliance into a World Cup victory. France won its host year in 1998, and came tantalizingly close again in 2006, until Zinedine Zidane's red card–generating headbutt of Marco Materazzi in extra time of the final match—seen as the turning point in a deadlocked contest Italy would go on to win on penalty kicks—made *coup de boule* the lament of French fans everywhere. Spain, despite its two primary feeder club teams enjoying an era of European dominance that goes back to 2005, has won just a single title, which came in 2010.[4]

That's eight victors in all, over twenty-one World Cups. All eight are European or South American nations where soccer is arguably the most popular sport, with long histories of player development and well-established domestic soccer leagues. The Americans, by contrast, have never come into a World Cup tournament as favorites, and their best result remains the third-place finish at the inaugural World Cup that featured a mere thirteen teams.

Indeed, the United States once went four decades between World Cup appearances, making the 1950 edition and then failing to qualify for nine straight cycles before emerging once again for the 1990 edition. Ever since their return to the tournament, soccer observers around the world have been amused by how such a dominant nation has forged a global soccer identity as a scrappy underdog, known for guile and heart rather than the technical prowess and superior athleticism American athletes display in so many other sports.

Based on their 2010 and 2014 World Cup performances alone, the US was establishing itself as a team that could (and indeed did) get past the tournament's initial winnowing and into the Round of 16. The new expectation of the Round of 16 as a baseline for 2018 coupled with the team's failure to make even the initial stages of the 2018 World Cup led many who care about American soccer to see the failure to qualify for the World Cup as a systemic one, rather than just the collective unlucky shortcomings of a few players.

This understandably has not sat well with fans and media in the months following the final CONCACAF qualifying matches for 2018. The immediate, collective cry for human sacrifice—in the form of USMNT head coach Bruce Arena and US Soccer Federation president Sunil Gulati—began on social media and in countless conversations between soccer pundits. Comments from both targets, made immediately after the loss in Couva, only fueled the fire.

"There's nothing wrong with what we're doing," Arena told reporters. "Certainly as our league grows," he added, referring to MLS, a league he knows well from his years coaching in it, "it advances the national team program. We have some good young players coming up. Nothing has to change. To make any kind of crazy changes I think would be foolish."[5]

Gulati even suggested that had the seventy-seventh-minute attempt by perennial American hero Clint Dempsey snuck inside the post rather than clanged off it, the USMNT would have drawn against Trinidad & Tobago and qualified, thus erasing the need for a conversation on what changes missing out on the World Cup should foment.

"You don't make wholesale changes based on the ball being two inches wide or two inches in," he said.

"We will look at everything, obviously," he then granted, "all of our programs, both the national team and all the development stuff," before echoing Arena by saying, "We've got some pieces in place that we think are very good and are coming along."[6]

In a conference call US Soccer hosted three days after the loss—and just several hours after Arena's anticipated resignation was announced—many representatives of the American soccer media grilled Gulati about US Soccer's role in the debacle. At the time of the call, Gulati had not yet announced he was stepping down, although the media's initial questions centered on whether he should even stay.

When asked what he might say to those fans who are upset, Gulati responded, "What I say is all of us involved in the game are so passionate about the team, and we're extraordinarily disappointed in every possible way." He went on to express a desire to get the USMNT back among the teams playing in soccer's ultimate tournament, and called this particular failure "a shock to the system."

Gulati did eventually announce—in early December—that he would be stepping down from his post at the end of his term, setting the stage for a free-for-all election in February 2018 to determine his successor. The eight candidates included two American soccer-players-turned-TV-commentators, Eric Wynalda and Kyle Martino; an American soccer-player-turned-National-Premier-Soccer-League coach named Paul Caligiuri, who we'll learn more about in the opening chapter; soccer-player-turned-lawyer Michael Winograd; Boston-based attorney Steve Gans; longtime USWNT goalkeeper Hope Solo (whose tenure ended in a cloud of controversy stemming from the team's 2016 Olympics exit); Soccer United Marketing president Kathy Carter; and US Soccer vice president Carlos Cordeiro; with the last two more representative of the status quo and the rest of the field hinting at a desire to create swift if not specific change. Tellingly, Cordeiro was chosen by USSF voters to be Gulati's successor, in a race that ended up primarily between him and Carter, giving USSF a known entity for the new uncertain era.

In the initial days following the loss, fans raged in the comment sections of online articles and in venues like Sirius XM FC's *Counter Attack*, a satellite radio show geared toward American soccer fans. *Counter Attack* cohost Brian Dunseth, a former MLS player and US soccer Olympian, sees the loss as an opportunity to explore where American soccer is in developing players and how coaching education, scouting networks, high school and college soccer, and the current youth soccer network all might be lacking. But he also notes that the callers who have responded in the wake of the World Cup ouster, some educating themselves on the fly about the various debate points, have a very pointed opinion about the state of US Soccer.

"Everyone wants to burn it down to the ground," he says. "I think it's the obvious fan reaction and the frustration of the inability to win. It's the political climate we live in. And it's all of that combined with the technology where we're having this instantaneous gratification of making ourselves feel better by giving our own opinion out publicly, in some type of public forum. Everyone wanted a flamethrower, and everyone wanted to point it in a couple different directions."

Claudio Reyna, the former USMNT international and current New York City FC Sporting Director, labeled the loss a "wake-up call" rather than a "disaster," and characterized the American approach to the sport as cocky. As he put it, "You go to speak to a U14, U15 coach at FC Barcelona, and they want to learn more from you than you from them. If you go to the local clubs anywhere in the [United States,] the U14, U15 coach, youth technical director [...] have all the answers. They tend to be arrogant, they don't want to listen, they don't realize what they're doing isn't right."

At the same time, he also faulted a "blame culture" that tries to put responsibility at the feet of a Gulati or an Arena, when the job of fixing issues that are "more behavioral than structural" should be a collective effort.[7]

Some fans and critics see a system in rot. They see complacent players and multiple entities more concerned with making money than molding future national team players, especially when comparing American soccer to the incredible systemic overhaul in Iceland that led to qualification for the 2016 Euro Championship and the 2018 World Cup.

Others, like me, remain more optimistic—certainly not blithely unaware of the red flags that have cropped up over the last five to ten years, but also cognizant of changes already put in place which could put the USMNT back on course sooner than some might imagine.

For fans, players, coaches, and federation officials consumed by the question of how our nation stacks up against the other soccer-playing nations of the world, the World Cup provides a quadrennial means to chart the USMNT's progress. Missing the World Cup could be and hopefully will be an opportunity for Americans to collectively assess the system they've built, the improvements they've worked to institute and how those improvements might ultimately manifest in future victory—all of which this book details.

If we're to take the last two tournaments and say the Americans were a few unlucky moments away from playing in the quarterfinals—the stage of the tournament where three victories result in a trophy—and, if (with the realization that this is a colossal *if*) we regard the failure of the 2018 World Cup cycle as a motivating, Nietzschean making-us-stronger juncture from which the USMNT will emerge newly energized, the question begs asking: What will it take for the US Men's National Team to win a World Cup? And then, because we can't help ourselves: When will it happen?

It's a question that has gnawed at American soccer fans for a long time, and it's one that US Soccer has even, at times before now, sought to predictively answer. In 1998, it created an ambitious blueprint to win the World Cup by 2010, and named it, unambiguously, Project 2010. Carlos Queiroz, who managed the New York/New Jersey MetroStars during its inaugural season, and would go on to be a manager with Portugal and Real Madrid as well as an assistant under the legendary Sir Alex Ferguson at Manchester United, was commissioned to draft a plan (later dubbed the Q-Report) that would provide the foundation for US Soccer's ambitious run to the top.

According to soccer writer Michael Lewis, "Queiroz's blueprint for change included revamping the youth player coaching and development system (which would have trashed the Olympic Development Program), the establishment of a technical department, establishing a network of ninety-nine coaches at the national, regional, and state levels, upgrading coach education and the establishment of an Under-19 national league, among other recommendations."[8]

Some of these ideas didn't manifest right away, of course, but some of the suggestions found their way—in spirit, if not exactly to the letter—in some of what's happened in the twenty years between Project 2010 and Actual 2018.

Gulati told Lewis, "I don't think there were a lot of specific things that we said, 'OK, we'll take these 20 things and implement them.' It was really a long-term view and what he thought were deficiencies and where we might be able to improve. And in that sense, Project 2010 has really been a vision and goal that has been filled in along the way with any series of quantifiable actions." And while Gulati also quipped, "I don't think at any point we cleared any shelf space at Soccer House for a trophy,"[9] he did laud the big-picture thinking that motivated not only the hope of winning a World Cup but a plan to get it done.

The US Women's National Team has triumphed in its competitions largely through superior athleticism and an array of talented playmakers who can individually transform games. Their male counterparts, of course, don't lack for athleticism, but their emergent collective identity is decidedly different.

In a 2012 article titled "What Is American Soccer?" appearing in *Howler*'s debut issue, Matt Doyle wrote,

> A neutral observer of the last 22 years could be forgiven for assuming that the American style—to the extent one exists at all—is "try hard, run fast," and don't spend too much time thinking about tactics. That's what happens when you have players whose athleticism (with rare exceptions) exceeds their technical ability. But unsexy as it sounds compared to, say, "Total Football," US national team players did (and do), habitually try hard and run fast. They eagerly compress space. They work in groups defensively and love to break forward. It's a style that hasn't inspired poetry, but as they said in Rome, *Quod facis bene fac*. What you do, do well.[10]

Aside from the goalkeeper position—a longstanding, consistent strength—the US has produced an assortment of sturdy center-backs and diverse attacking players who individually show talent and high soccer IQs. Yet, as a soccer-playing nation, it has not consistently pulled together a full complement of players who can get into the Final Four of any given World Cup tournament. If you don't count 1930 (and for this discussion, it's wise to ignore that ancient history), the quarterfinal rung is the highest American teams have been able to reach. Certainly, everyone who cares about American soccer wants to see the USMNT win a World Cup, but even a semifinal appearance would be a next, admirable plateau.

To its credit, the USMNT recently reached the semifinals of a hemispheric soccer tournament: The US-hosted 2016 Copa America Centenario, the venerable South American tournament that invited six CONCACAF teams, including the US and Mexico, creating a sixteen-team field to celebrate its centennial. But, to its detriment, the team's performance against Argentina—though just a one-game sample size—illustrated a considerable gulf between the US and one of the world's elite teams. The US suffered a 4–0 drubbing in which the team was barely allowed to advance the ball past midfield. As US veteran midfielder Graham Zusi told me in February 2017, the game was a "perfect storm" in which "Argentina had one of their better days, and we had one of our worst days." Zusi said that the longer the match was scoreless, the better it would be for the US; Argentina scored its first goal in the third minute.

While it may not be fair to use a sole lackluster performance as evidence that the US is not yet ready to win a World Cup, the match did nothing to help American soccer proponents make the case that a winning run through the tournament is imminent—especially given the team's absence from the 2018 edition.

In July 2017, the US was near its lowest ebb in the FIFA World Rankings since the rating system launched in 1993, though the team did jump from thirty-fifth to twenty-sixth between July and August, thanks to its successful Gold Cup tournament for top CONCACAF teams.[11]

That Gold Cup triumph was the latest in a series of hope-giving performances to offset disappointments. The landmark 2009 Confederations Cup victory over Spain proved Americans have the ability to beat a top soccer power, and 2013 and 2015 wins over Germany in friendly competitions reinforced that belief.

It's also worth noting Americans weren't the only tributes to fall in the Hunger Games of 2018 World Cup qualifying. On the same day the US was ousted, Chile shockingly failed to escape a down-to-the-wire competition in CONMEBOL (the "abbreviation" for Confederación Sudamericana de Fútbol), the ten-member South American federation. Three days earlier, Ghana failed to advance as an African representative, thanks to a controversial offside call negating a late goal the team needed to advance past Egypt in its group. And if the Netherlands' failure to qualify out of Europe created tremors in the soccer world, Italy's was an outright seismic shock. Those two nations' respective football federations, the KNVB and the Federcalcio, face the same sort of existential questions as US Soccer in the aftermath of qualifying campaigns that fell short.

So, assuming the quest to win a World Cup resumes with the US's participation in the 2022 edition, where does that leave us?

What I can say—as a writer, a researcher, an interviewer of players, insightful observers, and the people working in sometimes-surprising ways to get American players closer to legitimate World Cup contention, but also as a fan—is, to borrow from the American soccer chant that gives the book its title, I believe that the USMNT will win a World Cup, and I believe it could even happen before my daughter, who will celebrate her first birthday two days after a champion is crowned in Russia, turns ten.

How can this possibly be, so soon after missing out on a World Cup altogether? My prediction for USMNT success in the 2026 World Cup is predicated on the assumption that the US wins its joint hosting bid with Mexico and Canada. It helps to be the home team at a World Cup; it's not a requirement for winning, of course, but it can push an already-good team into the rarified air needed to win. France failed to qualify for the 1994 World Cup, after all, before winning in 1998 at home.

But it's also predicated on the development of players who were (with one notable exception) too young to contribute to the 2018 World Cup cause. A number of the players who comprise what we may fondly recall years from now as a golden generation of Americans will be at or near or not quite past their primes when the tournament starts in June 2026: Kellyn Acosta and Paul Arriola will be 30; Justen Glad and Weston McKennie will be 29; Brooks Lennon will be 28; Christian Pulisic and Tyler Adams will be 27; and Josh Sargent, Andrew Carleton, and Timothy Weah will be 26. For reasons we'll explore as we meet them throughout the book, these are ten players who could make up the core of a team with talent to rival the world's most consistently elite squads. There could also be emergent players, playing for clubs affiliated with the new-and-improved US Development Academy—or with recently-opened or already-established MLS academies—whose names we don't yet know, who will be vital to the team's 2026 prospects.

There's also the wild-card factor of a forty-eight-team World Cup. FIFA announced, in January 2017, that they'd move to the expanded bracket starting with the 2026 edition of the World Cup. While FIFA maintains that the tournament will fit into the thirty-two-day window of prior World Cups, it will reconfigure the competition structure from eight groups of four to sixteen groups of three, with the top two teams surviving each group moving to a thirty-two-team knockout phase. With each team only playing two instead of three group matches, and with the increased chance that one of those matches is against a comparatively weaker team drawn into a group, luck appears poised to play a heightened role in 2026.[12]

In the current format of the World Cup, Zusi speaks of the importance of "grinding through those first three matches in the group stage," which then allows for the sports cliché, but a very real part of what has coalesced into the American soccer mentality, of "taking it one match at a time" and adopting the belief that "anything can happen on any given day." While there's obviously one more match in a thirty-two team knockout round than there is a sixteen-team round, there's less of an endurance test quality to the reconfigured group stages, and it will be worth seeing which teams benefit from the new format (and, indeed, if the new format presents unforeseen consequences).

Of course, if the US can win a World Cup in 2026, some may see the Americans as jumping their rightful place in line. But soccer doesn't account for rightful places in line, and the convergence of talent and home-field advantage may work to the USMNT's favor in the next decade. This is perhaps a remarkable thing to say given, as we'll soon review, where we have finished in the most recent competitions. But as we'll explore throughout the book, it's not outlandish.

In their groundbreaking 2012 book about world soccer, *Soccernomics*, authors Simon Kuper and Stefan Szymanski counted the US among their nations to watch. They noted that the US "has the most young soccer players of any country," lauded the expansion of MLS as a further indicator of potential future soccer greatness, and, in grouping the US with China and Japan, remarked that they are "fast closing the experience gap." They added, "In the new world, distance no longer separates a country from the best soccer. Only poverty does."[13]

Indeed, the great wealth and knowledge and science and nutrition and all else that goes into the creation of American athletes has paid dividends in most every sport on the planet—including soccer, if you look at the women's three World Cups. And yet men's soccer remains a perplexing frontier, where many more nations than just the United States have wondered why they can't hold aloft the most prized trophy in world sport.

With 211 current member nations of FIFA, 203 still await their chance. If each of those nations found a path to success in turn, and each won a World Cup in succession, the last one (let's say Gibraltar) wouldn't do so until 2826. Clearly, that's not going to happen—many nations will dream of merely qualifying for a World Cup, and teams with past World Cup titles will successfully seize upon aspirations to capture future trophies.

But the United States is part of a group of nations, probably numbering in the twenty-something range, with realistic aspirations of winning a World Cup before the end of the twenty-first century. Its path is complicated by the perceived head start that other nations have taken in developing the players needed for international soccer success, even though the US is in the midst of evolving how it develops its players. I believe that missing out on the 2018 World Cup is ultimately not a setback, but rather an accelerant to the further evolution the USMNT will need to make the next necessary leap.

If, for you, the identifying American soccer chant of "I Believe That We Will Win" extends to future World Cups, read on to add some evidence and some hope to that belief.

CHAPTER 1

HOW AMERICANS BECAME
WORTHY OF THE WORLD STAGE

In 1950, THE USMNT PLAYED IN THE BRAZIL-HOSTED WORLD CUP, WHICH was remarkable just in its very existence. It was the first World Cup in twelve years and only the fourth ever held, even though FIFA had launched the tournament two decades before. The US missed out on the 1938 World Cup after playing in the first two; in that Italian-won, French-hosted edition, only Cuba and Brazil represented the Western Hemisphere.[1] Then, there was a twelve-year pause in the tournament, thanks to World War II.

For American fans, the 1950 World Cup is most remembered for the USMNT's 1–0 victory over England. That match is invoked even today by Americans who relish defeating its colonial forebears and the sport's inventors. That year would also be the last time the USMNT would be part of the World Cup lineup for forty years.

Ed Farnsworth, providing ample US soccer history on the Philly Soccer Page website, noted that "in the nine unsuccessful qualification campaigns between the 1950 and 1990 World Cups," the US compiled an 11 win, 19 loss, and 9 draw record, outscored by their opponents seventy-eight goals to fifty-one in that stretch. They came close to qualifying for some of the intermediary World Cups, including the 1970 World Cup in Mexico (where they only had to beat Haiti to get to a play-in game but lost 2–0 away and 1–0 at home); the 1978 World Cup in Argentina, which the US missed out on by losing a tiebreaker match to Canada played in Haiti; or the 1986 World Cup, again in Mexico, where they needed a draw or better at home against Costa Rica and lost 1–0.[2]

The 1990 qualification cycle bucked this trend of near misses and embarrassments, to the relief of those with vested interests in United States soccer. By virtue of hosting the 1994 World Cup, of course, the US was guaranteed entry into that tournament. And starting in 1998, the first year that the World Cup field expanded to its current thirty-two teams, the US had successfully run the CONCACAF gauntlet to make it into the World Cup until this latest cycle.

The current World Cup qualifying process for CONCACAF includes a six-team, ten-match playoff known officially as the "Final Round," informally as the "hexagonal," and affectionately, for short, as "the Hex."[3] It takes place over the course of just over a year, during FIFA-mandated "international breaks" in which the top professional leagues in England, Germany, Spain, and many other nations stop play for a week to allow players to join their national teams. In the Hex, each team faces each of the other five opponents in home-and-away matches, for a total of ten games. The top three teams, primarily determined by the number of points accumulated in the standings—with three points for a win and one for a draw—automatically qualify. In the most recent cycles (save for this most recent one, of course), it's been either Honduras or Costa Rica joining the US and Mexico in the top three.

If the United States felt considerable pressure in the doomed post-1950 qualification cycles, it felt it even more acutely and fiercely leading up to the 1990 World Cup. On July 4, 1988, the United States won the right to host the 1994 tournament, but the bid was contingent on the nation organizing a first-division professional soccer league to replace the North American Soccer League (NASL), which unceremoniously folded in 1984. (While other American professional soccer leagues continued on after NASL's demise, they weren't considered first-division, certainly not in the way that England's Premier League or Germany's Bundesliga serve as standard bearers for first-division leagues.)

Despite that lack, there was international enthusiasm for the American bid, primarily due to its massive stadiums and the potential to make money, as showcased on a global sporting stage during the 1984 Olympics in Los Angeles.

The US had clear advantages over the competing bids from Brazil and Morocco that ultimately led to the vote going its way. But there was still one major caveat. As *The New York Times* noted in its story on FIFA awarding the World Cup to the US, "Soccer's lack of popularity in the United States was regarded as the one weakness in the American federation's bid. Billed more than twenty years ago as 'the game of the future' in America, soccer has struggled to fulfill its promise on a professional or world-class level. Leagues have come and gone, and the game has prospered only at grassroots and school levels. Americans, interested in so many other sports, have never been as attracted to soccer."[4]

Imagine, for a moment, if the US had been absent from the 1990 World Cup—and how its absence might have played out in the world soccer media, with sponsors for the 1994 World Cup who had to at least predicate some of its saleability on American fortunes, and on organizers like United States Soccer Federation head Alan Rothenberg, who saw the success of the World Cup as the necessary catalyst to propel an American professional soccer league to success and longevity. Bob Gansler, who coached the American team that qualified for and competed in the 1990 World Cup, was aware of lofty expectations by Americans for Americans in all world sport: "Some thought, we're Americans, and it should be like the Olympics, where gold medals rain down upon us."

On January 16, 1989, Gansler took over the helm of the USMNT from Lothar Osiander. As Farnsworth noted for a 2014 Philly.com article, Osiander was a part-timer "who had continued to work as a waiter in San Francisco during his time as national team coach."[5]

At the time, most players on top world teams were playing for clubs in England, Germany, Spain, Italy, or elsewhere, only coming together for tournaments and international breaks. The USMNT players, on the other hand, primarily trained together and even lived together, save for the few good enough to have landed overseas club assignments. This included defender Paul Caligiuri, who had played for German teams Hamburger SV and SV Meppen in the late 1980s, and Peter Vermes, who had landed club football assignments in Hungary and the Netherlands. As Gansler recalls, the rest of the team was composed of players who were in college or had just graduated. "We had a young team, but rather than bemoan what we didn't have—what we had were young players with talent, and we tried to choose players who we felt were resilient and passionate about this game, we went from there." In fact, as Gansler noted, the team that the US sent to Italy was the youngest in the competition, with an average age of twenty-three.

"It was a challenge because there was no league," Gansler says. "The last year prior to the qualification, the Federation assigned them to very small contracts so they could concentrate a little bit more. But basically, our preparation was you'd be with the team for a week, preparing for a game, and then you'd play that game, and we'd send them home for two weeks with homework. Some were a little more conscientious than others [about doing the homework], but it wasn't like going and playing with a top-notch team so you could go refine your skills."

"Winston Cigarettes were sponsoring a whole bunch of games," Gansler notes of the exhibitions that served as preparation between qualifiers. "More often than not, we were down in Florida, in Miami, in the Orange Bowl. We played Colombia umpteen times, we played some other teams. Again, the Federation didn't have the money to finance these kinds of things. A big difference now, and has been for the past decade now, and especially the past five years, is that people do want to come to the United States and play games. But they're also rewarded with a fee. Back then, we didn't have money to entice a name team to come play us or for us to play them. I'm not saying woe is us; that's just how it was. And by the way, it was a heck of a lot better than when we were trying to qualify in '68 and '69, when I was a player, and we were negotiating with the Federation to get a $5 per diem, because we were getting $2. We got 'em all the way up to $3!"

By the 1994 qualifying cycle, the American team was more of a close-knit squad, living in dorms in the team's Southern California base and preparing for a more robust schedule of exhibition matches—including the World Series of Soccer competitions that Kevin Payne (the future DC United GM and one of MLS's principal early architects) organized to help promote the coming World Cup. "They were paid fully by the Federation, so in a sense they were professionals—in the real sense," Gansler notes. "But they didn't play in a league, which is important, in games that you have to do well in, that you have to win." Regarding the relatively low stakes of an exhibition match, according to Gansler, "There's a difference between *you must* and *it's nice if you would*."

The USMNT's 1990 World Cup qualification ended up pivoting on a single match: an away match in Port-of-Spain, Trinidad & Tobago's capital, on November 19, 1989, with a World Cup berth on the line for both teams. US Soccer's site characterized the matchup this way in a 2015 retrospective on the match:

> The Soca Warriors, or "Strike Squad" as they were known back then, needed only a draw against a largely inexperienced American side that two weeks prior had made the match tougher on themselves with a scoreless home draw against El Salvador in St. Louis.
>
> As a result of that listless performance, the US would have to go into hostile territory and win a Qualifying match—a tall task, considering the MNT had only done it twice previously, with the last coming in a 1–0 win at Honduras 24 years prior.
>
> Then there was the supreme confidence of the Trinidadian side. The upstart soccer nation had gone 3–0–2 in home qualifying matches during the 1990 World Cup Qualifying cycle, making the team's self-assurance pour over to the entire nation.
>
> "Never before," said Trinidadian daily *The Guardian*, "has there been such an overwhelming, uninhibited display of patriotism and national pride as for our beloved Strike Squad, the sons of the soil who are set to add a new aspect to our claim to fame: 'Home of the steel band, calypso, limbo and the 1990 World Cup football finalists.'"[6]

The American media wasn't exactly brimming with confidence about the USMNT's chances. As John Bolster recounted in his 2014 MLSsoccer.com article, "On the eve of the match, one American scribe asked US coach Bob Gansler, 'After this game tomorrow, how badly are you going to feel about the opportunity lost for American soccer?'"[7]

But the US team had other ideas—specifically Caligiuri, slotted into a holding midfielder role for the match against Trinidad & Tobago. His thirtieth-minute goal was dubbed "The Shot Heard 'Round the World," but had Caligiuri heeded Gansler's advice during the match, it might have not even happened. As Bolster noted:

> Caligiuri was supposed to man-mark T&T midfielder Russell Latapy and prevent him from getting the ball to future Manchester United star Dwight Yorke up top.
>
> Caligiuri was specifically told not to attack, not to get forward.
>
> In the 30th minute, though, frustrated by the US's inability to generate any rhythm or create any chances, Caligiuri decided to "look for my one opportunity." He picked up the ball in midfield, hoping to "start getting something going" for the US, he says. He wasn't thinking about shooting.
>
> "I was thinking, I won't lose the ball, coach," he says, "and, don't worry, we won't get countered on."[8]

"That's Paul's version of it," Gansler laughs, adding, "He played it extremely well, like any intelligent midfielder would. On that play, he had a huge chunk of real estate in front of him, and made a good shot. In situations like that, you need a little bit of good fortune, which we were able to get."

Despite a late John Doyle foul on Yorke that might have resulted in a penalty kick and an equalizer—and likely would have in the less-foul-tolerant modern era—the US held on to win 1–0 and finally, for the first time in four decades, make the world's premier tournament.

(Incidentally, some Trinidadian fans have carried a twenty-eight-year grudge against the Americans for bumping them from a World Cup berth they were expecting to celebrate. Darryl Smith, the Trinidad & Tobago sports minister, told *The New York Times*, in its coverage of the October 2017 upset, "The [US] has been a rival since 1989 when we were stuffed out by them," while fellow Trinidadian Alvin Corneal, a commentator and coaching instructor, proclaimed, "They got the shock of their lives. I am happy that the [US] should realize that there are other people in the world who exist.")[9]

The US team came into the 1990 World Cup with belief in itself. Vermes, a forward on the 1990 team best known in modern soccer circles as the longtime coach of Sporting Kansas City, noted in Bolster's article, "We were all very excited to be there. But the makeup of the group was not 'happy to be there'–type guys. The makeup of the group was *very* much in line with seeing if we could sort of upset the apple cart, if you will."[10]

But reality came in the form of three formidable European foes drawn into the USMNT's group: Czechoslovakia, Italy, and Austria. Gansler says of the Americans' three-and-out performance, "We showed our potential," but he also acknowledges that the opening 5–1 drubbing the US took was a case of a young team experiencing what he termed "stage fright."

In the match against the Czechs, the US went down 2–0 at halftime and further compounded their issues five minutes into the second half by giving up a third goal. The US would close the gap with a Caligiuri goal in the sixtieth minute—just one of two goals they'd score in their entire World Cup run—but it would get more lopsided later, in part because they played most of the second half one man short.

In an article darkly titled, "World Cup '90: It Will Get Worse for US," the *Los Angeles Times*'s Mike Downey wrote, "It took only one game to confirm what many of us already knew: That the United States is more prepared to play host to a World Cup than to play in one." He assessed that the US was able to match up favorably against Central American teams but not the world's elite, and even struggled with the "at least nobody was seriously injured" silver lining he attempted to offer up, noting, "Goalkeeper Tony Meola did crash face-first into a goal post. Forward and serious scoring threat Peter Vermes did go down wailing with an injured hip. And midfielder Eric Wynalda did have somebody step on his toe, whereupon he gave the Czech a body check and promptly was excused from playing the rest of the game, making Wynalda either the most foolish or most fortunate man on the American team."[11]

Many expected the USMNT's worst match would actually be its second one, against Italy in Rome, and not their first match against the recently-sprung-from-behind-the-Iron-Curtain Czechs. Downey folksily observed, "A calf stands a better chance to win a rodeo"[12] than the US did against the hosts.

"But we caught ourselves, and in that second game, people thought that we would get a thrashing against Italy, and we didn't," Gansler says. "We were in front of 80,000, which is more than we'd played in front of in our games prior to that combined. I think there were maybe 300 or 400 Americans in those stands. There weren't many."

Giuseppe Giannini scored the game's lone goal in the eleventh minute, and when Gianluca Vialli missed a penalty kick eight minutes later to double the score, it let the US back into the match for what ended up being a smart, defensive, and noble—but ultimately futile—performance. As Farnsworth notes, after the match, Italian manager Azeglio Vicini declared, "The Americans proved they are an excellent team, nothing like the team that lost 5–1," while Gansler simply told the assembled press, "This is the US team I know."[13]

Gansler regards the match against Italy as a high point, in that the team "showed they could play the game in intelligent fashion against the team who didn't win the World Cup but were favored to win it." He adds, "The third game, I thought we were more dominant, against Austria, who was one of the dark horses for that tournament. I think we acquitted ourselves reasonably well."

In that match, marred by thirty-seven fouls and nine cards, Austria scored twice and the US could only muster a late, face-saving goal before exiting the tournament.[14]

Gansler sums up the whole World Cup experience by assessing, "Some people were keenly disappointed and thought we didn't do ourselves proud, and others thought there's some potential here." He notes, "If you look at the names of the guys who played most of the minutes in '90, six or seven were still starters in '94. I think we did pick some folks who had the wherewithal but also the psychological makeup to take those steps forward." Vermes was among these, as was Tab Ramos, who would go on to an instrumental role for the USMNT as a coach as well as a player.

The 1990 campaign, as best exemplified by the Italy match, showcased a defense-first, counterattacking style that the USMNT has cultivated over the years. For Gansler, it manifested out of necessity, in which "you see what you have, you try to maximize the positive and you try to camouflage the negative. And what we had at that time, we had to play a little more defense than some other folks. There are people who say defense and then spit after that, but defense is part of the game. It needs to be played. It's a cerebral part of the game quite often. Everyone wants to play artistically and score five goals. But you have to realize what you have before."

In 1994, the US was the host nation without having cultivated the longstanding home-field advantage that other more soccer-crazy nations already had. Alexi Lalas recounts that the American soccer landscape leading up to the tournament was a "Wild West environment," with the nation between top-tier leagues and the US team in an extended, years-long residency to prepare for the World Cup under head coach Bora Milutinović.

"We had so many caps," Lalas recalls, using the term for playing in a match for one's national team, "because all we did for two years was play international games. Every coach of a national team will always lament the fact that he or she doesn't have the players for enough time. That could not be said for Bora leading up to the '94 World Cup. I think he probably would have preferred to have the best of both worlds, in that he would have had players at his disposal for an extended period of time, but also with valuable club experience."

"You know, people forget that guys like myself and Cobi Jones, when we stepped on the field that summer, had never been on the books of a club team," he adds. "Traditionally, you come up with a club team, you do well, people recognize you, and you get invited on the national team. We did it completely backwards from the way you're supposed to."

And yet, Lalas maintains that the unconventional set-up helped the team prepare for what it saw as an important tournament. "It made us closer. I think it gave us an understanding of how we wanted to play. It certainly gave us a very clear and concise pathway; that summer, all our energy and resources were razor-focused on having us be successful in that summer, for what it meant to the future of soccer."

"There was a real worry that we were going to embarrass ourselves and therefore the sport and set it back by not doing well," he recounts. "We were the first host country in a number of years where it was really

worrisome if the host country was going to get out of group. And so we
wanted to make sure we got to group because that for a lot of people
was the defining thing of whether it was successful."

Happily for American fans, the host team improved upon its 1990
performance, advancing from the group stages in the twenty-four-team
tournament (as one of the four best third-place teams) with a win, a loss,
and a draw in the space of eight days.

The draw came in its 1–1 opener against Switzerland in the Pontiac
Silverdome. The win was against Colombia in the Rose Bowl, 2–1, with
Andres Escobar's infamous own goal (for which he was reportedly mur-
dered ten days later in Medellin) opening the scoring. The loss also came
in the Rose Bowl, by a 1–0 margin to Romania. But the results from the
three matches were enough to advance the US from the group stages to
the knockout rounds.

A week later—fittingly or tragically, on July 4—the USMNT lost 1–0
to the eventual tournament winners, Brazil, in the Round of 16 in the San
Francisco Bay Area's Stanford Stadium. But it wasn't quite that simple.

As Farnsworth recalled:

Although the final scoreline was only 1–0, Brazil controlled play
for the entire match and the US was unable to muster a single
shot on goal. This was due in some part to the fact that two of
the best US midfielders were unavailable for the match: John
Harkes was suspended after receiving two yellow cards in group
play, and Claudio Reyna missed the entire tournament with a
hamstring injury. Tab Ramos, who had started the match, left it
when Brazilian defender Leonardo elbowed him in the head and
fractured his skull just before the end of the scoreless first half.
Now down to ten men in the second half after Leonardo's ejection, Brazil nevertheless continued to attack. In the 72nd minute
they were rewarded when Romario found a way through the
packed US defense to lay the ball off to Bebeto, who scored the
only goal of the match. The US would be down to ten men after
Fernando Clavijo's ejection in the 85th minute. Minutes later, the
1994 World Cup would be over for the US.[15]

The day after the loss, *USA Today* readers were greeted with Gary Mihoces's article praising the US performance throughout the World Cup. His initial assessment of a "moral victory" in facing some of the best players in the world and showing respectably, coupled with coach Bora Milutinović's assessment that the team had a "bright future in soccer," captured the optimism that Americans had for the future.

The article surmised, "The US players who finally might win a World Cup someday might be among the 16.3 million the Soccer Industry Council of America reports are playing the game in the USA today (of that total, 12.1 million were reported under age 18). Maybe the memory of watching this Cup on television or in one of the packed stadiums in nine cities will figure in the decisions of some of those players to stick with soccer when they get to high school or college, instead of opting for the traditional mainstays like football, baseball or basketball."

The article closed with goalkeeper Tony Meola predicting if the US progressed "half as much in the next four years as we have in the last four, we'll win the World Cup."[16]

Of course, the US again had to qualify for the World Cup—the 1998 World Cup didn't come with automatic qualification as the US-hosted 1994 World Cup had. But the Americans found their way to France, losing only one of its ten final round matches (to Costa Rica in its Saprissa Stadium fortress) to qualify along with Mexico and Jamaica to represent CONCACAF.[17]

The US was drawn into one of eight four-team groups, in the newly expanded format, with Germany, Yugoslavia, and Iran. It would lose all three games, mustering just one goal to its three opponents' five, finishing dead last among the thirty-two teams. The most dramatic of these was the 2–1 loss to Iran, a match with a dramatically political narrative due to conflict born of the Iranian Revolution of 1979 (and the hostage crisis that dominated American newscasts in that era).

Between 1994 and 1998, soccer had changed dramatically in the US with the launch of Major League Soccer—the long-awaited solvent first-division professional league, which, in its earliest incarnation, featured the players who made the USMNT's improved 1994 run so memorable. In fact, twenty-one players from the league ranks found their way into the World Cup, including sixteen on the American squad.

Coach Steve Sampson—who had compiled the winningest record to date in US soccer history, yet resigned four days after the team's ouster from the 1998 Cup—was widely blamed for the poor American performance. Several players were critical of lineup changes. John Harkes, controversially left out of the squad that went to France despite being one of MLS's early stars, noted, "The sad thing is the rest of the world looks at us now and says we're not that good. But the talent was undermined. That was the decision by the coach."[18]

The 2002 World Cup came at a critical juncture for American soccer fans. Players were eager to cast the poor 1998 performance as an anomaly, while MLS was teetering on the brink of bankruptcy and extinction toward the end of the 2001 season. The league made two critical decisions to kick off 2002—it would contract from twelve to ten teams, with the Miami Fusion and the league-owned Tampa Bay Mutiny ceasing to be, and it would create a new marketing partnership with US Soccer called Soccer United Marketing (or SUM for short) to wed the struggling MLS to Americans' appetite for World Cup soccer.

2002 wasn't an optimal year for rolling that out, given that the World Cup was being staged in South Korea and Japan, two nations literally half a world away from the US. Despite a curiously high FIFA ranking that actually declared the Americans to be the best in their group, they drew a challenging set of group stage opponents in Portugal, South Korea, and Poland. With the thirty-two-team format established, and only first- and second-place teams advancing, it seemed unlikely to many observers that the US could repeat its 1994 accomplishment and advance from the group.

Not only did the Americans advance from their group, they went on a run, under the guidance of head coach Bruce Arena, resulting in their best ever World Cup since the inaugural 1930 tournament. In the group stages, they stormed out to a 3–0 lead after thirty-six minutes against Portugal and hung on for a 3–2 win, drew against South Korea, and lost to Poland. Yet, in the final pairing of Group D matches, a surprise 1–0 South Korea win over Portugal made the hosts group winners and vaulted the US to second in the group and into the Round of 16.

(Twelve years later, the USMNT would register the same win-then-draw-then-lose-but-still-advance "formula" to get them beyond the group stages.)

The US would face its CONCACAF rivals Mexico in the Round of 16, and won by the *dos a cero* scoreline that would come to be an essential part of the rivalry's narrative, with USMNT stalwart Brian McBride and emerging star Landon Donovan scoring in the match. Against Germany in the quarterfinals, Michael Ballack's thirty-ninth-minute goal was enough to end the American dream, though the end result was seen by many as undeserved. In the forty-ninth minute, US captain Claudio Reyna took a corner kick and connected with teammate Gregg Berhalter. His shot was deflected by German keeper Oliver Kahn toward the goal. German defender Torsten Frings knocked the ball off the line with his left hand—a potentially World Cup–changing call that the referee did not make.

"I took the corner and I had an angle that I could see it," Reyna told MLSsoccer.com's Simon Borg for a 2014 retrospective article. "And my reaction is that, 'If I saw it, the referee had to see it.' It's pretty clear that it could've changed the whole game with a penalty and a red card. It's something we'll never forget."

"The ref kind of ignored us," he added, "It was one of these things where I think the big teams get the calls and the little teams don't. I do believe in that, because of a lot of tradition with some of the bigger teams. Still, the reality is how could you not see that?"

"Some of the guys on the team knew the players from Germany," added forward Clint Mathis in the same article. "And the Germans said, 'Hey, you outplayed us and you were the better team.' That's something you don't usually hear from those guys talking to Americans [. . .] Win that game and we thought we could've made it to the final."[19]

Instead, Germany made it to the final, losing 2–0 to Brazil, with both goals scored by Ronaldo, then regarded as the best player in the game. Could the US have contained Brazil's potent offense in the finals and taken home a World Cup? The question will sadly and perhaps unfairly go unanswered, and yet American soccer enthusiasts saw the 2002 World Cup as a moment of unparalleled arrival and a source of great optimism.

As Michael Lev noted for a *Chicago Tribune* wrap-up of the US-Germany match:

> The American soccer establishment—from soccer stars to soccer moms—has been waiting for the game to break out of its niche status for more than 20 years, and there are hopes again that the game is ready to take off now that the US team has shown it can be played at the highest level.
>
> Friday's game offered that tantalizing possibility in such poster boys as the 20-year-old midfielder Donovan, whose baby face and coltish Jerry Rice deep patterns could inspire a million Saturday morning soccer kids to keep playing and loving the game.[20]

As Donovan told me in an interview, he began 2002 convinced he was on the "outside looking in" for World Cup roster consideration after the January camp that helps coaches determine who is ready. "My sole motivation in life at that point was to make the World Cup, and that's what every day consisted of for me." He certainly didn't foresee such a principal role for himself, noting, "I don't think until a few days before the tournament started that [Coach Arena] would even consider starting me. For me, I didn't really look past being on the team. I hoped I would get to play. Later in my career, I would have overthought it. Back then, I just enjoyed playing every day."

The successful World Cup run, involving twelve MLS players, gave the league an enthusiasm boost when those players returned to join a season well in progress. Donovan recalls playing a game in Spartan Stadium for the San Jose Earthquakes almost immediately after returning from Asia. "I could just feel the energy in the crowd," he said. "I could see the way people were looking at me. It was on a much smaller scale than it is now, but there was no question that had made an impact on the American soccer scene, and that we were going to be treated differently because of it. It was a welcome change for all of us. I had only played in the league a year, but for people who had been there a long time, it was pretty exciting to see that."

"When we got back from the World Cup, the reception that we got was excellent," adds DaMarcus Beasley, who returned to the Chicago

Fire from what would be his first of four successive World Cup journeys. "I didn't know that it was going to impact that many people. I knew we did well, but given that we didn't do well in '98, I wasn't sure that many people would watch it—but they did! It's a great feeling to have that support, even though we didn't see it, to know that it was there, that so many people were staying up late to watch it. It impressed us."

"If you don't like soccer, and you take the time to see a World Cup game and see what that's about, you can't help but be affected by it and impacted by it," Donovan said. "You may not come away loving it, but you're going to understand how special the game is. How we did in 2002 definitely had an impact. I wouldn't say it in and of itself saved the league, but it probably made huge strides toward making sure the league would keep moving forward."

The USMNT built on its 2002 momentum in the 2006 World Cup qualification process. The team was the first to qualify from CONCACAF for the 2006 games as the result of a strong early showing in qualifiers—the first time since 1934 they'd done so. The clinching game was a 2–0 win over Mexico in Columbus before a sellout crowd of nearly 25,000 on September 3, 2005.[21] The US finished the Hex atop the group with an identical record to Mexico's, and with the World Cup held in Germany and its relatively friendly time zone range for matches, a sizable American audience tuned in to see what they hoped would be a repeat performance of the deep American run four years prior.

It was not to be. Despite Arena bringing back eleven veterans from the 2002 squad, the US failed to make it past the group stages, drawn into a "Group of Death" with the second-ranked Czech Republic, thirteenth-ranked Italy, and a Ghana team regarded as one of the most talented in Africa.

It was shades of 1990 as the Czechs dominated the US 3–0 in the opener. That was followed by a tense, literally bloody match between Italy and the US that finished 1–1 on the scoreboard and ten vs. nine on the field; Daniele De Rossi was sent off in the twenty-eighth minute, shortly after the teams traded goals, with a vicious elbow that caught Brian McBride under the left eye, creating a cut requiring stitches. The US fared worse in the red card category. Pablo Mastroeni was dismissed for a slide tackle toward the end of the first half that he claimed "would be a yellow card anywhere in the world,"[22] while Eddie Pope was sent off two minutes into the second half for a slide tackle that *was* a yellow— albeit his second. The 1–1 draw, lauded by US Soccer's story on the match as "one of the all-time great performances in US Soccer history,"[23] kept the USMNT in contention for the final group match. A victory over Ghana, plus an Italian victory over the Czechs—not at all out of the realm of possibilities—would be enough to advance the Americans.

Ghana, however, had other ideas. Ghana defeated the US 2–1 and set a rivalry in motion that has now spanned three successive World Cups. As Jason Davis recounted in a 2014 ESPN look back at the match:

> Just 22 minutes into the game, Haminu Draman stripped the ball from US captain Claudio Reyna in the American defensive third, leaving the Manchester City midfielder crumpled in a heap. Draman charged into the box and fired a shot past Kasey Keller, beating the American keeper to the far post. It left the US captain injured, embarrassed and responsible for a goal.
>
> Reyna never recovered, eventually coming off in the 40th minute, when it was clear he could no longer continue. Still, the Americans fought on, leveling the match just a few minutes later. DaMarcus Beasley, then a winger playing in his second World Cup, played a perfect early cross for a streaking Clint Dempsey, who slammed a one-time shot into the net to bring the match even.
>
> Controversy eventually won the day for Ghana. The referee whistled defender Oguchi Onyewu for a penalty on a rather innocuous challenge in the box at the close of the half, sending Stephen Appiah to the spot. Appiah converted. American efforts to claw back another equalizer came up short. Ghana won 2–1, securing advancement.[24]

The 2006 World Cup, while not the capitulation of 1998, provided evidence that either the US was regressing back to a mean of World Cup futility, or establishing a ping-pong pattern between the group stage and the knockout rounds. And though Arena wanted to pick back up and prepare the team for 2010, US Soccer would opt to go in a different direction, announcing so just three weeks after the team returned from Germany.[25]

In a *New York Times*–produced video wrapping up the USMNT campaign in Germany, simply titled, "Not This Year," Roger Cohen credited the team for having "an extraordinary, valiant performance that was full of heart, passion, and composure." And yet, he observed, "In the end, it just came down to the fact that they don't have enough world-class players on this US team. In fact, I don't think there are any. Ghana today had Michael Essien, who is a world-class player. The Czech Republic clearly has several world-class players, and so does Italy. I think until the level of soccer rises in the United States, until MLS becomes a serious league, it's inevitable that when the US goes up against the great soccer powers, it looks mediocre—or even embarrassing."

Fellow *Times* writer George Vecsey provided a more optimistic counterpoint, predicting that, "Sometime in this century, the US will be a world-class soccer power. It may not be early in this century, but it will happen. Eventually those youth leagues will pay off, players will go around to the Champions League over in Europe, and we will produce better players." He also said that Arena, likely not eager to lead the USMNT through a third straight World Cup cycle, suggested there might be a replacement in someone "who lives in the United States, who speaks good English [. . .] how about Jürgen Klinsmann?"[26]

Though Klinsmann was reportedly under consideration, US Soccer opted to name Bob Bradley interim coach in December 2006, who then stayed on as coach for nearly five years. Bradley was an Arena assistant, first at the University of Virginia, and then at DC United when the team became the first ever MLS champs in 1996 and 1997. He went on to coach the Chicago Fire for five seasons (starting with its inaugural, MLS Cup–winning 1998 season), the MetroStars for three seasons, and the ill-fated Chivas USA for arguably its best season in 2006.

The USMNT qualifying for 2010 was essentially identical to the qualifying for 2006. The team finished first in CONCACAF, with its only two losses coming to Mexico at Azteca (again, by a 2–1 margin) and to Costa Rica at Saprissa. The US even beat Mexico by another *dos a cero* scoreline in Columbus.[27]

The 2010 World Cup draw took place on December 4, 2009, in Pretoria, South Africa, and both English and American media crowed about the group they had jointly been drawn into. Predictions of who would emerge victorious depended on which side of the pond the observers were on. Vecsey wrote, "The World Cup draw for the United States was not even so bad when England popped out first from the magician's hat. Then the draw kept getting better for the Yanks as Algeria and Slovenia materialized. This means the United States has a decent chance to advance to the second round in South Africa, as of now. 'A fair draw,' as Coach Bob Bradley put it, trying to keep his heels from clicking together in glee."[28]

As Donovan assessed in the *Times*'s primary story on the draw, "Any time now that we don't advance, we're going to be disappointed."[29]

The opening match featured the two group favorites, and Steven Gerrard got England on the front foot with a fourth-minute goal. But in the fortieth minute, the match transformed on a speculative Clint Dempsey shot that hit England keeper Robert Green's gloves and then skipped over the line for the equalizer. Whether attributable to Dempsey's opportunism or Green's unfortunate howler, it was good enough to secure a draw that, coupled with Slovenia's 1–0 win over Algeria, left an unlikely team in the Group C driver's seat.

Things got even murkier in the second match pairings: The US fell behind Slovenia 2–0 at halftime before engineering two comeback goals for the draw, while England and Algeria slogged through a scoreless affair. Any of the four teams had a path to the Round of 16 heading into the final pair of group matches.

Twenty-three minutes into the simultaneously played matches, Jermain Defoe put England up 1–0 over Slovenia. Were the scores to remain unchanged in those matches from that point forward, England (whose win and two draws would garner them five points) and Slovenia (with a 1–1–1 record good for four points) would advance past the United States (whose three draws would only bring them three points). The US had its chances to get on the scoresheet, including a nineteenth-minute Dempsey would've-been-goal wrongly ruled offside, and a fifty-sixth-minute effort in which Dempsey hit the post on a shot and then sent the rebound shot wide. But, as the match headed into stoppage time, it was still scoreless, and it looked as though both teams on the pitch would be playing their last moments of World Cup 2010.

Then, US Soccer delivered perhaps the most iconic American team victory since the US hockey team's "Miracle on Ice" against the Soviet Union in the 1980 Winter Olympics. On a break upfield, Donovan passed to a streaking Jozy Altidore on the right flank with Dempsey charging straight toward the near post. Altidore entered the box, and then skimmed a cross into Dempsey's path. Dempsey's shot was stopped by diving Algerian keeper Raïs M'Bolhi, and Dempsey's momentum carried him past M'Bolhi onto the ground in front of goal, next to a late-arriving Madjid Bougherra. M'Bolhi, still on the ground, helplessly watched the ball roll past his grasp to the six-yard-line, into the hard-charging Donovan's path and then, with Donovan's deft finish, into the net behind him for the game-winning goal.

"I knew when I got the ball and I looked up, there was a chance for us to score," Donovan remembers of the play that led to the goal. "99 percent of the time when you get the ball, you're not thinking this has a real chance to lead to a goal. This time, I could tell right when I got the ball that the numbers were in our favor, and it was materializing in a way that we were going to get a chance out of it. Other than that, it was instinct and it just unfolded the way it did. I'd never scored a goal like that in my career, and never scored one like that after that either." He added that it's the kind of goal that right-place, right-time players, like Dempsey, are more prone to score.

The aftermath that unfolded—Donovan's celebratory headfirst slide toward the corner, players and subs pig-piling on top of him, the incessant South African vuvuzelas pitching into an even more excitable higher gear than anyone thought possible, Ian Darke on the ESPN telecast memorably trilling, "Oh! It's incredible! You could not write a script like this!"—set off jubilant expressions all over the US. Many of the exultant fans were gathered at watch parties, held in bars that had opened their doors earlier than usual, to let patrons more accustomed to coffee than beer at that time of day immerse themselves in the world's sport.

A cynical observer might say that the US should've had the game well in hand before stoppage time, that Algeria was an inferior opponent in a relatively weak group, and given the course the tournament took, that it was an emotional moment ultimately of little import to the overall composition of how it all played out. These are perfectly reasonable assessments—but they're also bereft of joy and don't acknowledge the transcendence of the moment. Anyone professing to be an American soccer fan knows where they were when it happened and how they reacted to the 1–2 punch of Dempsey's blocked shot and Donovan's opportunistic finish.

"I didn't really understand it until the next morning," recalls Donovan, noting that during the 2010 tournament, he shied away from soccer media and even more traditional soccer news coverage. "I walked into our communication center, and they were showing us the video someone had made from all the celebrations across the US. But I didn't truly grasp it until I got back from South Africa, and the way we were treated, the way people had responded, how much more visible we were, how much more people recognized us. That's when it truly kind of sank in for me."

The magical moment (and its replays on TV and online) also galvanized a larger American audience who tuned in for the Round of 16 match, conveniently falling on a Saturday afternoon in American time zones. In fact, the largest US soccer audience to date, 19.4 million,[30] tuned in to see if the US could replicate its 2002 feat of getting into the quarterfinals.

Alas, they could not. They did take the game to extra time, after matching Ghana's fifth-minute opener from Kevin-Prince Boateng with a sixty-second-minute Donovan penalty that Dempsey forced, after Donovan put a deft touch on halftime sub Benny Feilhaber's pass from midfield. But in the third minute of extra time, Asamoah Gyan rifled in a shot from fifteen yards out, led into a dangerous area via a beyond-midfield pass from André Ayew. Despite some chances in extra time—including, cruelly, shots from Dempsey and Jay DeMerit in the match's dying moments that couldn't quite find the target—Ghana beat the USMNT for the second time in as many World Cups and ousted it from the tournament.

It's perhaps a spiteful consolation for American fans that Gyan transformed from hero to goat in a particularly cruel quarterfinal match with Uruguay. In the final seconds of extra time, what should have been the game-winning Ghana goal was blatantly punched off the line by Uruguay's Luis Suarez. Suarez received a red card, but was inexplicably allowed to linger for Gyan's penalty kick, which smashed against the crossbar, leading Suarez to a fairly disgusting display of joy and relief. Uruguay won the ensuing penalty kick sequence, eliminating the last African team in the tournament. (Uruguay, in turn, would lose to the Netherlands in the semifinals, resulting in an all-European final which Spain won.)

Though the USMNT's journey to South Africa was ultimately disappointing, it did result in a return to the knockout rounds and an increasingly tuned-in American audience who witnessed the joy and heartbreak that a tournament can bring. In the two decades since the US reentered the World Cup arena, it solidified as a nation and removed the doubt as to whether it even deserved to be on the World Cup stage. Despite several fruitless cycles within that timeline, the US also showed an ability to challenge perennial powerhouses and quickly ascending soccer nations.

Was Jürgen Klinsmann indeed the architect needed to bring the US into the upper echelon of world soccer? The US Soccer Federation thought enough of him to name him the head coach a day after firing Bradley in July 2011, five years after first courting him. The five years under Klinsmann that followed may not have directly propelled the US where it wanted to be as a soccer nation, but it most definitely accelerated the conversations and heightened the expectations attached to such aspirations.

CHAPTER 2

KLINSMANN AND THE
DUAL NATIONAL DEBATE

Jürgen Klinsmann was officially introduced as the USMNT coach at an August 1, 2011, press conference, which happened to be just nine days before a friendly with Mexico in Philadelphia.

Klinsmann was a coach who, to borrow from Walt Whitman, was large and contained intriguing (and European) multitudes: German-born, multilingual, seasoned as a player and a coach in the top European leagues. Indeed, he was seen by some as a sort of for-hire mercenary striker, playing for Stuttgart Kickers, VfB Stuttgart, Inter Milan, Monaco, Tottenham Hotspur, Bayern Munich, and Sampdoria in a nearly two-decade career—and excelling in World Cup competition for his native country both on the field and on the sidelines. Yet, at the time of his appointment to US Soccer's top post, he'd lived in the US for thirteen years—a particularly salient selling point that US Soccer Federation President Sunil Gulati made in his introduction of Klinsmann.

"Jürgen's experience, both as a player and coach, and as a resident of this country—and I think all three of those are important—we think are huge assets," Gulati said. "The latter solves whatever we think about having an international coach, and whether they'll know America, and know the difference between Duke [University] and the Portland Timbers, and all the things that are specific to the US, like the role of education, geography and so on."[1]

Klinsmann was a cavalier outsider at a time the program needed a new perspective—even his eventual detractors would surely grant that—

but he was a curious kind of maverick. A June 2014 *New Yorker* feature, titled "Jürgen Klinsmann's Soccer Mandate," characterized a failed coaching stop at Bayern Munich in 2008, using Klinsmann's predilection for having Buddha statues placed through its training center as a sign that he was "was too 'American' to properly coach Germany's most prominent club team," too "extravagantly emotional" for what he termed "Germany's rigid, bureaucratic soccer culture," and too prone to "pushing change in sweeping, sometimes reckless fashion."[2]

While the article did interestingly posit that "[o]ne of Klinsmann's qualifications to Europeanize American soccer is that, for most of his career, he seemed to be trying to Americanize German soccer," it also noted Klinsmann was guided by a vision that "step-by-step, over the years, we want to play with the bigger nations, to attack the bigger nations, and to possess more than them."[3]

Klinsmann also brought ideas about gamesmanship to the table. After a US-hosted 4–1 friendly loss to Brazil in May 2012, he said, "We need to get an edge, more nastier [*sic*]. Maybe we're a little bit still too naive. Maybe we don't want to hurt people. But that's what we've got to do. You've got to do that at the end of the day. So we've got to step on their toes more and get them more frustrated and make a case with the referee maybe as well, for us, not only the opponent." In an article that labeled him "a noted flopper during his legendary playing career," he opined, "You watch big teams in the world, what they do, and there's a call going against them—Barcelona is one of them—they come with 10 guys towards the referee. The referee is confused. He doesn't know even know who to show a yellow card."[4]

Though a 4–1 loss to Brazil is an odd occasion to find positives for a new, reinvigorated American soccer program, *Grantland*'s Brian Phillips nonetheless did so, excited about promises of a quicker style more reliant on short passes, which he summed up as the new coach "gambling that he can teach the USMNT to walk before it's really gotten world-class at crawling." He wrote: "Under the domed, doomed gaze of Bob Bradley, the USMNT often seemed to be raising its ceiling by small increments while focusing on the parts of the game that are supposed to raise the floor: organization, defensive cohesion, stamina, muscle, heart.

Klinsmann seems to have decided—spectacularly if not wisely—that the floor is actually a boring place to be, and that what we really ought to do is focus on technique, creativity, and speed, push the ceiling up into the exosphere, and let the ground take care of itself."[5]

And as Ryan Rosenblatt pointed out, covering the introductory press conference for SB Nation, Klinsmann's initial message "had little to do with the actual senior team he will be managing and more about the youth system in the country." Klinsmann, after all, was seen by many as a coach whose potential to find and develop new talent was perhaps even more important than inspiring the talent he inherited.

"When Klinsmann did talk about the senior team," Rosenblatt cautioned, "it wasn't particularly cheery, acknowledging how far the US had to go and the gap between them and their Mexican rivals. He called Mexico one of the top 10 teams in the world, while saying that if the US were to ever win a World Cup they would 'need maybe 10 Landon Donovans at different positions with different characteristics in order to one day be there.'"[6]

It did indeed help Klinsmann that his team tied Mexico in that first friendly; it helped even more that a year later—on August 15, 2012, to be exact—Klinsmann took an American squad to Estadio Azteca and beat Mexico 1–0. While it was another relatively low-stakes friendly match, a win in Mexico's hallowed home stadium was a result American soccer fans had been waiting literally decades for.

And, for a fan base using US-Mexico results as a measuring stick, Klinsmann's six straight matches against Mexico with a win or draw certainly helped generate goodwill.

Winning in Azteca is significant, even if the match is a friendly rather than a high-stakes qualifier. Azteca is, quite simply, a fortress for El Tri, and affords a home-field advantage unlike anything else in CONCACAF. The stadium sits at 7,200 feet above sea level, in the midst of a 25 million person metropolis with attendant air quality issues, with at least 100,000 typically cramming in a stadium that officially seats just 87,000. The fans are, in a word, bellicose. There is a long, storied tradition of American soccer articles detailing the treatment American fans get in Mexico: The police escorts they get as they enter the stadium and move to their section, in the stadium's upper tier, cordoned off with barbed-wire-topped fence, where they endure food, beer, and epithets thrown at them for the entirety of the match.

An *Outside* article ostensibly celebrating the 2012 friendly win, titled "Playing Soccer With a Plastic Bag on Your Head," observed that the US came into the match 0–8–1 in Azteca and 0–23–1 in all matches played in Mexico. It also assessed Mexico as a "good-unto-average-unto-good-unto-etc. soccer team, much like the US" but "by no means [. . .] a world power." The article went on to explore the physical effects when high altitude is multiplied by air that the American Lung Association awarded a failing grade, attributing Mexico's incredible record at Azteca—a mere nine lifetime losses in a stadium that opened in 1966—to a "real, scientific home-field advantage" in which El Tri players live and breathe in an ecosystem that other humans can't flourish in. One expert quoted in the article argued that it requires a human two full years to acclimatize to Azteca's caustic conditions.[7]

In overcoming the physical and psychological challenges of Azteca, the 2012 victory nearly a mile and a half above sea level represented a sea change for US Soccer. In fact, the win over Mexico helped the early Klinsmann era become one of possibility and optimism. So it was certainly no coincidence that two significant losses to Mexico plunged the late Klinsmann era into discontentment and seeming despair.

The first of those losses came in the 2015 CONCACAF Cup, a Rose Bowl–hosted match—what a cynic might term both a home and an away match for the US—pitting the 2013 and 2015 Gold Cup winners against each other for the right to represent CONCACAF at the dress rehearsal for the 2018 World Cup, the 2017 FIFA Confederations Cup in Russia. Through ninety minutes, the teams played to a 1–1 deadlock. In extra time, one of Mexico's most reliable forwards of late, Oribe Peralta, scored in the ninety-sixth minute. Then one of the US's most reliable forwards of late, Bobby Wood, matched his effort in the 108th minute, just ten minutes after coming on a sub. Mexican right-back Paul Aguilar scored Mexico's winning goal with just two minutes left, volleying a loose ball in the pinball aftermath of a set piece.

The first loss to Mexico under Klinsmann meant that El Tri would travel to Russia during a crowded summer that would include a Gold Cup and key World Cup qualifiers—not the worst opportunity to miss out on, even though ceding that meant some bragging rights and FIFA ranking points would go with it.

But it was another Mexico match decided by the same final margin, the opener for both teams in the 2018 World Cup qualifying cycle, that ultimately sealed Klinsmann's fate. Though the US Soccer Federation could tolerate a degree of uncertainty and mystery surrounding their controversial coach, it wasn't ready to face the uncertainty of missing out on the World Cup—something that the US had seemingly corrected for good throughout the 1990s. And what happened over the course of those five fateful days in November 2016, starting with the Mexico match, gave US Soccer officials ample reason for concern.

On November 11, the US played Mexico in Columbus's MAPFRE Stadium, as they have done in each World Cup qualification cycle since 2001, when it was still known by its original Columbus Crew Stadium name. It's the stadium where the USMNT clinched qualification for the 2014 World Cup, by the *dos a cero* scoreline that the team has serendipitously landed upon in multiple matches.

While many American fans associate the legendary scoreline to the 2002 World Cup Round of 16 showdown, a November 2016 Stars and Stripes FC article noted that thirteen of sixty-six matches prior to the November World Cup qualifier ended in that scoreline. Though Mexico was on the *dos* side of some of those earlier contests, Americans won notable 2–0 matches in the 1991 Gold Cup semifinals, during Landon Donovan's US debut in October 2000, and the original Columbus-hosted World Cup qualifier in February 2001, the first of four straight US-hosted World Cup qualifiers won by the celebrated *dos a cero*.[8]

Why does US Soccer choose to play the match in Columbus? Partially because the climate during winter months is less hospitable to Mexican players used to warmer climes, and partially, perhaps more cynically, to minimize the number of Mexican supporters who could potentially attend, compared to cities closer to the US-Mexican border accessible to Mexican nationals and numerous American-born El Tri fans willing to travel.

The Columbus assignment does have specific origins. A *New York Times* article previewing the November 2016 matchup noted that Columbus Crew GM Jim Smith hatched the plan for a Columbus-hosted winter qualifier in November 2000, working out how they could sell out the stadium, and then calling Crew owner Lamar Hunt for his blessing. The article noted that the American win streak, "along with a mix of unmatched ambience, undying support and—not surprisingly—a little bit of superstition, has turned this college-football-mad town in the Midwest into the de facto caretaker of what is the United States' biggest soccer match on home soil." Gulati even asserted in the article, "Until we lose, there may be someone who moves the Mexico game away from Columbus, but it's not going to be me."[9]

But on November 11, 2016, *dos a cero*, as we knew it, died. Mexico took a lead in the match's twentieth minute on a Miguel Layún header. As in he did in a prior, notable high stakes match against Mexico, Wood equalized for the US, doing so in the forty-ninth minute. But in the eighty-ninth minute, Mexico's thirty-seven-year-old veteran captain Rafa Márquez, who *Sports Illustrated*'s Grant Wahl noted was "a longtime goat in this series," became the unlikely hero by heading in a corner kick to stun those congregating in Columbus.

Wahl leveled criticisms that echoed two of the prime points detractors brought up regarding Klinsmann: adventuresome formations and puzzling lineup choices. "One of the keys to the US's surge this year was finding consistency at last under Klinsmann in lineups and personnel, so that the core group got larger and more unified," Wahl reasoned, before asking, "So why did Klinsmann change everything up and go with a 3–5–2 lineup in the biggest World Cup qualifier of the year?" He noted that the team seemed disjointed before reverting back to a more familiar 4–4–2 formation shortly after the opening goal, and questioned several of Klinsmann's choices to fill the starting roster.[10]

The loss, in addition to ending the USMNT's run of success against its bitter rivals, also notably ended its thirty-match home unbeaten streak in World Cup qualifying matches, dating back to a 2001 loss to Honduras at RFK Stadium[11] and a win over Jamaica at Foxboro Stadium the following month.[12]

Four days later, it got even worse. The second biggest test for the USMNT in recent World Cup cycles has been playing in Costa Rica. This was in part due to the Ticos' former home, Estadio Ricardo Saprissa, which soccer writer Noah Davis noted was a "loud, imposing venue nicknamed 'the Monster's Cave' that featured fans on top of the action and a pockmarked artificial turf made for tearing ACLs."[13] Though the Chinese-built new national stadium, Estadio Nacional de Costa Rica, opened in 2011 to replace it, Costa Rica has since emerged as a formidable CONCACAF opponent, qualifying for three of the last four World Cups, and advancing to the quarterfinals in 2014.

The US lost by an unconscionable 4–0 margin; though US Soccer's official account had the team "battl[ing] through a physical and feisty match but ultimately succumb[ing],"[14] other accounts were less charitable, including a *New York Times* account that diagnosed the US as having "no fluidity [. . .] no flow, no rhythm, no concentrated push, either early or late [. . .] no sturdiness or stoutness or resilience in a game that felt critical [. . .] no creativity," assessing it as the team's "single worst performance" in Klinsmann's tenure. A *Guardian* article piled on by observing that "the increasingly dissatisfied fanbase will have seen nothing to suggest that the team is on target for the 2018 World Cup."[15]

That dissatisfaction had been brewing for a while with some fans. On March 25, 2016, the unthinkable happened: The USMNT lost 2–0 to Guatemala in Guatemala City, leaving the Americans third in a four-team group in which only the top two teams would qualify, in the round winnowing CONCACAF's field from twelve to six teams. Though there was a return home leg scheduled in four days' time, that game—against a team that FIFA ranks right around the 100th best in the world—ended up gathering much greater import and even worry than American fans thought possible.

The New York Times's account of the match, and the post-match assessment, was a bit eyebrow-raising for concerned American fans:

> In fact, Guatemala, which was playing its first competitive game, and third overall, under a new coach, Walter Claveri, looked more cohesive than the United States, which has had nearly five years to get in sync with Klinsmann.

Klinsmann, who has come under increasing criticism, was asked how such a lack of focus could be present at the start of a game. He replied, "That's a good question for the players."

Later, when asked if he questioned either his lineup choices or his mode of preparing the players, Klinsmann said: "Absolutely you question that, and you kind of think how can we fix this, this and this. At the end of the day, these two mistakes, these two goals—you just have to swallow it, because those are individual mistakes that you cannot do at this level. That's what happened tonight so we'll take the blame. I take the blame."[16]

The Stars and Stripes FC website pointed out the loss was the first to Guatemala "since the Reagan Administration, a streak that had lasted 21 games over a 28-year span," and voiced the oft-leveled criticism that Klinsmann was being too clever with the lineups rather than picking the most appropriate and most evident lineup for the situation.

"There's tinkering, and then there are Jürgen Klinsmann's lineups," Roderick MacNeil wrote. "Playing guys out of position has been a hallmark of the Klinsmann era. You cannot predict his Starting XI, but you can predict it will only make sense to one person: Jürgen Klinsmann." After citing specific instances along the defensive line, and singling out the deploying of Mix Diskerud behind (rather than in front of) Michael Bradley, he assessed, "When the majority of your starting lineup is asked to perform a job it is not accustomed to doing, you're no longer thinking outside the box. You're dousing the box in gasoline, flicking a match, then acting surprised when it burns."[17]

The qualification train did indeed get back on track four days later, with a 4–0 victory in Columbus that put both the US and Guatemala in their expected places in the standings. And yet the episode was enough to cause concern in both where Klinsmann positioned his chess players on the field and how those players responded.

And while it was one thing to right the ship against Guatemala in the playoff series leading up to the Hex, it was another thing entirely to

exhibit the same tendencies and befall the repercussions of the same mis-
steps in the midst of the Hex.

Just six days after the catastrophic loss to Costa Rica in November
2016—leaving the US at the bottom of the Hex standings with more than
a four-month gap before qualifying play would resume—Klinsmann was
fired and replaced with Bruce Arena, a coach clearly familiar to USMNT
fans. The move to Arena signaled more of a stopgap, let's-worry-about-
qualifying impulse than finding another long-term architect and seismic
shifter along the lines of what American soccer fans hoped Klinsmann
would be, but it also signaled the seriousness of US Soccer's desire to get
to the World Cup by tapping presumably the best available person to deliver on that.

Reaction from USMNT captain Michael Bradley to the Klinsmann
firing was appropriately sober. "It's never a good thing when we have to
go through a night like we did in Costa Rica," he said. "The reality of
sports is that the coach is the one that takes the fall and again, as players,
that's not a nice thing. Because we understand that we're the ones on the
field and we ultimately have to look at ourselves in the mirror and be
very honest and just say that it's not been [what it's] needed to be this
last stretch. There's nothing else to say now. As captain, nobody takes
that harder than me."[18]

Bradley, of course, had notably stepped to Klinsmann's defense before—or, perhaps more accurately, to the team's defense—when it seemed
to falter under Klinsmann's guidance. It was during the prior World Cup
qualifying cycle, after an opening loss in Honduras, that Brian Straus inadvertently set American soccer opinion ablaze with a *Sporting News* article that ran three days before the USMNT's first home World Cup
qualifier match in 2013—now known in American soccer lore as the
Snow Clasico in Denver.

Straus's article started by recounting then-captain Carlos Bocanegra's
surprise omission from the lineup of players facing Honduras in the 2014
World Cup cycle's Hex opener, and what was seen by several players as
Klinsmann's "awkward, tone-deaf" appeal to Bocanegra to provide
pregame support—likened to "driv[ing] the knife in and twist[ing] it"
after the initial, injurious move of leaving him out of the starting

lineup. Straus then criticized the team performance that followed, writing:

> Sure enough, the US played like a team lacking leadership and an appropriate, coherent plan throughout an ugly 2–1 loss to Honduras.
>
> It wasn't the defeat itself that proved so troubling—the US always loses two or three matches during the 10-game qualifying gauntlet known as the Hexagonal. It was the manner in which the Americans capitulated. The final score flattered a US squad that spent the majority of the afternoon on its heels, devoid of the energy, possession and ideas Klinsmann intended to deliver.
>
> The performance that day, as well as a lack of obvious improvement during his 19 months in charge, has alarmed the American soccer community and unearthed considerable discontent. The US might have just set out on the road to Brazil, but confidence is on the wane on both sides of the locker room door.

To prepare the article, Straus talked to eleven current players and eleven additional individuals connected to the USMNT, and quoted them all anonymously, allowing for a candor that revealed several disarming themes. Players perceived Klinsmann as lacking tactical acumen, spending time and energy on initiatives that didn't translate to on-field success and changing lineups with a disorienting frequency.[19]

In a *Planet Fútbol* podcast recorded exactly one week after the firing, Wahl interviewed his *Sports Illustrated* colleague on what he declared the "most talked about" soccer story of Klinsmann's entire tenure. Straus noted that the blanket anonymity was given to sources in part because he didn't want to ruin anyone's national team career should Klinsmann avenge their candor.

"The primary trend was that of general confusion," Straus said of the litany of complaints he chronicled in the article. "Of things not being explained, of things being unpredictable, changing lineups, changing schedules, changing plans for training sessions. They didn't feel like they were being communicated with, they didn't feel like they know what to expect."[20]

To Straus's credit, he did interview Klinsmann two days before the story ran, feeling it was critical to the article to share the views of the twenty-two sources with him and gauge his reactions, to set up a framework of "here are the concerns, and here's what Jürgen said." (Also to his credit, Straus didn't run with any allegations from solo sources—everything in the article was confirmed by at least two people he interviewed.)

Klinsmann viewed the reactions as byproducts of his deliberate plan to take players out of their comfort zones, to have them, as Straus recalled, "swim in the cold water."

"He wanted these guys to be in a different kind of environment than they were used to," Straus noted, "where they weren't sure what to expect, where they had to be ready for anything, where they had to play any system, any position, take anything that the game throws at them and be comfortable and have the kind of dexterity that he thought international players should have. So what the story shined a light on at this time was that he really believed this stuff, and he hasn't shied away from it, and the players were having trouble with it at the beginning. They were really struggling."[21]

The overall tone and tenor of Straus's article led many American soccer fans to openly worry about the future of the team and how the team would fare in the crucial match just three days after the article went live. Fans during that Hex were fond of chanting "We Are Going to Brazil," yet Straus's article made them question the optimism that chant conveyed.

Straus claims that the story's timing was merely a function of when Klinsmann spoke to him and his final rewrite, yet some took to social media to accuse him of purposefully timing the story to have maximum impact on the team. The fallout was a little awkward for Straus, who was in Denver at the time the story broke to cover the match. "I'm standing there in the pre-practice mixed zone," Straus remembered, "and Michael Bradley is telling the reporters present it was shameful that players would talk to the media about their concerns. And I'm standing six inches from him while he's saying this to two dozen writers!"

And yet the Snow Clasico ended up, like the Donovan goal against Algeria nearly three years prior, an indelible and joyous memory for US soccer fans. The US won the match 1–0, and turned its World Cup fortunes around, and by playing in a swirling blizzard where the ball was skidding into snowdrifts by match's end, created real, resonant, lasting American soccer lore for the swell of fans who would make 2014's World Cup audience supersede all previous ones. "That's where The Legend of Jürgen began," Straus cracked, referring to those two matches. "We put one shot on goal in 180 minutes and came away with four points."[22]

In fact, the US rode the momentum from those two matches to finish first in CONCACAF qualifying. As an odd bonus that their Mexican rivals appreciated, the US gave Mexico a lifeline in the federation's final slate of qualifying matches by engineering a come-from-behind victory over Panama in Panama City. In the eighty-third minute of their match, Luis Tejeda's goal put Panama up 2–1, which would have elevated Panama over Mexico to fourth place in the CONCACAF standings and into a home-and-away playoff series with Oceania's New Zealand. But the USMNT scored two stoppage-time goals: a header by Graham Zusi to bump Panama to fifth in CONCACAF and out of World Cup contention, and the game-winning goal by Aron Jóhannsson to fully seal their fate.

Mexican fans on both sides of the border were jubilant, and in one of the most famous broadcasting calls in modern American soccer history, the team from TV Azteca—showing the US and Mexico games side-by-side in split screen format—exulted, "We love you forever and ever! God bless America! The US puts us in the playoffs!" before laying into the Mexican team for their relative lack of involvement in the outcome.[23] Zusi was christened "San Zusi" by fans grateful for his role in rescuing Mexico from a snakebitten qualifying campaign.

The draw for the 2014 World Cup in Brazil did the USMNT (and, ultimately, Klinsmann) absolutely no favors. In some World Cups, the idea of a "Group of Death" is merely relative to the rest of the field. In this case, though, it was legitimate. The US joined two European teams— eventual champions Germany, and the core of what would be eventual Euro 2016 winners Portugal—and also drew, in Ghana, the nemesis responsible for the US team's exit in the two most recent World Cups.

Against Ghana, the US opened the scoring comically fast, with Clint Dempsey pouncing on a Jermaine Jones leading pass at the thirty-second mark to make it 1–0. That should have eased some tension for the Americans, but when Jozy Altidore pulled up with a hamstring injury midway through the first half, tensions set right back in. Injury further complicated the American mission when defender Matt Besler had to be subbed for John Brooks at halftime, and a match beginning to pivot toward Ghana swung level when André Ayew scored a goal in the eighty-second-minute. But the Brooks sub paid unexpected dividends; four minutes after the goal, Graham Zusi (the third US sub) sent a corner kick in, and Brooks found it with his head from seven yards out, scoring what would be the game winner.

Straus recalls that after the USMNT's opening 2014 match, he wrote a column in which he assessed that, "after two years of [Klinsmann] telling us what the soccer was supposed to look like," the team had merely reverted to what they knew: "Absorbing a ton of pressure, and looking to score on a counter or on a set piece to win a World Cup game."[24] They were successful in doing that, but it would be their only win of the tournament.

The Portugal match, in steamy Manaus, opened with a fifth-minute goal from Nani, inadvertently assisted via a poor Geoff Cameron clearance. Yet the US looked the more threatening side overall. Leveling on a Jermaine Jones goal just over an hour into the contest, the USMNT pulled ahead on Dempsey's odd eighty-first minute goal, in which he ran onto a Zusi cross directly in front of goal and bounced it over the line with his midriff. But in the last instance of stoppage time, the man widely considered to be the best player in the world—kept in check for so much of the match—showed he had one great play in him.

Cristiano Ronaldo sent in a parabolic cross to Silvestre Varela in Portugal's last break of the game, and Varela headed the ball past Tim Howard for the tying goal. Thus, Portugal stayed alive in the tournament and kept the US from clinching a spot in the Round of 16 with what looked, until that last moment, to be a second win in as many matches.

Still, as Zusi recalls in my February 2017 conversation with him, the team was proud of their ability to contain Ronaldo. "Obviously you have to pay special attention to a player like that," he notes. "But I think our defenders just took it personally. Specifically, I remember Matt Besler just having a beast of a game in the back line and shutting Ronaldo down. I think that's a typical American mentality. It's the 'when the going gets tough' kind of thing with us—that's when we're going to shine."

"In Brazil, as usual, we were put into a Group of Death," Zusi says, reflecting on the entirety of the World Cup. "Getting out of your group is first and foremost the most important part of it because once you do that once you grind through those those first three matches then you can take it really one match at a time. And when you have that mentality of 'anything can happen on any given day,' that's when you can really press forward and get the results. It's all about getting the results. And when you do that, that's when you can find yourself deep into the tournament."

The USMNT's final, rain-drenched group game, against Germany, was closer and tenser than many were expecting. The US, clearly holding to an absorb-and-counter game plan, nearly scored midway through the first half when Zusi's speculative, edge-of-the-box shot curled just over the crossbar. But Germany, controlling the time of possession by nearly 2:1 throughout the match, scored the match's lone goal in the fifty-fifth minute, courtesy of Thomas Müller, who finished second in the 2014 World Cup Golden Boot race to Colombia's James Rodríguez. Yet the result, combined with Portugal's win over Ghana, allowed the US to join Germany in the Round of 16, and into exactly what I'd predicted at the start of the tournament: a hard-fought loss to a talented Belgian side to miss out on the quarterfinals.

But I didn't predict the heartbreaking way in which they'd do it. Tim Howard recorded sixteen saves, the most in a World Cup match since the stat was kept—necessary because Belgium took thirty-eight shots, twenty-seven on goal, approaching World Cup records themselves with that barrage. Remarkably, the match remained deadlocked through regulation, though in the final minute of stoppage time, Jermaine Jones, held by a Belgian defender six yards from the center of goal, found himself able to head a pass in the path of a fast-approaching Chris Wondolowski. A deft tap-in would have sent the Americans to the quarterfinals against Argentina. Instead, Wondolowski's shot from just three yards out went wildly wide and high.

Belgium would go on to score two goals in extra time, and even though Julian Green would come on in a late substitution role and score a 107th-minute goal to create a sense of hope, the Americans couldn't find the late goal they needed to send the match to penalty kicks.

Though Klinsmann did deliver the US to the World Cup, it would turn out to be his one and only World Cup at the US helm, and the overall assessment of the team's performance was mixed.

"Even though the US arguably got outplayed in three of those four World Cup games," Wahl observed in his podcast with Straus, "they did get out of a very difficult group, they exorcised the ghost of Ghana, and did better than most people expected they would do."

"Getting out of the group was important," Straus responded, "because you're trying to build the sport, and you want the attention and the momentum that getting out of the group generates." He then added, "But when you say that we're all about results at the World Cup, that's true, unless the coach comes in promising more than results. This coach came in promising an approach, a style of play, a dynamism, a proactive kind of way of looking at the game that was going to change the way that American soccer looked to people. And he didn't do that at the World Cup."[25]

In the immediate aftermath of the match, however, some Americans found hope despite the second straight Round of 16 defeat. ESPN's *SportsCenter* Twitter account optimistically opined, "USA's future is bright. Julian Green (19 yrs, 25 days) is youngest to score at World Cup since Lionel Messi in 2006," even adding a split photo of both of them in identical, index-finger-pointing goal celebrations.[26]

It's worth noting that Straus and Wahl credited Klinsmann for their ability to find talented players outside of the usual search zones, with Jordan Morris and Bobby Wood prime examples of that, though Straus did wonder if "turning over more rocks than his predecessors" is a laudable legacy.[27]

But Green—a German-born son of a US soldier—exemplified the dual national debate that was troubling and even uncomfortably bordering on xenophobia at times, but certainly ever-present throughout Klinsmann's tenure. Klinsmann, having obvious German ties, sought players who were the sons of US soldiers, born in Germany, and schooled in German soccer academies—with Jermaine Jones, Fabian Johnson, and John Brooks being the most successful, oft-capped examples.

"It's no secret that Klinsmann relies heavily on the sons of US soldiers, men who served in Germany at the tail end of the Cold War," wrote *The Guardian*'s Jack Kerr in December 2015. "He's not the first US coach to use this type of player, but under him, the practice has been ramped up."

"A soccer federation does not hire a manager known for his interest in youth development and knowledge of German youngsters then give him the role of technical director if they are interested in any other outcome," another *Guardian* writer, David Rudin, noted in a January 2017 retrospective on Klinsmann's ways.

"Klinsmann elevated the dual national to a fetishistic ideal," Rudin observed, adding that "the Klinsmann regime actively tried to secure the loyalties of young players eligible to play for multiple countries,"[28] citing the recruitment of young players like Green and Gedion Zelalem, both of whom had lived in both the US and Germany while growing up, and were sought after by both federations.

Zelalem, who may eventually find his way into the USMNT first team, injured his knee at the U-20 World Cup in May 2017 playing for the Americans, and so 2018 will prove a crucial year for him in both his physical recovery and his professional career. Expectation has surrounded Zelalem since he signed with Premier League side Arsenal in 2013 as a promising sixteen-year-old, and though he's still under contract with Arsenal, he's already been loaned out to both the Rangers of the Scottish Premier League and VVV-Venlo of the Eredivisie since arriving in London, in order to pick up first-team playing time in leagues more appropriate to his level of development.

Green has been a particularly curious case. Klinsmann's choice of Green over Donovan for the 2014 World Cup—while perhaps not the binary either/or choice for the final roster spot that some make it out to be—is at best a choice privileging the potential of the future over the legacy of the past, and could be more cynically seen as hubris in operation, with Klinsmann determined to prove people right about Green by throwing him into a World Cup—in the final minutes of a knockout match, no less—in just the scenario where Donovan might have flourished as he did four years prior.

Though many believed (or wanted to believe) that the goal Green scored against Belgium was a promising sign of things to come, it might have actually been the apex of Green's career for both club and country. Consider that in November 2013, Green signed a contract with Bayern Munich and made his first-team debut by subbing into the final minutes of a well-in-hand Champions League game later that month.

His move to the US in March 2014, under a FIFA rule that allowed for a dual-national youth player to make a one-time switch, was confirmed in a bright tweet by Klinsmann himself, who chirped, "We are absolutely thrilled that Julian Green has chosen to be a part of the US National Team Programs!"[29] USA Today's Nate Scott declared it "a coup for United States soccer,"[30] and the celebrations from fans on social media and in real life were reminiscent of how college football fans welcome news of a big recruiting commitment, because that's exactly what it was.

Yet upon returning from Brazil, Green's club career was anything but storybook. Green was loaned to Hamburger SV for the 2014–15 season—the club where Bobby Wood would succeed just two seasons later. At Hamburg, Green played just 113 minutes in five appearances and did not score the whole season. The next season, Green went to Stuttgart, a relegated squad at the time, faring slightly better with one goal in eight appearances.

Green's international career has similarly stalled. He wasn't capped for all of 2015, and only had three appearances the following year, including a pair of October 2016 friendlies against Cuba and New Zealand, where he logged a combined 168 minutes, scored a goal in each game, and added an assist in Havana.[31] The goals were his first in red, white, and blue since the World Cup goal and provided an encouraging glimpse at his brilliance, yet Green was passed over for 2017's slate of World Cup qualifiers and for the Gold Cup roster that serves as a platform for experimentation.

In a May 2017 article for Stars and Stripes FC, titled "The Miseducation of Julian Green," Charles D. Dunst lays out a provocative argument about Green's failure to meet perhaps-too-lofty expectations and how that failure (to date) reflected poorly on Klinsmann:

> Green's international and club career has been a disappointment to most fans. In his World Cup selection, Green was lauded as the American soccer messiah, much like Christian Pulisic is today. Although Green is a solid player, he never truly had Pulisic-like potential. Green's mythical talent was a narrative constructed by Jürgen Klinsmann and only furthered by his World Cup goal, which was most certainly an aberration.
>
> Green was Jürgen Klinsmann's big discovery—a youngster who could demonstrate the former manager's eye for talent and hopefully save his job. Klinsmann pursued a similar strategy with other German-Americans . . . but he deemed Green to have the best potential.

Dunst went on to observe "though Green was certainly a talented prospect, he never should've been coronated as the harbinger of American soccer success," or indeed even Pulisic's equal, arguing it was unfair and unwarranted to cast him, as some were quick to do post-2014 World Cup, as "the physical embodiment of America's promising soccer future."[32]

But Green's inclusion highlighted a facet of the debate over the composition of the US men's team about who should be a candidate to be that physical embodiment. *Slate*'s Jeremy Stahl, as part of a pre-World Cup series on irascible soccer personalities called "World Cup Jerk Watch," pejoratively stated about Klinsmann, "He doesn't believe in America. At least he said back in December that he didn't believe the US would win this World Cup. As a coach, you're supposed to boast 'I believe that we will win' even if your team's odds are vanishingly slim. He has so little faith in the US system, in fact, that he brought in seven dual citizens, including five German players, to his 23-man World Cup squad. That's more than one-third of all US field players."[33]

Abby Wambach, in one of a series of interviews tied to her December 2015 retirement from the international game, complicated this particular facet of the debate about her male counterparts further. She complained about the dual national practice, perhaps too bluntly, on *The Bill Simmons Podcast*. While she noted her appreciation for players like Jones and Johnson, she remarked of Klinsmann, "The way that he has changed and brought in these foreign guys, it's just not something that I believe in."[34]

Norwegian-born Mix Diskerud, first capped for the Bob Bradley–coached US senior squad in 2010 and playing for NYCFC at the time, took umbrage at the comments. He responded on Instagram by posting a photo of Wambach holding a giant American flag at the 2015 Women's World Cup, challenging her in a caption doubling as an open letter. Starting with the salutation "Wow Abby," Diskerud noted that there are "pros and cons in limiting the base for selection," asked Wambach why she's singled out specific players, and warned her: "Think about who you try to disenfranchise. Because if you see us as the group to disenfranchise, then at least let it be known who we are. Stats and history will show— 'our group' has more than others produced volunteer [*sic*] and defending soldiers for what, by us, is willingly chosen and gathered to be worth protecting: Your nation. Wish you would accept it as ours too."[35]

But Wambach would later double down on her criticisms about Klinsmann's player recruitment, telling *The New York Times* in an October 2016 article:

> It feels a little bit odd to me that you have some guys that have never lived in the United States that play for the United States because they were able to secure a passport. To me, that just feels like they weren't able to make it for their country and earn a living, so they're coming here.
>
> But do they have that killer instinct? I don't know. I'd love to sit down with Mix Diskerud and some of these other guys and talk to them about it. I'd love to understand how much they love their country. I believe they can have love for both countries, but I'd love to hear it, and I think so many other people would, too. If this is an ignorant opinion, I'll raise my hand in the end and say, "My bad." But I'd want to have that conversation.[36]

This echoed an argument that Donovan made at the time of her original comments back in December 2015. Interviewed on Eric Wynalda's Sirius XM soccer show, Donovan intimated that representing the US for the national team somehow meant more to players who grew up in the United States than those who grew up elsewhere.

I'll share something that I shared with Jürgen, actually when I got left off the [2014 World Cup] team. I said, "Jürgen, I understand, you're allowed to make your choice and your decision, but there's at least a few players that are on your World Cup roster that are going that don't care in the same way I do. I mean, I grew up as a part of this whole system, and I feel like it is a part of me, and I think there's players in that locker room who, if you go three-and-out in the World Cup, they'll go back to their club teams and won't even blink twice. Whereas, if we go three and out, I'll be devastated.

And I think that's a piece that's important because that shows up in the way you play. It doesn't mean you're not going to try as hard and you're not professional, but when you really feel it, when you hear the national anthem and you get goosebumps and your blood starts pumping because you're proud to be an American and you love this country, that's a much different feeling than, "OK, I'm playing for a national team in a significant, exciting game."[37]

Donovan's omission from the 2014 World Cup squad was the most notable and certainly the most controversial of Klinsmann's decisions. For those who remember Donovan's heroics in the 2010 match against Algeria—that is to say, everybody—it was unthinkable that the engineer of those heroics, with his leadership and experience, would be seen as surplus to the team's needs.

"Klinsmann never appeared fully comfortable with a player whose occasionally flagging will undoubtedly frustrated the World Cup–winning German,"[38] Wahl wrote in *Sports Illustrated* immediately after the decision. Donovan did take a three-month sabbatical in the first part of 2013, missing the critical first two World Cup qualifiers against Honduras and Costa Rica. And yet, once back with the team, he spearheaded a victorious Gold Cup run as one of eight squad players over thirty, on a B-team full of players with five caps or less.

Some weighing in even went as far as playing the "If you're not Native American, you immigrated from somewhere" card to make the case that multiple national influences might be good for a team that needs to cultivate and then develop a team identity. Jeremiah Oshan, sizing up the 2014 World Cup roster, wrote:

> Ever since Jürgen Klinsmann took over the United States national team, much has been made over his pursuit of dual nationals. While Klinsmann's predecessors called in their fair share of players without solid claims at being "real" Americans—how's that for a loaded phrase?—the former German national team player and coach has gone out his way to convince players who might otherwise represent another country to strip on the Red, White and Blue.
>
> A quick glance at the United States' World Cup roster illustrates the point: Seven of the 23 players were either born or raised outside of the United States. Although there's not an exact overlap, seven of the 23 players also expressed some openness to representing other countries before committing to the USA during this cycle. If there is a legitimate critique of the squad Klinsmann has assembled, it's that it lacks a certain history.
>
> Even that understates just how diverse this team is, and it's what I believe really makes it representative of this country. Dig a little deeper into the upbringing of the players and you'll see a group dominated by first or second-generation Americans who are often of mixed race. Jozy Altidore's parents immigrated from Haiti; Tim Howard's mother is Hungarian; Alejandro Bedoya's father is Colombian; Omar Gonzalez carries a Mexican passport; Nick Rimando is part Mexican and part Filipino; Chris Wondolowski is a member of the Kiowa tribe; DeAndre Yedlin is half Latvian and a quarter Native-American.

Close to half the team would at least have to give some thought as to which box they'd check on the census. It's surely the most ethnically diverse team in the World Cup. Klinsmann did not set out to do this on purpose, but it's beautiful nonetheless.

This group is the American dream.[39]

Straus spoke a hard but fitting epitaph for the Klinsmann era in his podcast with Wahl. It was a particularly striking statement considering that Straus is a self-declared fan of Klinsmann, who notes he never called for Klinsmann's firing even when soccer media colleagues were piling on in the dismal final days of his reign.

"In all of the ups and downs of the past five years, all of the headlines, all of the controversy, all of the hope, the headlines, stories, and memories we have, I don't know that anything was actually accomplished," Straus said. "And that's incredible to me, with all that time, all that money invested, all of us hanging on his every word for a long time, I think we're right back to where we started. The things Bruce [Arena] said in his introductory news conference about giving this team an identity and building some chemistry and some awareness—that's foundational stuff! That's stuff Klinsmann should have been working on in his first year or two. And here we are at square one, starting that again [. . .] I don't know that the program has advanced that much over the past five years."[40]

And yet, Klinsmann's departure hasn't stopped players born outside the United States are still being brought in to represent the red, white, and blue, and that might ultimately be the legacy he's left.

The 2017 Gold Cup roster provided US Soccer the chance to seal the first American caps for three dual-national players with decidedly different routes to making the team: Kenny Saief, an American-born player (to Israeli parents), who grew up in Israel and had to make the FIFA-allowed one-time switch as Green did to make him USMNT-eligible;[41] Jesse Gonzalez, the FC Dallas goalkeeper who rose through its academy's ranks while playing for Mexico's youth national teams, and also made the FIFA one-time switch;[42] and Dom Dwyer, the English-born striker who joined Sporting Kansas City from 2012 and scored fifty-eight goals in 134 appearances (including the 2013 MLS Cup) before moving to Orlando City SC in a surprise move in July 2017.[43]

Both Dwyer and Saief actually made their USMNT debuts before the Gold Cup commenced, in a pre-tournament friendly against Ghana, with Dwyer starting and scoring the match's first goal while Saief came on as a second-half sub.[44] Injury prevented Saief from playing in the tournament, but Dwyer scored twice in three matches in the group stages before being swapped out for more experienced players (including Altidore, Bradley, and Dempsey) in the knockout rounds.

While Arena did rely on an experienced cadre of players to bolster the 2017 Gold Cup roster and secure the victory, it's noteworthy that Jordan Morris—who Klinsmann took from the "obscurity" of Stanford University to the USMNT first-team—scored the winning goal in the championship game. And, of course, when it came time for the crucial post–Gold Cup qualifying matches in the fall of 2017, it was those same experienced players who disappointed everyone counting on the United States making the World Cup.

How the utilization of dual nationals will continue as the USMNT prepares for the 2022 qualifying cycle will be a crucial question for the coach entrusted with getting back to the World Cup. In a 2014 article on US Soccer's dual national policies inspired by Green's decision, *The Guardian* recalled that the 2002 and 2006 World Cup rosters were low on what it termed "immigrant" talent, and even noted that many "felt recruiting two-passport players with servicemen fathers was 'against the spirit'" of the FIFA rules that expand the notion of the nation or nations one belongs to when it comes to soccer.[45]

Arena, while caretaking the team, displayed an acerbic optimism and a bullishness on what he saw as developing talent across the whole spectrum of available US players. To the assembled throng of press after the US-hosted 2–0 World Cup qualifier win over Trinidad & Tobago in June 2017, Arena said, "I've been around a long time, and our young players are getting better. I've been watching our U-17s, our U-20s, their World Cup competitions. I see good players in Major League Soccer, in the academies. We have a tremendous amount of talent in our country. We just have to do a better job in moving forward. We have good players now;

there's no question about it. I think in 2026, we can challenge better in the World Cup. I really believe that."

He did, of course, say that with the belief that the USMNT would advance, and certainly without the knowledge that the Trinidad & Tobago team they'd handled sufficiently if not spectacularly in Denver would ultimately dispatch them in Couva.

And he said so from a perspective intertwining a considerable history with both the national team and MLS. Arena led DC United to become the first-ever MLS Cup–winning team in 1996, and before his most recent stint as head of the USMNT, he oversaw the evolution of the LA Galaxy over eight seasons, from what could cynically be called the David Beckham Traveling Roadshow into a legitimate MLS dynasty that is now ebbing in his absence. It's clear that Arena predicated much of his approach in managing the national team on the rapidly changing league where he spent the bulk of his coaching career.

And MLS is, for reasons we'll explore in the next couple of chapters, essential to the USMNT's development and its very identity. While it isn't and may never be the best soccer league in the world, it's undoubtedly— advantageously and disadvantageously—the most American soccer league in the world.

CHAPTER 3

HOW MLS WAS CREATED, SAVED, AND NURTURED TO RESPECTABILITY

WHEN BOB GANSLER LED THE USMNT TO ITS FIRST WORLD CUP IN FORTY years, the US was between full-scale, functioning, top-flight American soccer leagues. Gansler believed the presence of such a league was pivotal to the US national team's fortunes, and he wasn't the only one seeking a new league as salvation for American soccer.

The 1994 World Cup provided the catalyst for moving American soccer fans to its brand-new premier soccer league. It moved them beyond mourning the death of the North American Soccer League (NASL), where from 1968 to 1984, the likes of Pelé, Franz Beckenbauer, George Best, and Johan Cruyff improbably joined top American players in a collection of franchises largely defined (for better and worse) by Pelé and Beckenbauer's New York Cosmos.

It was during a week of pre–World Cup festivities in the undeniably American setting of Las Vegas, on December 17, 1993—two days before the drawing of teams into their World Cup groups—that US Soccer Federation head Alan Rothenberg announced the arrival of a twelve-team, first-division American soccer league.

The league that perhaps-too-ostentatiously labeled itself as Major League Soccer (MLS) was important for American players from its inception. In the years between the demise of the NASL and the launch of MLS, there were organized leagues fielding teams and allowing players to get game action—most notably the American Soccer League, which would morph into the American Professional Soccer League, with famil-

iar former NASL entities like the Tampa Bay Rowdies, Fort Lauderdale
Strikers, and Washington Diplomats calling it home, and the Major Indoor Soccer League, which functioned as a de facto top-tier league in
NASL's absence, even though its odd soccer/hockey hybrid cemented its
legacy in part by inadvertently inspiring arena football.[1]

Initially, stars from the 1994 World Cup team were recruited into the
new league and utilized in its marketing campaign. Rather than pit individual
owners against each other in a high-stakes financial arms race to secure players, which is where most of world football would eventually "evolve," MLS
operated as a single-entity league in which team owners were designated
"investor-operators" and controlled individual teams in a system where they
all were shareholders in the league with the resultant risks and rewards.

Tab Ramos, who'd been instrumental to both the 1990 and 1994
World Cup teams, was the first player brought into MLS. In a 2016 interview conducted for my book on Major League Soccer, *The United States
of Soccer*, Ramos told me that then–MLS deputy commissioner Sunil Gulati recruited him into the league. At the time, Ramos was locked into a
contract with Real Betis in Spain, but hadn't played during the early part
of the 1994–95 season due to the skull fracture that he suffered during that
summer's World Cup. He was interested in an opportunity to play for Tigres in Mexico once he recovered, and Gulati happened upon an idea to
enable this: sign Ramos to the league, in hopes that it would attract other
American players, and loan him to Tigres while the league moved toward
its opening match in April 1996. By virtue of being first, Ramos got to
choose between the franchise in New York/New Jersey and the one in DC;
he chose the locale closer to family members and went with the MetroStars.

Other American stars like John Harkes, Alexi Lalas, and Eric
Wynalda were also recruited into the new league, as were colorful Mexican goalie Jorge Campos and Colombian legend Carlos Valderrama.
While early critics of the league faulted its quality of play—in part because players had to navigate the oddly narrow fields in football stadiums
that served as some of MLS teams' earliest homes—league officials did
make the necessary effort to get talented and marketable American
players to serve in leading roles.

But it wasn't just the current stars who benefited. Young American players who would assume roles on future USMNT squads would get play-ing opportunities with MLS. The initial MLS draft in February 1996 was stripped of the biggest names available due to their pre-draft disbursement to teams, and the *Los Angeles Times*'s Grahame L. Jones, clearly under-whelmed by the college striker who became the #1 pick, asked,

> Ever heard of Brian McBride?
>
> Unless you're an avid soccer fan—really avid—the chances are slim.
>
> That pretty much sums up the way Major League Soccer's draft went Tuesday, when 80 players were selected to join 40 of their more illustrious colleagues in the fledgling league that starts play April 6.
>
> Like most first drafts, this one needed a rewrite.
>
> There would have been a lot more excitement had MLS not already assigned its "name" players to the 10 teams.
>
> As a result, those attending the draft in New York were left to ooh and aah over players who are hardly household names.
>
> Such as McBride.
>
> The 6-foot-1, 170-pound, two-time All-American forward from St Louis University was the first player chosen, instantly be-coming the answer to a trivia question.[2]

(McBride would go on to star for the Crew for eight seasons, give them sixty-two goals and forty-five assists in 162 appearances, be named to the MLS All-Time Best XI team, and leave MLS in 2004 to play with then–Premier League side Fulham for five years; one could do worse with a #1 pick.)

Assembling full team rosters to complement the stars and top draft picks was one of the league's initial challenges. DC United general man-ager and MLS board member Kevin Payne, who likened the league's early days to "building an airplane while in flight," noted, "You're building your roster on the fly. We had no idea how different players were going to respond to whatever environment we ended up having in terms of level of play in our league. Our roster, in particular, underwent pretty dramatic revision in the first few months of the season."[3]

A fascinating oral history longform article on MLS's birth, published in *Sports Illustrated* just before the 2015 MLS All-Star Game, chronicles amazing stories of some of the players that league and team officials corralled into MLS: *Melrose Place* actor Andrew Shue signing with the LA Galaxy and eventually appearing in five matches as part of a "player-marketing" deal; Bosnian refugee Said Fazlagić, who reportedly showed up to a combine with a worn pair of soccer shoes and a photo of him from a Bosnian newspaper clipping; Jorge Campos, who Gulati cornered in a San Diego stadium as the Mexican national team was coming out to play an exhibition match; and Steve Ralston, who would become MLS's first Rookie of the Year, being picked up in a car by a member of Tampa's front office to talk terms and then signing a contract on the hood of his car.[4]

In its first years, MLS got off to what could be retrospectively and correctly called a rocky start. Before the start of the second season, Doug Logan, the league's first commissioner, predicted an average attendance of 20,000, which would have required a considerable jump from the first-year totals to meet that milestone. As I noted in *The United States of Soccer*, top league officials differed in their view of Logan's proclamation. While deputy commissioner Mark Abbott saw the 20,000 goal as optimism from an optimistic CEO, Payne saw the milestone as a "millstone around [their] necks."[5]

Ultimately, the second-season attendance numbers felt short of predictions, and Logan had created a perception of a league that couldn't reach its attendance goals, and therefore failing solely based on that metric. As Payne noted, "For years, every MLS game story started out, in the first paragraph, there was always a mention of the attendance [. . .] it was always part of the story about MLS games. It took us a long time to lose that."[6]

The league did expand from ten teams to twelve in its third season. The Chicago Fire franchise proved an immediate success, drawing an ethnically diverse cross-section of fans to Soldier Field and winning an MLS Cup and a US Open Cup in its debut season. The Miami Fusion was dogged with inconsistent attendance numbers and a well-intentioned but struggling owner, Ken Horowitz, who puzzled over the too-modest results of his marketing efforts and cursed the stormy South Florida summer weather for keeping potential fans away. The Fusion enjoyed on-the-field success, particularly in a historic 2001 season under the direction of broadcaster-turned-coach named Ray Hudson, who told me in a 2016 interview that his training regimen for the team oscillated between days of intense workouts and days of hanging out at the beach with their girl-friends. That team, as it turns out, may have been the best team in MLS history to not win an MLS Cup.

Alas, the hopeful promise of "there's always next season" turned out not to be the case for Fusion fans. The 2001 season came to a close with two teams (Dallas and Tampa) still owned by the league itself rather than investor-operators. Horowitz felt as though he couldn't proceed losing money fielding and marketing the Fusion. Attendance numbers had picked up in response to the team's improved play, but not to the level Horowitz needed to forge on.

The relatively new league commissioner who took over for Logan in the middle of the 1999 season, Don Garber, conferred with his board and developed a plan to save the league. MLS would contract both Florida teams, accept Phil Anschutz's offer to assume control of addi-tional teams (bringing his allotment to six), and place control of the for-merly unowned Dallas Burn with Lamar Hunt, adding to his franchises in Columbus and Kansas City. Furthermore, the league would adopt aus-terity measures to allow teams to right themselves financially until they could become attractive to new investor-operators once again.

There was also one important facet to the plan which significantly involved US Soccer: the Soccer United Marketing partnership I mentioned in Chapter 1, which initially sought to generate money by shopping the American broadcast rights to the 2002 and 2006 World Cups, as well as the 2003 Women's World Cup and select MLS matches.

I also remarked in Chapter 1 that young, ascendant MLS players like Landon Donovan and DaMarcus Beasley entered the 2002 World Cup as relative unknowns, and returned as national heroes, able to play before American soccer audiences with their MLS teams immediately upon their return. As both Garber and deputy commissioner Mark Abbott acknowl-edged in interviews with me, that World Cup and the audience it drew was vital to MLS's survival.

While its audience was reined in some by the high hurdle of time zone disparity, the USMNT's successful tournament run made the 2006 World Cup—especially with what Germany offered in the way of time zone and logistical possibilities—a hotter commodity for potential broadcast advertisers. In the interim, the presence of recognizable American heroes in MLS made those televised matches more enticing for viewers who wanted to stay acquainted with them.

In part thanks to the gains made by SUM, and in part thanks to the austerity measures actually working, MLS survived its near-death experience, returning to relative health and even, by 2005, expansion. That year, the league added two teams. One was the oddly named Real Salt Lake, a paean to the Real Madrid team that owner Dave Checketts felt a special kinship toward. The other was Chivas USA, initially an American offshoot of the Liga MX powerhouse team Club Deportivo Guadalajara (best known to fans by its nickname "Chivas," Spanish for "young goats"), but also the unlikely launching pad for Brad Guzan, who became the team's first SuperDraft pick in 2005, winning major minutes that season en route to becoming the league's Goalkeeper of the Year in 2007 and a reputation-making move to then–Premier League team Aston Villa the following season. In its second season, Chivas USA also helped bolster new coach Bob Bradley's reputation, making the playoffs under Bradley's tutelage following a historically moribund inaugural season.[7]

In 2007, a little more than a decade into its existence, MLS was still a welcome landing place for American players to get regular, first-team soccer in games with stakes—the very thing that Gansler and others like him had been hoping for when the nation was between first-division leagues. But its reputation was about to change dramatically with the arrival of David Beckham. The iconic English soccer star who had played with Manchester United and Real Madrid, perhaps the two most beloved *and* reviled, wealthiest, most famous clubs in the world, came to the Los Angeles Galaxy at age thirty-one, presumably with at least five good years remaining in his already remarkable career. Some speculated that the LA location and its potential for business and branding was as much or even more of a draw than the soccer, but the announcement of his arrival sparked genuine curiosity and excitement from Americans who had previously regarded MLS with peripheral attention at best.

A 2012 ESPN article, looking back at the five-year anniversary of the signing, labeled Beckham the "world's most marketable footballer," detailed his struggles to get into the Real Madrid starting eleven as a salient plot point leading to the move to America, and noted the immediate enthusiasm boost he gave: "His reception in LA saw the season ticket sales for the club's 27,000-capacity stadium, the Home Depot Center, jump by more than 3,000 by February. The Galaxy also had to restrict their annual trials to 800 people—each of whom paid $130 (£65) to try to win the one place up for grabs in the squad—after thousands had applied."[8]

Beckham's arrival didn't result in immediate success on the field, though. The Galaxy didn't win an MLS Cup until 2011, with the championship game's lone goal symbolically involving all three of the Galaxy's stars in the buildup to the goal: Beckham; Irish striker Robbie Keane, arguably the final missing puzzle piece to turn the Galaxy into true contenders; and Landon Donovan, the goal scorer, who came to the Galaxy in 2005 and became the team's talismanic player (even aside Beckham) for nearly a decade. Despite Don Garber's proclamation upon the 2007 signing that "people are going to feel really good about David Beckham spending the rest of his career in the US,"[9] Beckham ended up leaving Los Angeles after the 2012 season, and another MLS Cup triumph, to close out his career with Paris Saint-Germain.

But it wasn't just Beckham the player, in his six seasons with MLS, who had an impact on the league. The league created a mechanism to allow Beckham to be signed and for the team to engage in the financial intricacies needed to make the signing work under the league's salary cap rules. The Designated Player Rule (or "Beckham Rule," as it's colloquially known) allows an MLS franchise to accommodate a star player whose salary might otherwise push an entire team's salary cap past its limits. The rule has been modified in subsequent years, allowing each MLS team to have up to three designated players, and in some cases, to effectively sign a fourth designated player by paying and demoting an existing designated player at the time of the new player acquisition through what is called "targeted allocation money."

As Garber told me in 2015, the Designated Player Rule was borne of a desire from MLS fans to bring more recognizable "name players" to the league following a 2006 World Cup in which more American fans than any cycle prior watched name players on the world stage. The fact that it was initially activated to bring in someone with Beckham's brand name wasn't just happenstance. Over time, the rule has built a perception that MLS serves as a "retirement league" for past-their-prime European players, and there have indeed been even recent, prominent examples of players with long, storied careers overseas finishing their careers in MLS. New York City FC named English international Frank Lampard one of its initial three designated players; he entered the league in 2015 along with fellow English international Steven Gerrard, who the Galaxy brought in under the same circumstances. The legends retired within three months of each other after completing their second MLS seasons in 2016.

And yet, overall, the retirement league moniker is becoming less and less true. Keane, in a November 2013 *Daily Mirror* article delightfully titled "US soccer is no doddle," on the occasion of extending his time with the Galaxy via a two-year contract, dismissed the "retirement league" notion, noting that designated players weathered more pressure due to their status. "Over here, when you're one of the three designated players, the pressure is on you more because players look up to you," he said. "They expect you to do something on the field if things aren't going right but in the Premiership you could have seventeen players who can do that. In America, if you're struggling in games, they'll look to you to do something so, in that respect, there's a lot of pressure."[10]

A cursory look over the 2017 MLS list of designated players shows general managers are locating players who can withstand that pressure and make the contributions expected of a player for whom rules around salaries and salary caps have been established.

Atlanta United FC, not content to ease into its inaugural season, signed three young South Americans—Paraguayan midfielder Miguel Almirón, Argentine striker/winger Héctor Villalba, and Venezuelan striker Josef Martínez—to push the new franchise beyond mere relevance into full-on excitement.

The Chicago Fire brought Bastian Schweinsteiger to MLS in March 2017, after the World Cup–winning anchor of the German national team, also a core player at Bayern Munich for more than a decade, completed a two-year experiment with Manchester United. The move transformed one of 2016's most moribund franchises into one of 2017's best. (Though the Fire's December 2016 acquisition of Serbian-Hungarian striker Nemanja Nikolić from Legia Warsaw, a lower-profile move at the time, turned out to be arguably as instrumental to their success. Nikolić scored twenty-four goals in his debut MLS season, winning the league's Golden Boot trophy.)

The two expansion teams in 2015, Orlando City SC and New York City FC, used designated player announcements to generate enthusiasm around the club as well as to anchor their rosters. Kaká arrived via Real Madrid and AC Milan as the Florida team's first designated player, while New York City FC made a splash in a city well accustomed to splashes by signing Spanish legend David Villa and Italian legend Andrea Pirlo, in addition to Lampard, with their three slots. (Villa has flourished, scoring at least eighteen goals and making the MLS All-Star team in each of his first three seasons in the league.)

Nicolás Lodeiro, a talented Uruguyan midfielder brought in from Argentine super-club Boca Juniors on July 27, 2016, propelled Seattle Sounders FC, improbably, to its first-ever MLS Cup. Three days prior to his signing, the Sounders suffered a demoralizing 3–0 loss to Sporting Kansas City that left the team ninth out of ten teams in the Western Conference, seemingly out of playoff contention. Two days later, the team and longtime coach Sigi Schmid agreed to a mutual parting of ways. Even before the Lodeiro-led Sounders completed their destiny by beating Toronto FC on a frigid Ontario night to claim the Cup, MLS players, management, and media voted Lodeiro as MLS Newcomer of the Year, over Columbus Crew SC's Ola Kamara, the Galaxy's Jelle Van Damme, and the Colorado Rapids' Shkëlzen Gashi.[11]

But a number of MLS clubs also feature key US national players in designated player roles. Graham Zusi, one of Sporting Kansas City's designated players, has been with the club his entire career, starting in 2009 when they were still the Kansas City Wizards. Both Michael Bradley and

Jozy Altidore came to Toronto FC, from Roma in 2014 and Sunderland in 2015 respectively, to play out the second halves of their twenties in MLS as opposed to overseas. Alejandro Bedoya made a similar move in 2016, at age twenty-nine, foregoing a professional career in Europe (peaking with three years at Ligue 1 club Nantes) to join the Philadelphia Union.

But of course, even before those oft-capped American players returned to MLS from abroad, Clint Dempsey's 2013 move to Seattle signaled a change in the perception of how top American players should and did regard MLS. When Dempsey was transferred from the New England Revolution to Fulham in December 2006, it was seen as the very move that ambitious American players should be making.

And yet, MLS declared Dempsey's return to Seattle to be the league's Story of the Year on its website. "If you're the type who tracks notable milestones in the beautiful game's slow but inexorable spread across the North American sociocultural landscape, those heady days at the beginning of August won't soon be forgotten," wrote Charles Boehm on MLS's website. The year-end retrospective acknowledged that Dempsey's addition to the Sounders didn't pay immediate championship-winning dividends on the field, for Seattle was ousted by its Portland rivals in the conference semifinals that year. But Boehm argued having a top-tier US international was invaluable for generating enthusiasm about the league, and the fact that the Sounders were able to sign and pay a player of Dempsey's caliber sent a powerful message about the financial health of the league.[12]

At the time of the signing, MLSsoccer.com's Jeff Bradley noted, "We've never seen a move like this in MLS, with an American player who'd made it big in one of Europe's top league, still in his prime, coming home to play in the league."[13]

But would the league provide enough of a test for Dempsey? Klinsmann was skeptical that MLS—certainly, at least, in 2013—prepared players as adequately for international play as the Premier League or other top European leagues.

Even before Dempsey's move back to an MLS club, Klinsmann controversially told the *Wall Street Journal*, as part of a larger article on the culture of mediocrity Klinsmann was trying to transform: "[Dempsey] hasn't made s——. You play for Fulham? Yeah, so? Show me you can play for a Champions League team, and then you start on a Champions League team. There is always another level. If you one day reach the highest level then you've got to confirm it, every year."[14]

The freewheeling interview also criticized those who still lauded the 2002 World Cup run, with Klinsmann saying, "Just because you won a game in the World Cup in the knockout stage, you haven't won anything."[15]

The article contrasted a German populace that seemed to live or die with their national team's performance with a more relaxed attitude from American fans and players. But the comment about Dempsey was still resonant, and definitely on Graham Ruthven's mind when he interviewed Klinsmann the week after the Dempsey signing was announced. Klinsmann told Ruthven, regarding the sentiment of that comment:

I've not changed my mind, no. I'm always there to push them to the next level. That won't change.

In Clint's case there are different views on his move. On one hand it's fantastic for MLS to have him back in America. He'll inspire kids to play soccer. The challenge for him is to keep up his standard. He has to maintain the level he's set for himself over the past two years and I'll be there pushing him to do that. We won't let his game slip.

We always take personal circumstances into consideration, and with Clint and Landon that's a factor. But I'll always challenge my players to push for the next level and that means playing in the big European leagues.[16]

Jeremiah Oshan, commenting on the Ruthven interview for the Sounder at Heart blog, remarked, "No, Klinsmann isn't exactly bashing Dempsey's move, but you don't have to read too far between the lines that he wouldn't have recommended the move if he'd been asked. Of course, Dempsey didn't ask Klinsmann and he shouldn't feel as though he had to. Dempsey obviously felt this was a good time to return to MLS and there's every reason to believe that he'll remain sharp while he's here." He added, "One of the ongoing themes of his media tour yesterday was that Dempsey rejects the idea that playing in Europe is automatically better for a player than being in MLS. He pointed out that plenty of teams don't play 'good soccer,' that taking the winter off may actually be good for him and playing meaningful minutes is probably better than fighting for playing time."[17]

The debate over Dempsey reminded Jeff Bradley of Donovan's return to MLS from the Bundesliga in 2005. "I can tell you that Bruce Arena, then the coach of the US national team, was not thrilled," he wrote. But Arena also realized he could not control where Donovan would live and play. Arena's oft-repeated line back then was: 'Landon seems to play his best when he's happy. He's happy in MLS.' And then Arena would talk about how Landon was 'the guy' in MLS and how that was a unique challenge in itself."[18]

The question reactivated by Dempsey's decision remains one of the great quandaries of American player development: If a player joins a team in the Premier League or the Bundesliga—the two upper-tier leagues that have invited in American players in recent decades—is it better for that player to learn and practice with what is believed to be the higher grade of player there, or is there more value in playing for MLS and getting more consistent playing time?

If you're a once-in-a-generation talent like Christian Pulisic, you get to bypass the debate entirely by earning ample playing time in both the Bundesliga and the Champions League for one of Europe's best teams. If you're one of Pulisic's contemporaries—Bobby Wood comes to mind here—you can have a meaningful experience even at the bottom end of the Bundesliga table, as he did with Hamburger SV in the 2016–17 season, performing well enough to renew his contract.

And yet, choosing MLS no longer has the "settling" connotations it once might have had. As we'll explore in the next chapter, MLS has been taking cumulative evolutionary steps, even in the four years before the 2014 World Cup qualifying cycle and the 2018 World Cup qualifying cycle, that are narrowing the gap between Premier League–quality and MLS–quality.

Dempsey, though talented enough to fare well in the Premier League, as evinced by his fifty goals in 184 matches at Fulham, chose more regular playing time with Seattle over what he experienced in his final full Premier League season, with just seven goals in twenty-nine matches. Since returning to MLS, Dempsey has been a consistent performer when healthy; while his goal and assist totals aren't quite as eye-popping as Villa's, they've been on par with the league's top echelon of players, and numbers don't account for the disruptive effect his offensive movement has on opposing teams.

He did, however, develop an irregular heartbeat in August 2016 and was sidelined for the remainder of the season, missing the MLS Cup–winning run fans pictured him leading when he arrived in Seattle three years prior. Dempsey only returned to action in February 2017, but in the pair of World Cup qualifiers the month after he scored a hat trick in a 6–0 rout of Honduras and scored the only American goal in a 1–1 draw with Panama, bringing him one goal from tying Donovan's all-time USMNT goal-scoring record. The fifty-seventh and tying goal would come in the team's Gold Cup semifinals win against Costa Rica. The anticipated, tiebreaking fifty-eighth goal never came during the USMNT's qualifying run; certainly, an equalizing goal against Trinidad & Tobago to send the Yanks to one more World Cup would have cemented Dempsey's legacy—and maybe even his case as the best American player ever.

Sebastian Giovinco, Toronto FC's diminutive striker, provides evidence—perhaps in confounding fashion—that MLS is a league where talented European players in their prime can thrive. Giovinco came to TFC as a designated player in January 2015, broke the league's record for combined goals and assists in his debut season with twenty-two goals and sixteen assists, and followed up in 2016 with a nearly-as-impressive seventeen goals and fifteen assists. A product of the Juventus youth system, he debuted with its senior team in 2007—when it was uncharacteristically in second-division Serie B, and not the top-tier Serie A it has dominated in recent years. He was developed on loan spells to two other Italian clubs, as well as by getting playing time with the team quaintly known as the Old Lady.

He also debuted for Italy's senior international team in 2011, which is precisely what you'd expect promising young strikers playing for Juventus to do.[19]

Giovinco's move to MLS has not endeared him to Italian coaches; in fact, they've expressed a bias against Giovinco and fellow Juventus-turned-MLS-player Pirlo strictly for their decision to play their club soccer in North America. In May 2016, then-Italian coach Antonio Conte snubbed both Giovinco and Pirlo for the thirty-man Euro 2016 roster, saying, "It's normal that if you choose to go and play there then you can pay the consequences in footballing terms." Giovinco was passed over for Graziano Pellè, Eder, Ciro Immobile, Lorenzo Insigne, and Simone Zaza, then all playing with top European teams.[20] (Italy would go on to lose to Germany in the Euro quarterfinals in a penalty shootout, including a historically and comically bad attempt by Zaza, who'd actually been subbed on late in extra time, specifically with his participation in a penalty kick in mind.)

Six months later, after Conte moved from the Azzurri to shepherd Premier League giant Chelsea, new Italy manager Giampiero Ventura passed over Giovinco for World Cup qualifiers for the same reason as his predecessor. "I have done everything to help him but the reality is that he plays in a league that doesn't matter much," he said. "And the number of goals he scores is less important because with the quality he has got, he is bound to make a difference in that league. The problem is that if you play in that type of league, and you get used to playing in that type of league, it becomes a problem of mentality."[21]

Two days later, Giovinco's agent, Andrea D'Amico, came to his defense. He expressed surprise, and said that "without knowledge you can't have confidence," intimating that Ventura needed to do his homework and monitor not just those Italian national players in Serie A. D'Amico noted that "for an attacker, the numbers speak for themselves, and Sebastian is scoring a lot—more than many other of his fellow Italian players." He also pointed out that "MLS is a league full of top-level athletes," as competitive as the Russian Premier League where two other snubbed Italian players were plying their trade.[22]

The criticisms of the Italian coaches more likely reveal an uncomfortable xenophobia not too far afield from Americans who look askance at dual nationals for not being American enough than valid concerns about the relevance of MLS to international play. Indeed, Spain saw fit to call up a thirty-five-year-old Villa for two September 2017 World Cup qualifying matches, three years after he'd last represented them in competition.

"I think it's opened the door," said New York City FC manager Patrick Vieira—who is, like Villa, a member of a World Cup–winning team. "I think David going back to the national team just shows that you can make a decision to come to MLS and still have a big ambition, still have a chance to play for your national team. I think it will open doors for young international players and experienced international players. The league is competitive. Coming here, you will still have a chance to keep your place on the national team. This is a massive step forward for MLS."[23]

Regardless of the conclusion reached after weighing both Italy's shocking snub of Giovinco and Spain's equally shocking validation of late-career Villa, a fundamental question remains for both MLS's defenders and detractors: How good is MLS, in comparison to the rest of the world's leagues?

"My general feeling is that it's somewhere in the top twelve, maybe even the top ten at this point," said Matt Doyle, who has been with MLS since 2010, now serving as Senior Writer and author of MLSsoccer.com's Armchair Analyst column. "The longtime knock on the league has always been that the bottom tier of players are worse than you'd see in, say, Argentina or the Eredivisie or the Championship, but I don't think that holds true any longer. Even if it does, though, the top of the league is now so much better and deeper than it was. There aren't players like Giovinco or Villa or Almiron or Bradley in the Championship, right? So even if you want to point to those leagues and say 'they're deeper," you can point to MLS teams and players and say, 'Yeah, but this is better.'"

The league has also elevated play throughout CONCACAF. The Houston Dynamo, for example, ascended to the playoffs in 2017 with an international lineup including four Honduran international players, with Romell Quioto and Alberth Elis among them, and Panamanian international player Adolfo Machado, a key member of that World Cup bound–team. While Houston is currently the highest-profile MLS team with Central American talent, starters for the top tier of CONCACAF teams feature on a number of MLS rosters.

And more than one MLS player thinks that its teams—at least, its best teams—could compete respectably in one of the world's best leagues. ESPN conducted a survey of 123 MLS players in March 2016, asking them an array of questions and publishing results and comments under cloak of anonymity. One of the questions was, "Where would the best MLS team finish in the Premier League this season?" While none had the MLS team in the top four and winning one of the coveted Champions League places, 17 percent had them in fifth through ninth place, 50 percent had them in tenth through fourteenth, and 33 percent had them in danger of relegation (or outright relegation) in spots fifteen through twenty. The same survey did have 66 percent willing to leave MLS for a European league, though as one respondent qualified, "If the Premier League called tomorrow, of course. If it's to go play in the Finnish second division, I might as well go to the USL,"[24] referring to the second-division US league.

But FiveThirtyEight—the website best known for its presidential polling aggregation, but heavy on sports statistics and now an ESPN property—created a Global Club Soccer Rankings list in August 2017 assessing more than 400 club soccer teams from a number of leagues around the world. In their initial listing, the top eighty clubs were all European, starting with Champions League favorites and working down toward mid-table Premier League and La Liga teams, Turkish and Russian powers, and an assortment of Spanish and German squads. The top Western Hemisphere team was Boca Juniors from Argentina at #81, with its bitter rivals River Plate at #107, and Brazil's Corinthians is at #88. It wasn't until the #117 spot that CONCACAF got a shout out via Liga MX's Tigres. The best MLS team was even further down the list: Toronto FC, at #171.

The site's resident soccer expert, Michael Caley, explains that the index figures in the strength of individual leagues, "based on how well clubs from different leagues have done in direct competition with one another, such as in the Champions League," as well as the estimated market value of the teams' players.[25] Based on those metrics, MLS is at a marked disadvantage from top European leagues.

Despite the belief displayed by MLS players in the ESPN survey,

Caley observes that "MLS teams would generally fall in either the second or third divisions in the English pyramid. [New York City FC]—the second-highest ranking MLS side, at 259th—rates below the top 10 teams in the Championship." He concludes, based on the results of the survey, that "MLS still has a long way to go to match up with the top levels of club soccer."[26]

MLS teams do compete in one notable cross-league tournament, the CONCACAF Champions League, which started in the 2008–09 season to replace the CONCACAF Champions Cup. Currently, twenty-four teams from the federation's countries, with four each from Mexico and the US, compete in the tournament. Mexican teams have won every edition of the newly cast competition, although the prior version of the tournament was won on just two occasions by MLS teams: DC United in 1998 and the LA Galaxy in 2000.[27]

This track record led Caley to note, "The continuing failure of MLS clubs to advance in the CONCACAF Champions League leaves American and Canadian sides behind the best teams in Mexico." Ten top Liga MX teams appear above the MLS-topping Toronto FC in the ratings.[28] MLS has come close of late: The Montreal Impact got to the 2014–15 finals, losing 5–3 on aggregate to Mexico's America, even drawing in the initial leg in Azteca, before losing the return leg 4–2 at home. FC Dallas looked to be en route to the 2016–17 finals, but in their semifinals match with Pachuca, Hirving Lozano scoring a stoppage-time goal in the return leg match on Mexican soil, en route to winning an all-Liga MX finals over Tigres.

Those performances play into perceptions, fairly or not, about how the leagues compare.

"Despite moving on an upward trajectory, MLS isn't quite as technically proficient as Liga MX," says soccer journalist and self-proclaimed Mexican soccer fan Maxi Rodriguez. "Where Liga MX generally favors a bit more of a tactical game, I still think it's true that MLS is a bit more oriented towards an athletic approach. That's a stereotype, and there are teams in both leagues that that are either better or worse than the stereotype might assume, but that's the general truth in my opinion. It's not a bad thing either. People get stuck on which is better or worse, but ultimately, they both offer a unique product."

"Obviously, Liga MX has had a leg up on MLS," says former US international player and current ESPN analyst Hérculez Gómez. "Liga MX is ninety-something years old and has some teams that have been around for more than 100 years."

Gómez played in both leagues—he started in MLS in 2002 with the Galaxy, played for several American teams until 2010, when he journeyed from the Kansas City Wizards to Puebla to start a five-year Mexican tour including stints with Pachuca, Tecos, Santos Laguna, and Tijuana. Certainly, the league he returned to in 2015—for a Toronto team featuring Giovinco, Altidore, and Michael Bradley, before finishing his career in 2016 with the MLS Cup–winning Seattle team—was different than even the one he'd left a few years prior.

"Anybody who tells you MLS was better back then is a fool," says Gómez. "There are two different versions of MLS, pre-Beckham and post-Beckham. Post-Beckham, everything started changing. You had the designated player, you had more money to spend on players, the salary averages went up, you had academy systems sprouting up. On average, the average player got better, which is good. What I noticed when I got back, which was a big difference, was players were younger and they were better at a younger age, and that showed me huge progression."

In August 2017, another American-born, USMNT-capped player who found success in Liga MX, the then-twenty-two-year-old Paul Arriola, made a high-profile leap from Tijuana to DC United in what turned out to be the most expensive deal in DC United's history. In addition to paying Tijuana $3 million, DC United had to play allocation money to the LA Galaxy, which owned Arriola's MLS rights due to his involvement with the team's youth academy.[29]

"Liga MX is a wonderful league on the field," says Arriola. Though he alludes to challenges on the business side of the equation—as he quipped, "Sometimes you get paid on time and other times you wouldn't get paid on time"—he feels he's developed because of the quality of Mexican and South American players he faced, as well as his competition within Xolos to get starts.

"One to thirty, they're great players, and you really have to fight and perform to keep your spot," he says. "It's easy for the coach to put another guy in your position. And I think that that really helped me raise my level." That has suited Arriola well, as he describes himself as a "young and hungry player"—so much so that he relished the opportunity to go to a franchise that was dead last in its conference at the time of his signing.

"I wanted to improve a team; I didn't want to be the cherry on top of the team. I still have a lot to prove to myself, to the league, to my team-mates, to the national team. I wanted to make an impact. In Liga MX, I had decided to go down there knowing you had to prove yourself every time. The pressure was more internal."

"Here, as far as performing now in MLS, I come to a team where I was the highest-paid transfer in the club's history, and there's a lot of ex-pectation on me," he notes, adding that using the challenge to turn around a once storied, currently struggling club, to propel himself to the next level of his development, was, "in the end, an easy decision."

Arriola's determination to help DC United return to the playoffs is made possible, in part, by two features that keeps MLS slightly out of lockstep with top world leagues—its use of playoffs to determine the league champion, and its promise that every team that is in MLS will be allowed to stay in MLS the following season.

The idea of a team being expelled from the NFL or NBA just for hav-ing a bad season might seem ridiculous, yet that's what a number of American soccer fans want for MLS, insisting it won't make the next leap in its evolution until it adopts the promotion-relegation system that many other top soccer leagues around the world use.

In the Premier League, to use the most familiar example of such a system to American fans, the three worst teams in the twenty-team league drop into the second-tier league, the confusingly named Championship, at the end of the season, replaced by Championship teams who play their way into the Premier League. To get back into the Premier League, a de-moted team must spend at least one full season in English soccer's equiv-alent of baseball's AAA-level minor league and can only get back the way its replacement did: By finishing first or second and winning automatic promotion, or finishing anywhere from third through sixth and success-fully navigating a two-round playoff.

The relegated teams theoretically use parachute payments plus their own resources to marshal squad improvements, though relegation motivates some players to find new top-tier teams to sign with rather than going down with the ship. This puts those teams at an initial, additional disadvantage. Plus, the parachute payment system has received recent scrutiny, with some Premier League shareholders concerned that owners of relegated teams might just be pocketing the funds rather than investing them in players.

Some players are in favor of it—ESPN's March 2017 player survey revealed that 54 percent of the respondents favored promotion-relegation, compared to 49 percent in 2016 and 64 percent in 2015[30]—and at least one coach, the New York Red Bulls' Jesse Marsch, in an August 2017 interview with ESPN's Taylor Twellman, has come out in favor of it, expressing a belief that it "just raises the stakes and gives so much hope to some of these smaller clubs." He also, in the interview, endorsed the narrative that Premier League shareholders are beginning to question, saying that owners "should have to continue to put money into it and invest in the right areas and do the right things to continue to be in MLS."[31]

MLS has been resistant to adopting a promotion-relegation system because of how the league was initially set up—as a single-entity structure with investor-operators overseeing individual teams—and with franchises going for $150 million for the current round of expansion, a hefty climb from the original mid-1990s fee of $5 million. Garber has made it clear that he's not interested in asking a new ownership team to buy into the league at such a sum, only to jettison those owners from the league for an indeterminate period of time should they finish at the bottom of the standings. And it's simply unthinkable that an MLS team could drop into one of the lesser leagues, as a typical NASL or United Soccer League (USL) stadium holds about a third of what a typical MLS stadium holds.

While passionate promotion-relegation advocates are dismissive of Garber, his vision, his leadership, and his sticking to a difficult austerity plan in the 2000s have all helped the league come a long way from its beginnings. Both Beasley and Donovan, who were teenagers debuting in the league and then featuring in the World Cup that would help lift it out of crisis, marvel at its transformation from when they first became part of it.

"When I came back in 2014, I was blown away," says Beasley, who'd left MLS in 2004 for a ten-year world tour that took him to PSV Eindhoven, Manchester City, Rangers, Hannover 96, and Puebla. "Even the media coverage now is not like it was then. Everything has changed: The stadiums, our training facilities, the product on the field is 100 percent better. You get a lot of young international players here now and it wasn't like that back then. The quality of the league is getting there. Obviously, it's not there yet, but it's getting better, on the field and off the field. It's a whole different ballgame."

"The changes are dramatic and drastic," says Donovan, reflecting on all that happened over his lengthy MLS career. "We played in massive football stadiums around the country with very little crowds. We paid to be on TV, or paid to produce the telecasts. There was very little sponsorship, player salaries were $15,000 a year in some cases. The product on the field was at times pretty slow. When you juxtapose that with today, with sold-out soccer specific stadiums, huge sponsorship deals with the Adidas one they just signed"—here, Donovan refers to the six-year, $700 million that dwarfs the league's previous sponsorship deals[32]—"huge personalities coming to play and to coach in the league, franchise fees that will now go for $150 million-plus, it's night and day the way things have changed. For those of us who have been there for a long time, it's really exciting to see."

And it's not just the economics and the infrastructure—Doyle sees the quality of play improving greatly. "MLS is better than it was in 2015, and much better than it was in 2012," he notes. "All the indications are there that it will continue to improve over the next five years, and that improvement is, in my opinion, much more important than a somewhat arbitrary opinion about where the league fits big picture among what are considered the best leagues in the world."

An improving MLS is the proverbial rising tide that lifts all boats—while more robust competition brings challenges and growth opportunities to the American players in MLS, it will also give those same advantages to the USMNT's CONCACAF rivals and the growing number of South American players testing their talents in MLS—especially with the league poised to expand to at least twenty-eight teams in the next decade.

And the league's improvement isn't just limited to what's seen on the field right now. The growth of MLS academies has allowed teams to take promising young players and develop them, over the course of years, into players capable of starting in MLS and even in European leagues currently regarded above the MLS tier.

CHAPTER 4

MLS ACADEMIES: THE NEW TIP OF THE SPEAR

THE RELATIONSHIP BETWEEN MLS AND US SOCCER PLAYER DEVELOPMENT, enabled in large part by the MLS academy becoming *de rigueur* over the last decade, became more intertwined than ever before in February 2017. That month, US Soccer announced the second-largest-ever expansion for its Development Academy (DA), the network of MLS academies and local independently run soccer clubs for youth players, launched in 2007 as part of US Soccer's efforts to oversee and support player development throughout the nation. The seventeen new member clubs would bring DA's roster to nearly 200 member clubs. In the fall of 2017, as an indication that the model initiated for the boys was working, US Soccer launched a separate Girls' Development Academy for aspiring USWNT players.[1]

The inclusion of Minnesota United FC's academy was arguably the most significant addition of the seventeen, indicating the growing influence of MLS academies on player development. With Minnesota's new academy on board, the academies for all MLS teams (save for Toronto FC, which provides training for aspiring Canadian national players and chooses not to align with its southern rivals) were affiliated with the DA.

Even the academies for the other two Canadian MLS teams, in Montreal and Vancouver, are US Development Academy members. Even the academy for expansion team Los Angeles FC, which was up and running even before the team officially started play in 2018, added a U-13 and U-14 division to its already-operational U-12 division as part of the February 2017 expansion movement, presumably with plans to add players older than 14 as committed U-14 academy players aged into the U-15 category.[2]

While independent youth soccer clubs are still involved in player development—as they have been for decades—MLS academies have taken on a more defined and prominent role in developing players since the DA was first launched. Academy-developed players aren't just finding their way onto MLS first-team rosters. Nearly every MLS team either fields a second team or has a relationship with a team in the United Soccer League (USL), giving those teams a place for U-20 and U-23 academy-trained players to get seasoning if they're not yet ready for MLS prime-time. And significantly, for US Soccer, these players are also developing to the level of making USMNT U-20, U-23, and senior team rosters.

MLS teams didn't launch academies when the league started in 1996, according to league Executive Vice President Todd Durbin, for two major reasons. As Durbin explains, the first was a purposeful strategy to "allocate top young players across the league through a draft." Durbin asserts that the guiding principle of competitive balance has always been core to MLS—specifically, "the notion that, on Opening Day, every team has a chance at winning MLS Cup." Durbin and the other architects of MLS, including future US Soccer president Sunil Gulati, saw the draft as the best vehicle available for helping teams at the bottom of the standings to improve themselves.

The second was simply the economics the league faced as it was trying to attract and keep players and fans. "If our owners had a decision to make between putting an extra million dollars into the players on the field or the stadiums or into infrastructure [. . .] at least, at the time, the thinking was we had more immediate needs." Plus, the league didn't initially need to create its own players; Durbin notes that between college soccer and the existing youth club soccer system, MLS was able to populate its draft. (Though it's important to note that college soccer programs today have a decidedly more diminished role in producing MLS players compared to when the league started.)

Yet MLS has sought a role in player development for almost its entire history. The Nike Project 40 program initiated in 1997—now sponsored by Adidas and called Generation Adidas—identifies top college players and youth national team players. MLS then signs them to contracts, making them available in the annual SuperDraft, with those players drafted not counting against those teams' salary budgets.[3] Several players selected for the 2017 SuperDraft through the program made an impact in their rookie seasons. These include Minnesota United's Abu Danladi, who came to the US via Ghana through the Right to Dream program creating a pipeline from Africa to MLS, and New York City FC's Jonathan Lewis, who was also a 2017 US U-20 national team call-up.[4]

Even though that program brought its share of quality players to the draft, Durbin and other league officials realized the draft might not be enough. "If you want to improve the quality of players in your league, there's only two ways to do it," Durbin said. "One is to go out and import players, and the other is to produce players. And so we realized that this is an area that we should be involved in, and quite frankly, we should be rewarding teams for their participation in this."

This led them to examine the landscape of American player development, and they determined there were what Durbin called "systemic issues" in the youth club system interfering with what they wanted out of the process.

"One of these issues was the 'pay for play' model where players are on teams on the basis of their ability to pay," Durbin notes, concerned that the fees associated with becoming to a club team "does certainly remove not an insignificant segment of the population."

The second issue, according to Durbin, was a "priority on winning." As he explains, "If you are trying to win, if that's what you are about, you do two things. You dictate your training during the week on the basis of winning. You also pick your players based on winning, as opposed to trying to pick players and coach on the basis of what those players are going to look like five or 10 years down the line. And so, the benchmark for youth clubs before we got involved was how many trophies [they win] and how successful they are, as opposed to our very important goal, which is how many quality professionals are we producing. And when you have that goal it will make you, or should make you, behave differently."

This led MLS to make what Durbin terms a "fundamental sea change" and to tell clubs, as Durbin voices it, "If you start a youth academy, and you develop those players, then you will actually get the benefit and the reward of having those players on your roster." That benefit manifests most obviously in the league's Homegrown Player Rule—both in how MLS develops its own players and how MLS is impacting US Soccer. Started in 2008, the rule encourages teams to sign players being developed in its academies, rather than placing them into the MLS SuperDraft where they could conceivably be drafted by any team. To further incentivize teams, the rule notes "there is no limit to the number of homegrown players a club may sign in a given year. Players that are signed as homegrown players are not counted against the team's salary budget."[5]

A club whose academy trains a player for at least a year, provided that player has accumulated a set number of contact hours, can claim that player as a homegrown player. The club can use up to $200,000 of its targeted allocation money (which clubs use to improve their rosters per MLS's tangle of rules) to sign homegrown players.

As of August 2017, there were a record 101 homegrown players in the league according to MLS's front office, with goals, assists, and minutes played numbers also reaching record levels. Eight of those players received at least one cap for the USMNT. Illustrating that MLS is also a Canadian league, twenty homegrown players have been capped at least once for Canada's national team.

MLSsoccer.com analyst Matt Doyle sees the Homegrown Player Rule as one of two MLS innovations allowing the league to better fill its key roster spots and making the top-to-bottom talent pool in the league approach the levels of the world's best leagues, with the Targeted Allocation Money Rule being the other.

"FC Dallas plays better soccer because they have guys like Kellyn Acosta," Doyle says. "Seattle won the 2016 MLS Cup, and the US won the 2017 Gold Cup in part because of Jordan Morris. Basically, if there's no homegrown initiative, there's no future for MLS."

Doyle sees an impact even for teams who aren't regular playoff contenders, noting, "Philly's academy will come good sooner or later, and

we've seen Real Salt Lake start to get results with the kids playing prominent roles." He predicts over the next five years, as more local, academy-
developed players break into their first teams, the impact of the
Homegrown Player Rule will become more and more apparent.

It's even helping expansion teams out of the gate. Atlanta United debuted in MLS in 2017 to massive, enthusiastic crowds, and debuted its
first homegrown player—U-17 national youth team standout Andrew
Carleton—two weeks before his seventeenth birthday.

Carleton thinks about playing in Europe, noting, "Definitely, at some
point in my career, I want to play overseas; it's always been a dream of
mine." But he's finding the chance to play first-time minutes in MLS,
while still in his teens, invaluable to his development. As he observes,
"With Atlanta, I just want to truly be able to break into the first team,
and to keep moving up and getting more playing time. In a couple of
years, I'd like to be starting and playing more games. I love it in Atlanta,
and the fans here make it ten times more fun. To be able to play in front
of them just makes me hungrier to do it more."

The rule's importance, however, is felt beyond the players who stay
and the teams that keep them.

Doyle notes that the Red Bulls turned a sizable profit in developing
defender Matt Miazga and selling him to Premier League powers
Chelsea—for a reported $5 million, enough to land him in the top ten
for transfer fees involving American players.[6]

Those market forces impact the decisions of players as well as teams.
For instance, Tyler Adams, the emerging young Red Bulls star and US
youth national team player, was swayed to sign a homegrown player deal
in part from seeing what happened with Miazga. "It made my decision
even easier," he told ESPN FC's Jeff Rueter. "There's always the option
that, if you do well in the system you're at, there could be a bigger move
later on in your career."[7]

"Even the smallest MLS market has so much local talent that producing successful pros should be very, very repeatable, and therefore prof-
itable," Doyle observed. "At some point, MLS teams have to jump into
the world market with both feet and sell these guys at a profit. I'm not
sure everybody in the league understands that, though."

Plus, as he notes, there's the occasional player who can only go so far in MLS. For instance, he sees Acosta as a player who could develop new facets of his game in Germany or Italy. Conversely, he sees some young American players who moved from tutelage at MLS academies or US Development Academy-affiliated programs to English clubs—namely, Emerson Hyndman and Lynden Gooch—as players who would benefit from a return stateside. He also notes that Cameron Carter-Vickers, a US international center-back born in England who trained through the Tottenham Hotspur academy system but couldn't find meaningful minutes with the London team's first squad, "would do well to find any team in any league that would actually play him in real games," be it MLS or elsewhere. (In the fall of 2017, Carter-Vickers was loaned to Sheffield United, and then, in January 2018, to Ipswich Town for just that purpose.)

At the time that the Homegrown Player Rule was launched, most MLS teams didn't have academies. Now, they all do. What's more, as Durbin notes, "They are now in it aggressively and are now thinking about player development as a as a business unto itself. That is, they are in the business of producing professional players. You can imagine that is a very different goal than most of the other youth academies across the country."

Durbin believes that MLS "offers a pretty unique situation" for young American and Canadian players facing the quandary of where to launch their careers. For those players, he believes "your best chance for being a successful professional long-term is to start your career here in MLS, and whether that means stay here, or decide to go someplace else [later], I think it's a secondary issue."

The attractiveness of MLS, to Durbin, has a lot to do with the designated players the league has attracted. This gives young players, as he sees it, "the ability to be play in matches with players that are World Cup veterans and have played at a high level internationally. I would argue it is the absolute best training environment they can be in."

But it's also important for players to have the foundation that an MLS academy can give them—to be, as he observes, "in a system that actually truly knows you better than anybody else, knows what your strengths are, knows what your weaknesses are, and is in the best position to help you progress."

When you move clubs, irrespective of age, even the teams that do the most scouting haven't seen you train day and day out for four years," he continues. "They haven't seen you play in fifty matches. They don't know your temperament. They don't know your psychology. They don't know any of that. They're just not going to be in the same position to help you grow as a professional player."

Ultimately, Durbin feels that the Homegrown Player Rule is important because it helps develop players that raise the level of the league's overall play. "We understand that if we want to be among the best leagues in the world, that the quality of our player pool is going to be a function not only of the players that we sign internationally, but also the quality of the players that we produce domestically," he says. "That is the very backbone of our league. We need to be producing high quality players and we need to be producing them in sufficient numbers so that we can achieve our quality."

Because all MLS teams now have academies, the league has given each team its own designated territory. If a player lives in a team's territory, that team has the rights to recruit him as a homegrown player—incentivizing clubs to recruit players who could legitimately be seen as local. In fact, a team wanting to recruit a player in another team's territory can only do so if it gets permission from that team first.

While some sections of North America are open to whichever team wants to scout them, much of the US and Canada's population fall within the zones allotted to MLS teams.

Most of the territories are simply drawn as seventy-five-mile radius circles with the team's home stadium or training facility in the center. When Los Angeles FC came on board in early 2018, its circle made a Venn diagram with the Galaxy's, and those Angelenos inside the zone where both circles meet will get a choice. Some teams' territories aren't exclusively local, though, particularly if they're in markets that aren't densely populated beyond those team's urban cores.

The Sounders, for instance, get Hawaii as well as all of Washington, whereas the Timbers get Oregon, Idaho, and share New Mexico with the Rapids. Real Salt Lake gets Arizona as well as Utah. Minnesota United FC was naturally granted Minnesota (as it is the only MLS team to date named

for a state) and also awarded Wisconsin, save for parts of Milwaukee and
its surrounding regions within the seventy-five-mile radius belonging to
the Chicago Fire. Sporting Kansas City gets both Kansas and Missouri—
appropriate since its crest incorporates the state boundary bisecting its
hometown, though the team also gets Oklahoma, even though FC
Dallas's USL affiliate is based in Oklahoma City.

It's now possible for players who start as fans of a local team to get
to play for that team's academy, learn their system, move up the ranks,
and then get signed as a homegrown player. This, in Durbin's view, allows
both teams and players to "form connections in the community that are
deep and meaningful."

"We're the only sport in the United States and Canada where you
can train in the shadow of the very stadium you play in," Durbin notes.
Indeed, some of the league's stadiums are directly adjacent to multiple
fields on which academy players run through drills, scrimmage, and, for
certain select players and certain select times, get called into practices
with the first team.

FC Dallas Academy, one of the oldest MLS academies and widely regarded as one of the best, exemplifies Durbin's vision. Academy players
train on multiple grass and turf fields directly north of Toyota Stadium's
main concourse in Frisco, encountering North Texas's baffling array of
climes, with temperatures ranging from the twenties to the nineties (and
worse) throughout the year.

FC Dallas started its first development program, FC Dallas Youth,
in 2005, and launched the FC Dallas Academy under the FC Dallas
Youth umbrella three years later. The club "made it a point to start from
the ground up, beginning with teams at the youngest age brackets and
building their way up from there," MLSsoccer.com's Scott Sidway wrote
in his 2016 feature on the academy. "The strategy helped establish FC
Dallas as more than just another outlet to play soccer. They were able to
inculcate from an early age a culture of love and respect for the club with
an entire generation of players."

As Academy Director Luchi Gonzalez noted in that article, the initial
goal for the academy—aside from the obvious goal of finding and developing players able to play for FC Dallas—"was to create a community

of soccer, and from that, develop a community of lifelong fans for the club, family members that are going to grow up fans."

Sidway explains:

When Dan and Clark Hunt sat down to craft a new long-term strategy for the next phase of the club's development and carry out the vision of their late father, they knew they wanted to establish a model that encouraged young soccer players to come to Frisco to be part of something groundbreaking and potentially great.

Ultimately the FC Dallas owners tabbed [Óscar] Pareja, a former captain for the club from 1998 to 2005, to execute that vision and they named him Director of Player Development in the academy's inaugural year in July 2008. He spent the next three seasons building the academy from scratch, working on developing players in a system that was still unproven. And after three years, Pareja had elevated the academy to best-in-class among 70 other programs in the USA, and in the process earning him a reputation as one of the best coaches nationwide and his first senior head coaching job in Colorado.[8]

Pareja has been head coach at FC Dallas since 2014, and is one of the most respected and successful in the league. (He's also mentioned in some circles as a possible future coach for the USMNT.) While he's now responsible for the fortunes of the first team, he's still engaged with the Academy that he built his reputation on, and he sees it as the foundation for what FC Dallas is seeking to achieve.

"We're not just coaching them, but teaching them about every angle of the game," Pareja says of their approach. "We are getting these guys in international competition earlier. We're playing them as much as we can. The frequency of training here is just more aggressive. And then, the connection with the first team is crucial. We need to provide to them a real path, not as a romantic idea. It needs to be real."

Kellyn Acosta—heralded as the best player to come out of FC Dallas Academy to date—started there as a fourteen-year-old; four years later, in 2013, he'd worked up to making his first start for the first team, initially slotting in at right-back before working into his preferred deep mid-field role. He signed a homegrown contract with the club in July 2012—both showing commitment to the team that helped him develop and potentially setting himself for a Miazga-type move to Europe.

While Gonzalez understands why playing in Europe would appeal to Acosta, he also notes that Acosta's commitment to FC Dallas has better prepared him for following that path.

"He made a U-17 World Cup, he made a U-20 World Cup, he played in two of those because he was so young when he played in the first one," Gonzalez boasts. "He's a senior national team player now at 21 years old. He's got caps, he's got a high international transfer fee value [. . .] he's the perfect prototype for us. He's a player who maybe wants to play in Champions League one day. He wants to play in a World Cup. But he did it through our pathway, earning a contract with our first team, and knowing that's the springboard to playing overseas."

Gonzalez feels Acosta exemplifies what FC Dallas teaches, because he rates so highly in the five criteria by which the academy judges a player. And talent isn't one of them.

"No kid in our academy lacks talent," Gonzalez says. "They all have talent. Kellyn had phenomenal raw talent."

The five specific items the Academy team looks for are, in their estimation, how talented recruits cross over and become professionals. Gonzalez has pondered them enough to rank them.

"Fifth is athleticism," which he differentiates from raw talent by noting, "I'm not just talking about speed or size, I'm talking about coordination, balance, explosiveness. All of those characteristics you need to be a soccer player, whether you're a six, or a two, or a nine, depending on your position." He notes that although FC Dallas midfielder Michael Barrios is one of the league's most diminutive players, "he's super powerful, he's strong, [and] he has the athleticism to meet the criteria."

He ranks personality, which encompasses leadership, as fourth. "This doesn't mean you have to be vocal," he clarifies. "You can be a leader by example. You make an impact and make your teammates better. It's a subjective criterion. It's one that we have to look and hear and feel." He adds that players exhibit certain characteristics: "They want the ball, they're active, they face adversity in a positive way. They're always trying to impact their teammates and the group, on and off the field."

Third is technical execution, which is essentially taking athleticism and focusing it into knowing what do on a soccer field. As Gonzalez explains, "Those are your motor skills, your ability to take your athleticism and your coordination. How do you receive a ball? What's your first touch like? What's your pass like? Your short range pass. Your long range pass. Your heading. Your control with your upper body, with your lower body. How you use the outside of your foot. How you use your opposite foot." While objective data can figure into assessing that, Gonzalez notes that a lot of this is subjective, dependent on seeing how players move and react in practice and in games.

Tactical decision-making is second, which he summarizes simply as "soccer IQ." It takes into account where a player moves when he doesn't have the ball, on offense as well as on defense. "You need a high proficient soccer IQ to be a player at this club at the highest level," Gonzalez notes.

But the most important quality of all, in Gonzalez's view, is what's between the ears.

"Number one is mental strength," he states. "You can have two through five, phenomenal technique, amazing decision making, athleticism, personality, and you impact the game. But what happens when you don't make a roster? When you get injured? When your aunt passes away? What about when you win? Are you consistent when you win?"

What also distinguishes Acosta from other recruits, according to Gonzalez, is a work ethic that helped him apply the lessons they were teaching, and an attitude that made him not only a good individual player, but also a good teammate. "He does all of the intangible things," Gonzalez says. "He doesn't feel entitled. He doesn't feel like he's better than the next guy. He just wants to earn it. He's the model."

Acosta didn't originally seek out the academy; he'd been playing with a club team in his native Dallas, and checked it out on the recommendation of a friend who was playing in the academy. Once there, he says, "I knew it was the place I wanted to be. The following week I joined in the training and I fell in love with everything. That was all she wrote."

Acosta was impressed by the emphasis on professionalism; it was an atmosphere in which "they treated us like we were professionals" and where "people weren't just there to play; they were there to get better."

The intensity of the experience was especially eye-opening. "We wouldn't just watch video of games. We'd watch videos of us training, and I thought that was really different. I wasn't really accustomed to seeing myself train. I thought it was really cool to do that. Some people might just use training to let the foot off the gas. For us, training felt like a game. For us, every single chance to get out there was a chance for us to get better. That was one of my biggest takeaways. Even with the national team, I hadn't experienced watching training."

"We always got feedback about practices," he adds. "There were always little bits of advice, about taking an extra touch in the final third, creating goals, helping teammates, positioning, little aspects of the game. They were always in our ears trying to better us, and to make our team successful as a whole."

Acosta knew there were certain aspects of his game he wanted to work on in the academy: one-on-one defending, defending in the box, tactical spacing, being more clinical in his passing in the final third. Ultimately, he was looking to "be more polished," and he says the academy gave him the opportunity to put in the repetition necessary to improve his game across the board.

"We had tactical practice, we had finishing practice," he says. "Every little thing we could better ourselves on, they hit every checkpoint. I think I became a more well-rounded player in the academy."

Acosta was also, incidentally, part of the Spring 2011 residency class at US Soccer's Under-17 Residency Program in Bradenton, Florida (which we'll delve into in the next chapter) that also included US-capped and DC United midfielder Paul Arriola and Colorado Rapids midfielder Dillon Serna.

"I think the MLS academies are better now, but at the time I was at Bradenton, when some of the MLS academies were just starting up, I think Bradenton was up a step higher for me," Acosta recalls. "I think being with players my age who were the best of the best in the country helped my growth. Don't get me wrong; the academy was great. It was really, really beneficial. But with Bradenton, on the field and off the field,

I think I really matured as a person. I had to do everything on my own. Practices were really intense, the whole training regimen was. We had to practice really early, at 7 or 8 o'clock, and we had school afterwards. The whole day was different. I'd never really experienced that before."

Even though Acosta graduated from the academy several years ago, he's proud of how the U-17 team did in the most recent Generation Adidas tournament, an MLS-sponsored event that brings academy teams from all of the world to the FC Dallas Academy fields. In the April 2017 tournament, FC Dallas only finished seventh in its sixteen-team division, with Argentine super-club River Plate beating Brazilian powers Flamengo in the championship game. But in a head-to-head match with Real Madrid's U-17 team, billed as the marquee match of the tournament, Brayan Padilla, one of FC Dallas's most touted Academy players, delivered the win by scoring the match's only goal.[9]

"I mean, Real Madrid is one of the most renowned clubs in the world," Acosta says. "It shows that what we're doing here at FC Dallas Academy is really paying off. It really takes a lot of sacrifice to be in the academy. I know I didn't experience high school or middle school like other kids. It's a big sacrifice, but I know that what it takes for kids to get to the next level, and that's really been shown to me. These kids in the academy now, some of them train with us, and they're really holding their own."

If Gonzalez has his way, Acosta won't be the only success story coming out of the FC Dallas Academy. Coy Craft, who was part of the US U-20 roster for the 2017 CONCACAF U-20 Championship (but not the subsequent U-20 World Cup) signed a homegrown contract in July 2014. He's seen first-team minutes as early as 2014, but hasn't regularly broken into the squad as a teen in the way Acosta did. Craft, who will turn twenty-one a month before the 2018 World Cup, has spent 2017 in a perfectly-age-appropriate setting for development—FC Dallas's USL affiliate in Oklahoma City, OKC Energy FC.

Gonzalez's gut reaction to Craft, after seeing him grow and develop in the Academy, is, "He's explosive, has speed, has great technique. He's developing personality. He's a winner. He's young."

He then elaborates:

You won't really have a complete player until twenty-three or twenty-four. Coy's still developing. He's still developing with his decision making, and he's improved a lot. That's why he's making a U-20 roster. That's why he's now fighting for a first-team spot here. He's improving his decision making with and without the ball. He's more connected with teammates, and off the ball, he's making a lot more dynamic movements to separate himself.

Though some might consider being passed over for the U-20 World Cup squad and moving to Oklahoma City as setbacks, Gonzalez actually sees them as positives that may make him a better player in the long run. When Gonzalez says that Craft has "improved a lot with his mental strength," part of that has to do with how he responds to spot tests. "I've put him in physical duels with a really good defender, knocking him down," Gonzalez says. "And he gets back up."

But it also extends to the adversity of not making rosters and the relative adversity—given his brief, tantalizing tastes of MLS—of playing in USL. "He went to the OKC Energy on loan, to get minutes, and had a great attitude," Gonzalez notes. "He scored goals. His confidence grew. Now he's one of their best players."

FC Dallas has an obvious success story going, but they're not the only team in the league that's gained widespread recognition for their academy. The Philadelphia Union, which has struggled to attain much on-the-field success since entering the league in 2010, has developed one of the most comprehensive academy systems in all of MLS, and many expect that the investment they've made in development will eventually pay dividends.

How comprehensive is it? Starting with a program they call Union Futures, players can get in at the U-7 level and progress all the way to the U-18s. Players at the U-7 to U-12 are registered with their local youth clubs and participate in supplemental training that the Union offers. Players at the U-12 level and above can become full-fledged Union Academy members.[10]

The Union also offers residency, and they've developed a partnership with YSC Sports, a Philadelphia-area soccer training facility, to create the YSC Academy, which MLS's Charles Boehm called "a bold vision of progressive education and world-beating player development" in a September 2015 feature on MLSsoccer.com. This vision, as Boehm explained, is "one whose founders believe holds the key to the future of not only the Philadelphia Union, but all of soccer in North America."

The article noted that YSC founder and Union minority owner Richie Graham "fused a rigorous player development program with a customized college preparatory school of 66 students—all boys, all talented soccer players—from the eighth to twelfth grades."

"Here, soccer and academics are interwoven as snugly as anywhere in the United States, perhaps even more than US Soccer's Bradenton Residency program in Florida," the article continued. "MLS game balls are likely to be used for velocity and kinetics lessons. Union communications staffers occasionally visit to introduce the kids to dos and don'ts of interviews and social media. And to remind students of the high stakes and need for performance in both spheres, one of the school's rooms is even shaped like a stadium, with a table surrounded by swooping, pearlescent walls modeled after Allianz Arena, home of Bayern Munich."[11]

The YSC Academy also puts an emphasis on training. Part of the justification for this, according to the Union's website, is that the early exercise "works to release dopamine, essentially waking up the brain and activating the learning centers, which in turn enhances productivity in the classroom." Yet part of the justification also has to do with "dramatically increas[ing] the annual training units (hours) for each player."

"Typically in the US, elite-youth-soccer players train between 2 to 3 units a week," the site explains. "In Europe, and other parts of the world, elite youth train between 8 to 10 units a week. Our morning sessions enable our players to match their global peer group in terms of total training units while providing them an opportunity to work on their technical skills by improving key fundamentals."[12]

The Union's dedication to its academy programming also came through in reporting that revealed just how much of an expenditure the Union was making in improving through its youth system.

Will Parchman, in a March 2017 article on TopDrawerSoccer.com, focused on an aspect of Grant Wahl's annual Ambition Rankings, which measure how much individual MLS teams are gearing toward success. Nine of the twenty active MLS franchises in the 2016 season reported their spending on their academies. The total outlays ranged from $1 million at the lower end for the New England Revolution; a $1.5 to $2.5 million tier including, in ascending order, DC United, the Montreal Impact, the Chicago Fire, and Columbus Crew SC; FC Dallas and the Portland Timbers at $3 million each; and the LA Galaxy and the Philadelphia Union at $4 million each.

"The most intriguing positioning on this list is undoubtedly the Union's," he said. "As a caveat, their answer was that they spent an *average* of $4 million over the past few years, so they could've technically spent less than the Galaxy in 2016, but it also could've been more." He went on to note, "In any case, the Union have made more strides to outspend their competitors than anyone in MLS since its YSC Academy opened its doors in 2013. They're to be commended for the effort. Names like Matthew Real, Derrick Jones and Auston Trusty are proof positive the wheel is turning, too."[13]

Perhaps it's serendipitous that Parchman uses a wheel analogy. Union Academy director Tommy Wilson, when I interview him about his philosophy in running the academy, relies on a wheel analogy to describe the holistic approach they've adopted.

"We try to address all aspects of a player's development," he says. "Imagine a wagon wheel when the spokes point to the center. The center is the player and all at the end of each of the spokes of the wagon wheel as a service. It could be medical, it could be technical, tactical, athletic development, nutrition, education. It could be some administrative component, or video analysis, [or] data analytics. You think of all the things that go together to make up an elite sportsman. We are trying to address every aspect."

"It's a lofty goal we have; we're trying to develop world class players. It's not just us: It's other MLS academies and other academies across the USA. I don't think that's beyond our capabilities given the talent pool in the country."

Wilson came to the Union from the Rangers Academy in Glasgow. He left the esteemed Scottish club four years ago when it was in the midst of bankruptcy and soccer purgatory; the team had to claw back from Scottish football's fourth division to its rightful place in the top-tier Scottish Premier League. Wilson, with an opportunity to help forward the Union's development ambitions, seized it.

"I think we're all striving to develop players, initially for our first teams, and beyond that, the US national team," Wilson says. "Who knows? Maybe the next Lionel Messi is lurking somewhere in Philadelphia! I would love that to be the case."

"I think what we've been able to do is, because of our commitment to excellence and our commitment to education, is to develop players," he adds. He's realistic about the task before them, noting, "Not everyone's going to be a first team player. Not everyone's going to play for the national team." And yet, he still believes that their work has positive implications on soccer in the US, noting, "A lot of our boys will become college players, they may become administrators in the game, referees—who knows where they'll end up? We try and instill a love of the game, first and foremost, and our commitment to education is second to none."

The Union Academy, like the FC Dallas Academy, offers residencies to a select group of students who can't commute to practice session from their homes. For the Union, it's twenty-five academy students, including some who aren't within the Union's designated homegrown territory, but are from parts of the United States that aren't on MLS's map: Detroit, Alabama, parts of Florida not granted to Orlando City SC. Two of the residents, within FIFA's relatively new, tighter limits on how many non-US nationals can be in a residency, are Jamaican dual nationals.

"We've got a scouting network that covers the whole country," Wilson notes. He still relies on recommendations from agents to locate some players, and says that he'd like the network to be even more substantial than it is, but he's fully committed to getting talented players into the academy. As he says simply, "We find them wherever we can. I have no problem taking the boy off the street and putting him into the academy."

This extends to outreach in African American, African immigrant, and Latino communities of all economic stripes in the Philadelphia metro area and beyond, no matter how unconventional the background. Which brings us to perhaps Wilson's most significant find for both the Union and US Soccer thus far: Derrick Jones.

As Wilson recalls, he became aware of Jones when he took a composite team of U-14, U-16, and U-18 boys to play Junior Lone Star FC, a Philadelphia-based minor league soccer club competing in the fourth-tier National Professional Soccer League. Wilson noticed Jones, who was then just fifteen years old, playing alongside young men up to twenty-four years old.

Jones says of that experience, "When we played them, I wanted to do my best. I wanted to play for the academy, knowing it was my age group. I was hoping to do my best and get a trial with them. A lot of the players on my team played well that day. I didn't know I was going to be called in to try out with them. It was a little surprising."

Jones, who was born in Ghana but represented the US at the U-20 World Cup in 2017, reminded Wilson of Ivory Coast international and longtime Manchester City midfielder Yaya Touré. "He's an attacking midfield player, very creative, but strong, with physical presence," Wilson says. "He's really tall. He has the ability to get forward and move with the ball, to take the ball under pressure, and to hold players off with that body strength that he has. And you can still see that today in his game."

Jones made club history in March 2017, becoming the first Union Academy player to start a match for the Union first team. He was able to make the transition, in part, because of the residency program. As the Union's website recounts:

> When Jones became a member of the Academy, the technical staff and coaches became immediately impressed at the level of play Jones exhibited. However, it was tough to get him to training with Jones living with his family rather than in a residency house like most of the Academy players live in. Wilson said once he moved into with his teammates, everyone saw another level of play on the field and excellence in the classroom.
>
> "I used to take Jones to the train station on Friday nights and pick him up Monday mornings, and that's how he and I built a

great relationship," Wilson said. "The difference in him living in a residency house as opposed to living at home has made the difference now. And that's not a criticism of his home life, he comes from a good home. He was living in West Philadelphia, and he couldn't always get here. It was about controlling his environment. It was a professional and personal long-term investment.[14]

Though not everyone at the Union Academy is on the same trajectory as Jones, academy training does allow them more options than they might have had a decade earlier.

"We're starting to see the transition from young kids playing club and academy soccer to get the opportunity to go to college to now they are being told they play academy to become professionals," Wake Forest University head coach Bobby Muuss told Brotherly Game for a March 2017 article. Muuss had two recruits, who had trained at the Union Academy, de-commit from Wake Forest in the eight months prior to the article publication. One went to Bundesliga club Werder Bremen, and one went to the Union's USL affiliate, Bethlehem Steel FC.[15]

Durbin sees the emergence of the USL as a positive, noting it is "why we're beginning to see such an acceleration in the development," adding that players "now have the ability to get into a professional environment at the age of 18 or 19 and really exponentially drive their development in what is, in many ways, the most critical part of their career." Some MLS clubs have arrangements with independent USL clubs to place academy players on their rosters. The Houston Dynamo organization has an innovative relationship with the USL's RGV FC Toros that team officials bill a "hybrid" affiliation, like those pioneered in the NBA's D-League (now G-League).[16] Others field a reserve team literally borrowing from the parent club's name, like Portland Timbers 2, Seattle Sounders FC 2, or LA Galaxy 2—cleverly nicknamed "Los Dos."

One criticism of the MLS academy system is that clubs don't get worldwide rights to players by committing those players to the academy. That only happens when an academy player signs a homegrown contract, and in most cases still, that contract is a commitment the team values primarily because it has invested time and energy in training that player, and believes the player can mature into a first-team starter.

But a team doesn't initially own the rights to an academy player who might want to move overseas. A July 2015 article on Red Bulls website Once A Metro bemoaned the loss of Red Bulls Academy player Russell Canouse (who we'll learn more about in Chapters 7 and 8), who "slipped through their fingers" when he seized an opportunity to play with the German club Hoffenheim.

"It's one of the big problems with the academies here, there is no protection," former Red Bulls Sporting Director Andy Roxburgh told writer Rob Usry. "How can you invest in an academy or in your fringe young players if they can just walk away?" As an example, he said, "We lost a 17-year-old goalkeeper a year ago," referring to Aleksander Gogic. "He just walked and he went to Reading. His mother wrote a note: 'Thank you very much.'"

"Not only do the Red Bulls have to worry about clubs from all over the world poaching their young talent," Usry continued, "they have to fend off advances from their own ownership group who may have different plans in mind." He cited examples of players who went on trial with a Red Bull-sponsored affiliate team in Austria, asserting that "a reserve team under the Red Bull umbrella had free reign to poach the players New York strove to develop." The article also fretted about the possibility of Matt Miazga leaving without the Red Bulls being compensated, as he'd been brought in by the Red Bulls' German affiliate RB Leipzig for several stints.[17] (This article was, of course, written before the deal with Chelsea that allowed the Red Bulls to handsomely cash in on training Miazga.)

Durbin notes that a player in training with an MLS academy becomes eligible to be sign a homegrown contract after twelve months at the academy. Once the club initiates the process with that player, it retains its rights to the player in MLS, even if the player doesn't sign a contract with that club and instead opts to sign with an overseas club. For example, Arriola trained with the LA Galaxy's academy in 2012 and 2013, then joined Liga MX's Tijuana in May 2013. When he returned to MLS in the summer of 2017, it was with DC United, but United had to work out a deal with the Galaxy in order to obtain his MLS rights.

Canouse, by contrast, didn't stay the requisite full year with the Red Bulls Academy for the Red Bulls to claim his homegrown rights, and therefore he was free to sign with DC United upon returning from Hoffenheim.

MLS has an additional mechanism in place, called the Discovery List rule, which helps govern the signing rights to unsigned players "who are not yet under contract to MLS and who are not subject to another assignment mechanism," such as the SuperDraft. Each team can place up to seven unsigned players on its discovery list, giving that team the right to sign the player if it wants to and (in cases where a player might hold out) if it can.

Like many MLS rules, it is a bit on the convoluted side. A team can offer $50,000 in general allocation money to obtain the rights to sign that player from whichever team is holding those rights. For a player to be eligible for the discovery list, he has to be at least eighteen years of age and can't be on the U-17 or U-20 national team rosters, as MLS determines after those players' eighteenth birthdays whether they're placed into the SuperDraft or on the allocation ranking list.

There's also this contingency: "If one or more clubs submit a discovery request on the same day, then the club with the lowest points-per-game in the current MLS regular season (all clubs must have played a minimum of three regular season games) will have the priority right to sign the player."[18]

While the principal aim of the MLS academies is to ready players for MLS, having so much activity around player development in multiple American markets affects both club and country.

For Jared Micklos, Director of the US Soccer Development Academy, the MLS academies are ultimately helping the US create a larger and better pool of players. "What you see is a continued commitment and a further interest in investing and developing [players]," he says, marveling at the change from the start of the DA in 2007, when just a handful of MLS teams had its proto-academies emerging, to the full buy-in of academies today.

In particular, he's amazed by the breadth of the age range the academies are reaching—U-12 programs reach players as young as ten, and players in their late teens and early twenties can be involved even if they're not quite yet first-team candidates through USL affiliates.

"It's not just the opportunity," Micklos says of what attracts players to academies tied to MLS teams. "It's the player being surrounded by the environment every day, where they see themselves being able to go from one step to the next. So we've seen investment from them. We've seen commitment. We've seen an attraction of players. We've seen a number of different things outside of just the field. You've seen the creation of residencies, school-based programs, that flexibility. You've seen the integration with first teams, and now you've seen a connection with the second teams in USL or otherwise at the oldest age. There's a real commitment [from the academies] to create that pathway for players."

For US Soccer, of course, the MLS academies provide an invaluable service. They scout players and identify those players worth developing, then take them through the process with hopes of having them play in the United States or Canada. If there truly is a burgeoning golden generation of American players, the MLS academies are playing a major role in finding and developing many of its marquee names.

It could be said that the MLS academies are now the tip of the spear that is American player development, but to fully understand the trajectory American soccer is on, it's necessary—as we'll do in the next chapter—to study the whole spear.

CHAPTER 5

BEYOND BRADENTON: THE DEVELOPMENT ACADEMY REINVENTS ITSELF

In March 2017, US Soccer declared the end of an era.

Specifically, it announced that its Under-17 Men's National Team Residency program, at the IMG Academy in Bradenton, Florida, would be closing after its Spring 2017 semester ended in May.

Bradenton had, over its history, played a crucial role in US player development. Its inaugural class in January 1999 included five USMNT World Cup–capped players: DaMarcus Beasley, Kyle Beckerman, Bobby Convey, Landon Donovan, and Oguchi Onyewu. Over its life, it was a destination for promising young American players, designed in the best-case scenarios to develop them into USMNT first-teamers. This happened thirty-three times as of the announcement to close, though given the number of current youth national players whose paths wound through Bradenton, this number will eventually increase. It furthermore had an impressive track record in that more than a third of its 450-plus graduates went on to either MLS teams or professional teams in Europe.[1]

Of the thirty-three who'd graduated from Bradenton to the first team, ten earned World Cup caps up to and including the 2014 tournament in Brazil.[2] (At least three others, Kellyn Acosta, Paul Arriola, and Christian Pulisic, would have likely been locks for the 2018 World Cup team had there been one, and still yet may win those caps in 2022.)

"One of our main hopes when establishing the US Soccer Residency Program was that at some point advancements in youth player development would make its existence no longer necessary," said then–US Soccer

President Sunil Gulati in the announcement, adding declaratively, "We believe that point has been reached."

That comment implies an admission that Bradenton wasn't meant to be forever. The idea certainly had its merits—taking twenty promising players at a time into a semester-long residential camp where they could have a full, focused, immersive experience. And at the time it was created, MLS teams weren't far enough along in their development to run the full-scale academies that they're actively maintaining now. But US Soccer saw it fit to keep Bradenton running for a decade after the Development Academy was launched.

"Not only did the program develop a number of key players for our National Teams, it served as a model for academies across the country to follow," said Gulati, acknowledging the good that Bradenton did. But he also acknowledged the obvious—that a single residency program, on its own, is not enough. Though the level of immersion varies widely among its nearly 200 member clubs and academies, US Soccer characterizes the Development Academy as taking "the Residency Program model down to the club level," able to reach what is currently more than 10,000 young players.

"With the US Soccer Development Academy having achieved high standards in preparing our young athletes," Gulati said, "We are now able to impact future American professionals on a much larger scale."[3]

The final Bradenton class had a last hurrah of sorts at the CONCACAF U-17 Championships in April and May 2017. The US got to the finals against Mexico in Panama City and acquired a 1–0 lead in the sixty-second minute, with Atlanta United FC's Andrew Carleton volleying in a shot following from a poor clearance from the Mexican keeper. But Mexico equalized on a header in stoppage time, and edged the US 5–4 in penalty kicks to claim the trophy. (The U-17 squad did go on to the U-17 World Cup in India that October, where they advanced to the quarterfinals and ran into the eventual championship-winning England team. Though they lost to England 4–1, they showed fight in that match and promise throughout the tournament.)

Landon Donovan got to Bradenton, as part of the first class of twenty to enter the residency, via the Olympic Development Program that US

Youth Soccer launched in 1977 to develop a pool of potential US youth players, and then to national team tryouts from there. "I had the opportunity to go to residency," he remembers, "and after a lot of conversations with my parents, we decided it was the right thing. In retrospect, it was absolutely the best thing we could have possibly done at that time in our careers."

In this time before MLS academies, Donovan recounts that playing with a club team meant two training sessions a week and one game on Saturday. "That was not a good way to develop," he asserts. "At that time, and for many years, [Bradenton] was the only option if you wanted to take soccer seriously at that age. It served a great purpose in the development of US Soccer's history."

While he acknowledges that daily training at MLS academies has now superseded what a semester-long residency can offer, the sixteen-year-old Donovan found Bradenton an invaluable stepping stone to becoming an eighteen-year-old senior team player and a twenty-year-old World Cup starter.

Donovan praised John Ellinger, the program's coach, who Donovan describes as "a professional coach with real men." Ellinger would most notably do that as the first-ever Real Salt Lake coach when the new team launched in 2005.

"He understood what the game looked like at the next level. The biggest thing he taught us, aside from all the training and putting us in good environments to get better was how to be a professional. None of us understood what it was like to be a professional around the world. For us, we didn't know that. We did a lot of growing up in a short period of time, and that was the biggest benefit."

Beasley was also in the inaugural class of what he called, simply, "*the program.*"

"It was an opportunity to play with the best players in the country at your age, to play every day, to be a professional." Like Donovan, Beasley praises Ellinger for regarding them as professionals, adding, "He taught us that to be professionals, you have to put in the work. To get better on the technical side of things, you have to work with the ball every day, every day, and I think that's why we were so successful."

Though the immersive quality of a full-time residency program might seem intense for high school students, Donovan found it exhilarating. "I loved it," he said. "For me, it could not have been more enjoyable. And I was always sort of independent. I just wanted to be around people who wanted to be around sports all day, I wanted to play soccer all day. For me, it never felt taxing. It was hard waking up early and going to school for four hours, but again, we were young. Often, we'd go after training and we'd go back to the complex and play soccer or tennis for an hour or two, go run around and do things. It never felt too tiring, but there were mornings where you'd say, 'God, I don't want to go to school now.' Training was a full-time job already."

Based on his time at Bradenton, Donovan wasn't sure who would end up making the senior team, but he was certainly taking mental notes while there. "We all had ambitions, obviously," he said, "I knew Beas was special and different. Kyle was an incredible player, but I never would have guessed at that point that he was going to have the career he had. That shows just how much he put into this whole thing to have the career that he has. Gooch always had physical tools you thought would give him a chance, but I would have never envisioned that from that team, that five guys would end up playing for the national team. That speaks about how good of a job John Ellinger did with us, because he made us believe we should be there."

"We were like a family," Beasley said of the inaugural class, "We were brothers, and we still are."

"It's mixed emotions," Donovan said of the residency program going away. "It was such a big part of my life, and helped so many kids, not just from a soccer perspective, but it was a great time in my life, where I got to socialize with other kids who had the same dreams and ambitions I did. It's hard to find that in a normal high school. But it shows the progress and development. It's an exciting day knowing that US Soccer no longer has to be the sole provider of development for kids, that Major League Soccer can take over. I think it's the right step. It'll be sad the residency program go away, but that's the evolution of sports, and I think it's a good thing."

The closing of the residency program isn't the only major change US

Soccer has made of late. On August 1, 2017, US Soccer officially installed the Player Development Initiatives that it first announced in August 2015, revolving around two policies to help American soccer development line up with what's working for the rest of the world.

One simplified the math involved in determining which age group a player can be in. The US now calculates this the way most FIFA member nations do: By using a player's birth year. So, in an example they give for the 2017–18 season, a player born in 2006 is a U-12 player, because 2018 − 2006 = 12.

The second, more involved initiative transforms how the game is played at an early age. The changes mean that young players won't see full-field, 11-on-11 action until reaching the U-13 level. From the U-6 to the U-12 level, players will play games on small-sided fields and with smaller squads, starting with four-on-four games at the U-6 to U-8 levels, moving into to seven-on-seven (with goalkeepers) at the U-9 and U-10 levels, and graduation to nine-on-nine play by U-11.

US Soccer characterizes it as "creating an on-field game environment that allows players to have a stronger opportunity to develop heightened soccer intelligence and on-the-ball skills," more in tune to a young player's developmental needs than full-field soccer. It also allows for a more uniform, systematic approach that, given the very specific guidelines published on its website, should be easily implementable across the nation.

At the American Outlaws rally I attended in Austin in May 2016, Ramos spoke candidly in front of an invested audience of American soccer superfans about the then-forthcoming changes that were starting to be adopted by DA-affiliated clubs.

"Over the last twenty-five years, we have not had one American be in the top ten in Player of the Year voting in FIFA," Ramos pointed out. "When you look at the top ten, you can go down the line with Messi, Ronaldo, Suarez, and say, well, the top ten is a lot to ask. But it's not so much to ask when you realize over that period of time, over twenty-five countries have had at least one player, and we have not. And so we have a lot of homework to do."

"We start with that every day," Ramos continued. "When we wake up in the morning, if we're in youth development, every day we're think-

ing, 'How can we get better?' At the end, we always get judged by what
the senior team does. But we have to go past that. If the senior team goes
out there and has a bad game, or has a bad qualifying tournament, or
they have a poor Gold Cup, it sort of trickles down to everybody else
[. . .] that maybe youth development's not getting it right."

"From when I played until now, we have a lot of good players, but
other countries do too," he said. "Other countries aren't standing still
waiting for us to get better. As we have gotten better, so has everyone
else, so it's a lot harder to close the gap at the top."

The Development Academy's founding in 2007 actually came out of
the impetus to close the gap. A year prior, according to Development
Academy Director Jared Micklos, US Soccer researched how to improve
player development, looking at the landscape of American soccer at the
time at looking at other countries for comparison. They found a gross
imbalance between the number of training sessions and the number of
games played. "You'd often find the teams are training one or two times
a week and playing two, three, four games on a weekend," Micklos
says, "That added up to over 100 games a year, an astronomically large
number."

That realization led to US Soccer evaluating how players develop and
learn how to manage game situations, and it determined that it would
address these concerns with a select group of clubs and players. Initially,
about sixty clubs with U-16 and U-18 players were identified to be members, with the hope that they'd serve as role models for other clubs.

They've been able to course-correct in the decade since the Development Academy started. Micklos notes a developing player's week now
involves about ten hours a week: about seventy-five to ninety minutes
per practice session four times a week, and then two games a week would
account for an additional four hours (counting pregame warmups on top
of ninety-minute matches. "But there's a lot more that happens outside
of that, that players need to do in an unstructured environment to sup-
plement that," Micklos says.

While the smaller-sided games called for in the latest Player Development Initiatives aren't exactly a new innovation for American soccer,
Micklos notes that what is new is the decision to make one uniform set

of guidelines for age groups for coaches to follow, or what he calls "alignment."

"What we did was really intensely study the landscape and try to create what in our country we thought was the best that each for the age from a learning standpoint, and then made it consistent," Micklos says. US Soccer wanted a plan that was the same for each age group regardless of location and league, to allow players to develop elements of their overall game at the four-on-four level, at the seven-on-seven level, and at the nine-on-nine level.

As Micklos notes, "You introduce more numbers when the player's more nuanced, and they can understand tactically other concepts in the game. So what's really important is that it's consistent and there's alignment."

The uniform rules will also help make sure that players are playing in age-appropriate situations. "You have kids who are nine or ten years old, playing eleven vs. eleven on a full-sized field," Ramos told the American Outlaws gathering. "You have kids who can't even reach the ball from one side to the other, who have to take a double touch on a corner kick. We're changing all that."

As he explained to the eager-to-hear-it group, "We're trying to increase the number of touches on the ball. We're already hearing complaints about how the fields are going to be too small, that the ball's going to go out of bounds. The object of this is to teach the players so that the ball doesn't go out of bounds, and so that they can keep it in bounds!"

They're also instituting new rules for the younger age groups to help players—particularly, defenders—develop their decision-making skills. As the new rules state:

> Starting at the U-9 level, games will use build-out lines. A horizontal line drawn from sideline to sideline 14 yards in front of each goal, build-out lines will encourage possession and playing the ball out of the back. When a goalkeeper has the ball in hand or takes a goal kick, the opposing team remains behind the build-out line until the ball is put into play. This line also indicates

where offside can be called, as teams cannot be called for offside between the midfield and build-out line. As part of small-sided standards, there will be no offside infraction before the U-9 age group. New rules also ban headers as well as punts and drop kicks from the goalkeeper.[4]

Rather than the goalkeeper hoofing a ball down the field, hoping to get the ball to an advantageous spot on the field, the goalkeeper will play it out to a defender, who will then have to navigate pressure from incoming players.

"So now, players as young as eight or nine will have to learn to play out of the back," Ramos said. "We're trying to promote faster decisions for the players. On the smaller fields, players are going to have a man on and they're going to have to turn and use their bodies a little better."

The changes have been in the works for a while. In fact, the Development Academy had some early adopter clubs and academies utilizing the new rules prior to the official August 2017 launch. Ramos noted that the sheer number of state associations and youth organizations touched by the new uniform guidelines made for extensive discussions. "I don't think the plan is perfect," Ramos admitted at the American Outlaws rally, "but I think it was a plan that everyone was happy with nationwide, and I think it's one that's going to work for the players."

Certainly, negative perceptions exist about youth soccer development in the United States. A number of critics make generalized charges about it being too costly for working-class—or even middle-class families—and being ineffective in truly finding all of the best players in the country.

Some of the criticisms stretch across the entire youth sports landscape: A September 2017 report from the Sports & Fitness Industry Association and the Aspen Institute, as covered in *The Washington Post*, characterized youth sports as being "in the midst of a crisis" born of high costs and a lack of qualified coaches. Author Jacob Bogage noted that "athletic participation for kids ages 6 through 12 is down almost 8 percent over the last decade, according to SFIA and Aspen data, and children from low-income households are half as likely to play one day's worth of team sports than children from households earning at least $100,000."

Tom Farrey, executive director of Aspen's Sports & Society program, noted in the article, "Sports in America have separated into sport-haves and have-nots. All that matters is if kids come from a family that has resources. If you don't have money, it's hard to play."

The article went on to point out that only 37 percent of American children ages six through twelve play a team sport regularly, a drop of 8 percent from 2008 levels. "Experts blame that trend on what they call an 'up or out' mentality in youth sports," Bogage noted. "Travel leagues, ones that can sometimes cost thousands of dollars to join, have crept into increasingly younger age groups, and they take the most talented young athletes for their teams."[5]

A *Time* cover story released in the same month declared youth sports to be a $15.3 billion industry, where "practice and tournaments overtake nights and weekends like kudzu," where dedicated parents look to help even young children get a competitive edge, and where "a range of private businesses are mining this deep, do-anything parental love" with "everything from travel to private coaching to apps that organize leagues and livestream games."[6]

While these perceptions stretch across all of youth sports, they're definitely embedded in perceptions of soccer. Critics dub the "pay-to-play" system one that weds national team discovery to a youth club soccer system requiring parents to cover travel and other expenses, invariably pricing out talented players from poorer families.

The subject came up in the conference call US Soccer hosted three days after the World Cup 2018 ouster. There, Gulati contended, "It would be great to say that no one playing soccer, recreational or competitive soccer, will pay anything. That's not going to happen in the current environment. And, by the way, it doesn't happen in most countries that players pay nothing, that's a misnomer. Now, what we have to do is make sure that players aren't prohibited from playing, but if you can afford it, you pay for it, whether it's a piano lesson or soccer."

Gulati did go on point out steps that US Soccer is taking—both in tandem with MLS and on its own—to address pay-to-play. He started with the admission that, "as things become more expensive, where there's a roadblock, you'd like to do something about that," and cited some pilot programs US Soccer has initiated, showing both a measured concern and a willingness to take on the issue, if not the immediate prescription that so many fans were looking for in that moment.[7]

But the piano lesson analogy was not the most judicious choice, given that Gulati was seemingly seeking to make a point about affordability and access.

While the Development Academy's Player Development Initiatives are ultimately about the getting club teams on the same page, helping US Soccer to better develop players who will ultimately be wearing the crest in World Cups, they also have a proactive public relations value. Judging from the tone-deafness of Gulati's piano lesson comment, and at least one recent article on youth soccer in the US, PR is still needed to sell American soccer fans on how player development is evolving (or, at least, attempting to evolve).

"Imagine for a moment that you are an octopus," ominously began Will Parchman's Spring 2016 article in *Howler* on youth soccer development, which then continued:

> Your sinewy tentacles are extended before you into the jet-black deep, your movement clearly directed in a general heading, but there is something awkward about your progress. Each tentacle operates entirely on its own, dragging you in directions sometimes congruent with the goal you've set and sometimes on an errant course.
>
> Now imagine the holistic apparatus of soccer in the United States. There is a head—that is, the United States Soccer Federation —and there are tentacles branching off from the nerve center, each carrying the ganglion to vaguely defined destinations that may or may not be what the brain had in mind. This is the organism responsible for youth soccer development in America today, and it is every bit as slippery, complicated, and prone to working at cross-purposes as that octopus groping its way through the darkness.[8]

Parchman went on to use the octopus analogy to critique US Soccer's ability to scout all the players, calling US Club Soccer (USCS) and US

Youth Soccer (USYS) two of "the most muscular tentacles." He explains, describing the landscape in early 2016 as he saw it:

> All non-DA players younger than 18 play for clubs that are members of either USCS and USYS, the two biggest youth soccer organizations in the US. Together, they encompass hundreds of clubs and millions of players from U-6 to U-18. This scale is what makes the prospect of a single technical director benevolently ruling over all this territory with the assistance of just nine full-time scouts so comical.
>
> But that's the task Klinsmann has assumed. He, along with his scouting staff of nine plus roughly 100 part-timers, is expected to keep tabs on the brightest talents at every stage of youth development in our continent-sized country. Many smaller European nations have many times that number of scouts with far less ground to cover.[9]

While Micklos acknowledges the limitations Parchman identified, he cites improvements to the system since the article came out (and certainly, from the beginning days of the Development Academy when there was just a single scout), and characterizes their network more hopefully than Parchman does:

> As it's evolved from an individual to a scouting network, you have ten full-time technical advisers that live in major markets. Those technical advisors have a direct working relationship with the clubs that are part of the Academy. And that's the group that someone like myself or Aloys [Wijnker, Boys' Development Academy Director] has communication with every single day. There are over 100 people working in a scouting network identifying players, consistent with our technical advisors, who are full-time. It's evolved to now where some of the clubs, just a small number still, but some of the clubs are doing it on their own, whether it be through their coaches, or they've actually hired someone in the talent ID department, or their own scouts. Pro clubs are lead-

ing the way because there's now a benefit to them scouting with their own eyes for players that fit their system and then attracting them to a residency or to come and play with their club.

Parchman is still concerned that "if a promising 11-year-old player surfaces in Missoula, Montana, he is far more likely to wither on the vine than be picked for the harvest." Yet, as Micklos sees it, that player might attract the attention of a scout from Real Salt Lake, which has residency capabilities in its academy, or Seattle Sounders FC, which offers a home-stay program in which host families volunteer to take in academy players, with the reward of a monthly stipend to offset costs, plus two season tickets.[10]

A tweet from the US Soccer Youth National Team account, sent on September 22, 2017, and meant to generate interest in the U-17 World Cup team, boasted that the team featured twenty-one players from twenty-one cities—with a map showing most of the players from Texas and points east. That led Stars and Stripes FC to do a deep dive on U-17 rosters dating back to 2011, and openly questioning whether "125 scouts who report to 10 full time technical advisors" are sufficient in finding players from sea to shining sea.

The article opined that with ten scouts ultimately responsible for 41.2 million eligible players, they "all need to continue to pay more attention to their regions in finding future USMNT stars from all corners of the country," and while "mining the growing MLS academies will help in that area [. . .] the only way to find the best talent is to increase the number of scouts and technical advisors. This will allow the scouts with large territories to focus on smaller segments and focus in on some of the MLS clubs that are already developing future young stars. Then, they can find more diamonds in the rough. Once all this change happens, future U-17 teams can truly reflect the best talent from all across the United States."[11]

Micklos emphasizes that it's ultimately about finding quality rather than quantity:

By adding more academies, you're adding more players that can be seen on a week in, week out basis. [. . .] It's not necessary to add *more* players to the pool; it's necessary to add *the best* players to the pool. So if you have more scouts watching more games with more players in it you have hopefully a better idea that you're pulling the best players out of the system. So it's really been the opportunity to see players multiple times, to have a more dedicated network that can cover more games, and then most importantly, to be able to start to identify talent not just at the older age groups, but in these formative years before they're seventeen and eighteen tracking players who are thirteen, fourteen, and fifteen.

Micklos also emphasizes that US Soccer wants to develop more scouts, in order to "educate scouts on what it is that we're actually looking for, how you identify a player, what the trends are, and [. . .] get[ting] into things like relative and biological age." He even goes as far as saying, "We're looking to educate scouts in the way we're educating coaches."

US Soccer has a licensing program for its coaches, which was initiated in the early 1970s and evolved over nearly half a century to where it is today. It now offers eight different levels of licensing, from the two-hour Class F course intended for beginning coaches at the U-6 and U-8 level, up the alphabet to more complex courses requiring a mix of online and classroom instruction. Separate senior and youth tracks are necessary for a Class A license. There is also a top-of-the-ladder pro course, providing twelve months of ongoing instruction and evaluation for coaches who are already with the national team, coaching in MLS, NASL, or USL, or their counterparts in the top-flight National Women's Soccer League.[12]

"I think one of the most exciting things that has happened in the past decade is that US Soccer has taken a look at coach education," says Joe Cummings, former president of what is now United Soccer Coaches (formerly the National Soccer Coaches Association of America), a 30,000-strong network of soccer coaches across the United States. "By extension, that means player development, because better coaches make better players, which make better teams." He calls the pro license in particular a "dramatic change."

"The highest level of coach education that we [had] in the United

States just a few years ago, whether it was through the NSCAA [National Soccer Coaches Association of America] or whether it was US Soccer, was one week," he explains. "Just seven days. If you look at coaches' education across the world, those programs were far superior to what was being offered in the United States. In making the changes that they've made, not methodology changes, necessarily, but curriculum changes, and then the reinforcing of that curriculum and the observation of those coaches in the specific work environment, that's where the changes have been most felt and where they're most beneficial."

The recent changes to Class A, B, and C courses are now, in Ramos's view, "a little bit more in line with the rest of the world," and therefore more beneficial to the coaches and the players they coach. US Soccer's A License for youth coaches, for example, puts candidates through a six-month pathway that includes four five-day instruction blocks and three six-to-eight week sessions with the teams they coach. US Soccer sets the five-day sessions up in one centralized location like San Diego, St. Louis, or the Seattle suburb of Tukwila, where the candidates travel and stay for the duration. Candidates do one five-day session, then work on specific coach training assignments, with the youth players they're coaching, in a six-to-eight week block, before returning to the central location for the next five-day session. Cummings sees, in these expanded education schedules, the chance to take a topic that might have been covered in an hour lecture and a ninety-minute field presentation in a past era, and into more substantive territory.

Cummings sees technology, especially with video, increasing the capability of what today's better trained coaches can do. He notes:

Coach education, if you think of it as a science, like the science of becoming a teacher—there's so much information that's now available to us over the past ten years, specifically on the video side, the match analysis, the observational side.

Now, being able to say to a player, "Come on in, sit down, let's take a look at the hundred touches that you had in the game this past Saturday night. Let's talk about them." Just that! Something that sounds as simple as that my ability to convey to a player now, as a coach, what I feel he needs he or she needs to work on it is much, much easier to convey through the video analysis programs that we have available to us.

Though other countries obviously share the ability to access and analyze video, Cummings does believe that the US can narrow the player development gap because of it. He even believes that the incredible access American soccer fans now have to global soccer is acting as somewhat of a leveler, in that aspiring American players can watch idols in action from dawn to dusk (and beyond) on weekends if they so choose.

Many still have concerns about how coaches are developed in the US. A July 2016 article in Top Drawer Soccer called "The High Cost of American Coaching"—another critical look at the system by Will Parchman—contends that the A and B-level courses that are "arguably the two most crucial in the coaching oeuvre" are more costly in the US than they are in Germany and Spain—priced more on par with the English courses. The correlation Parchman draws is that the US only has one B-licensed coach for every 3,000 players and one A-licensed coach for every 6,000 players, putting it at a competitive disadvantage with Germany, Italy, and Spain, which has less expensive A and B courses and a better ratio of A- and B-level coaches to players. As Parchman put it, "The U.S. has largely emulated England in this, and I dare say that is not the track most of the country would have us on."[13]

The ongoing evolution in coaching and scouting, though it's not yet to the level all American soccer fans would consider ideal, is ultimately is in service to creating a better national team. "Everything we do in youth development is to make the senior team better," Ramos said, adding that the transition been the youth teams and the senior team "needs to be seamless" for the players.

But not everyone who plays within the DA has the national team in mind. Take Jakob Nordstrom. I first met him when he was eight years old, jumping into the mostly adult scrimmage games at Austin's Zilker Park involving players on an over-thirty rec league team his dad and I helped start. He's been playing soccer since age three, and aspires to win a scholarship to play soccer for an NCAA Division I school offering a good education. (He's eyeing Stanford, Duke, the University of North Carolina, and UCLA.)

He considered playing select soccer at age eleven with Austin's Lonestar Development Academy to be his big step up, in part because he was fortuitous enough to have coaches from Spain who gave him perspectives he didn't have previously.

"They were a lot more possession-oriented," Nordstrom says of those coaches. "I learned a lot more about the technical side of things versus conditioning and endurance. Obviously, those are big aspects. But they focused more on shoring up essentials, like when you're making a pass, focusing on where it's supposed to go every single time you make the pass."

Nordstrom graduated into Lonestar's Development Academy program, and he has since had the opportunity to play in Germany and regional and national tournaments. His team has faced the like-aged FC Dallas Academy team on multiple occasions and has even won on multiple occasions. "They work amazingly as a unit," he says of the MLS academy team. "The way that they're coached, they're very fluid in their game. They're very connected. They have great chemistry, that's their defining point."

By contrast, Nordstrom calls his Lonestar team "a lot more physically oriented, being able to play throughout the entire game, tiring out the opponent." He adds, "We've very good on counter-attacks, whatever that says about us." He likens their style to the 2015–16 Leicester team that won the Premier League, though he's quick to point out that he's not actually comparing the Lonestar players to those players.

Lonestar does feature two promising prospects who have captured US Soccer's attention. Nordstrom's U-15 teammate Kaya Ignacio is part of the US's U-15 pool of roster players and has been assessed by AS Roma coaches through Lonestar's affiliation with the Serie A team. Julian Gaines, playing a year above his age as a U-16 for Lonestar, featured in the CONCACAF U-15 championships for the US Boys' National Team, scoring in the semifinals win over Panama[14] that sent them through to the finals against Mexico (which they would lose 2–0). Julian's older brother McKinze, a Lonestar product and a US youth national team player, had a successful run with Wolfsburg's U-19 team in Germany. In June 2017, he moved to Darmstadt to play alongside fellow American Terrence Boyd.[15]

Nordstrom took part in the US Soccer Development Academy's 2017 Summer Showcase and Playoffs, the tenth annual event featuring more than 300 games on a sprawling thirty-three-field complex near Indianapolis. While the showcase is built around the U-15/16 and U-17/18 Academy Playoffs, featuring the thirty-two teams in each category who fared best during the regular season, there's also a 150-game showcase for invited U-14 teams.

Players notice the presence of scouts there, and when a player not already on the radar has a breakout game, they notice the presence of additional scouts at their subsequent games. Scouts keep rosters during games and keep notes on which players impress them.

Nordstrom notes that while players themselves don't see that list, their coaches do, and then it's up to the coaches to filter that feedback how they see fit. "The coach will basically list off what the scout said, without naming any specific players," Nordstrom said. "They'd tell you what they saw that was good, and what needed to be better. For our team, they liked our side-to-side movement in the back, and our ability to penetrate through the middle. But they wouldn't say that specific players did badly or did well."

Being with a Development Academy-affiliated club, Nordstrom says that the US Soccer philosophies for player development, including smaller-side, smaller-field games for younger players, were in operation when he played at those levels. However, the build-out line wasn't as familiar to him. He remembers games in his youth where goalkeepers would just try to kick it as far as they can.

Nordstrom also went through the US Youth Soccer's Olympic Development Program starting at age eleven. There, they specifically taught the build-out line as something US Soccer wanted in order to help prepare players. "They would talk about effective ways to build out of the back and release pressure," he recalls. "And if you weren't doing that, they'd call you out on it."

So, ultimately, has the Development Academy been doing what it set out to do? Is it creating players able to play with the youth national teams and the USMNT? According to Ramos, during 2015 and 2016, 89 percent of the youth national team call-ups were players who'd been trained at a Development Academy–affiliated club or academy.

And, as of September 2017, twenty-four players with Development Academy training have earned at least one USMNT cap, dating back as far as 2010. Kelyn Rowe became the first 2017 DA-to-USMNT player,[16] activated for a Gold Cup tournament where he performed well. He then returned to club play with the New England Revolution, injuring his knee before a crucial group of qualifying matches where he might have been called up.[17]

Based on the numbers, the Development Academy-to-youth national team pathway looks well established, and the next World Cup qualifying cycle should bring more of those players into the senior team to add to that tally.

In the meantime, despite the establishment of a coaching, scouting, and player development network seeking to improve on the past, some aren't entirely willing to be content with the status quo.

"We're looking for players everywhere," Ramos insists. "Whether it's in parks or in MLS, we have people all over the country looking for players."

But even he admits, "We're missing some for sure, so we have to get better." And, for more than a few concerned observers, the players that US Soccer are missing are the very ones US Soccer can't afford to miss if they're looking to create more diverse representation on its national team squads.

CHAPTER 6

BIENVENIDO AL FUTURO: ON FINDING AND DEVELOPING LATINO PLAYERS

THE US LATINO POPULATION IS APPROACHING THE SIXTY MILLION MARK. IT has never been a monolithic group; it encompasses multiple national identities and spans the breadth of the economic spectrum. Unfortunately, the prefix "under" comes into play when US Latinos are talked about as a group, sometimes as "underprivileged," or sometimes somewhat more euphemistically as "underserved."

And, when it comes to US Soccer, particularly in who has ascended to the Men's and Women's National Teams, some perceive Latinos to be an underrepresented entity. Were they more thoroughly scouted and recruited, the thinking goes, they could be brought on to the national squad as difference makers. That line of thinking has been in operation for a while—at least, long enough for Powers That Be to have seized upon it more than a decade ago.

In 2007, MLS partnered with Univision to launch a reality contest called "Sueño MLS." Aired as a segment nested within the popular sports show *República Deportiva*, "Sueño MLS" lasted ten years—and in its first year produced Jorge Villafaña, who emerged during the 2017 qualifying campaign as the long-awaited reliable starting left-back that seemed to elude the USMNT for a number of years.

According to Gabe Gabor, MLS's Miami-based Senior International Communications Consultant, the idea for the show came from a conversation between MLS Commissioner Don Garber and then-Univision president David Downs, who was also Executive Director of the US's

2018/2022 World Cup bid. Together, they realized, "There are so many great unknown Hispanic players out there; why don't we do something to try to discover one?"

The first year, 2,000 hopefuls tried out in Los Angeles, with Chivas USA coaches helping the show producers coordinate the winnowing process. As Gabor points out, the actual "prize" was just a trophy—offering a pro contract would run afoul of NCAA rules and interfere with a winner's college eligibility. As the show and MLS academies evolved, though, the MLS club involved with each particular season would be able to offer an academy spot at the age level appropriate for the winner.

Gabor loves to tell the story of Villafaña—then Jorge Flores—remarking:

> It should be made into a movie! He's a seventeen-year-old high school student who's playing in local leagues and is a good player, but he's not somebody that is well known to everybody. He's at Anaheim High School and for his job, he helps his uncle clean churches. His uncle watches *Republica*, convinces him to get out there and try out. And he didn't want to try out. As a matter of fact, he had a tryout at one point with Chivas USA's youth team academy and didn't make it. But his uncle convinces him to go and he gets picked by the scouts. He goes to the next round, and the next round, ultimately beats out 2,000 kids, and gets a spot on Chivas USA's U-19 team even though he's just seventeen. Three months later, he gets a professional contract; they say, you're so good, we're going to sign you to the team.

Villafaña—who changed his last name on Mother's Day to honor his mother, a detail Gabor says makes the story all the more Hollywood—played with Chivas USA for seven seasons, moved to the Timbers for two seasons (winning the MLS Cup with them in 2015), and then moved to Liga MX team Santos Laguna in 2016. Gabor notes that along the way, he's acquired the nickname "Sueño."

And yet, Villafaña would have to wait a while for a first-team call-up, having not featured for any national team since playing for the

U-23s in 2012. "It's not up to the player," he told MLSsoccer.com's Steve Brisendine in June 2016. "The player just does his work, and things come up. I'm just working and seeing what the future holds."[1] Villafaña never got his chance when Klinsmann was coaching, but was called up to the January 2017 camp in Southern California—known in US Soccer parlance as "Camp Cupcake"—and finally got his first cap against Honduras two months later.

Even as the show evolved over the years to incorporate multiple markets, it kept its unmistakable Univision flourishes along the way. Gabor recalls that Villafaña, when he was revealed as the winner live on a *Republica* telecast, came on to the set wearing a *luchador* mask to keep his identity secret.

Alan Gaytán may be the last of the "Sueño" winners. The fifteen-year-old Mexican-American midfielder, from Troutdale, Oregon, was invited to join the Timbers Academy in 2016 after four days of competition involving fifteen finalists in Southern California, featuring oversight from the likes of Luis "El Matador" Hernandez and Eric Wynalda.[2]

"Sometimes, programs run their course," Gabor said of the decision to not bring "Sueño MLS" back for an eleventh season. "I do believe that because the league, with its academies, developed so much in ten years, there wasn't so much of a need for something like 'Sueño MLS' for recognizing players or building academies. That job was done."

Even though "Sueño MLS" is no more, there's still a path to a *sueño* available for Latino players with aspirations to greatness, courtesy of Alianza de Futbol.

Alianza de Futbol was started in 2004; Brad Rothenberg, the son of US Soccer trailblazer Alan Rothenberg, was one of the cofounders. As Managing Director Joaquín Escoto says of Rothenberg's group, "They saw an opportunity in the Hispanic market. Nobody was doing high-quality events for this audience."

Today, Alianza programming includes corporate-sponsored national soccer tournaments for youth teams (the Copa Coca-Cola) and for adult three-on-three soccer teams (the Telemundo Deportes 3v3). The latter involves thirty-two teams per city, with up to seven players a team, in an eleven-city tour, culminating with a national champion winning a

$10,000 prize. Now, though, Alianza de Futbol—under the banner of "*Pasión por la comunidad*" ("Passion for the community")—is best known for its Powerade Sueño Alianza program, functioning as an *American Idol* of sorts for aspiring young soccer players.

"As the years went on in Alianza, it was pretty clear that the Latino was being alienated from the best soccer in development, because of the pay-to-play system," Escoto says. "The better you are, the more expensive it is. It shouldn't be $100 to do a tryout."

And so, Alianza has created a tryout program even more robust and expansive than "Sueño MLS." In the interest of "wanting to give Latinos a fair shot if they want to be pro," Alianza does tryouts for the eleven-city tour, with hopeful players traveling to one—or more, in some cases—of the cities on that summer's schedule to try to get noticed.

"It's an open tryout," Escoto says of the process. "They show up at 7:30 in the morning, they line up by age, and we do eleven versus eleven matches. The first goal is to filter and get to the top twenty-five or twenty-six players in each age group: U-16, U-18, U-22." The filtering process is done by professional scouts. "From there, they'll take the best eighteen in each age group. By that Sunday, when we play the local academy team, we'll have the best eighteen players that we've found, and then we'll guarantee at least one person per team in our national showcase. Basically, from the 500 we have any given weekend, we'll cut it down to the best fifty-four, and from there we'll get it to the best three. So it's a pretty tough filter."

"It's 100 percent soccer," he adds. "We don't do fitness tests. And for Alianza tryouts, it doesn't matter if you're Latino or not Latino, if you have papers, if you don't have papers. We don't look at that. We look at your age and how well you play."

The program has gotten more popular. Escoto notes that more than 1,000 hopefuls showed up in the program's first year, compared to more than 10,000 players this year. "The growth has been exponential," Escoto says. "And the talent? When you come to Alianza, you're already a soccer player. We just help you. We boost you to be seen. This is a showcase."

Escoto feels that they've been able to build up a trust level that has helped them grow the program throughout the US Latino community.

They decided specifically to not act as a player agent for any of the players they discovered because, as he notes, "We wanted the community to trust us; we didn't want to get into the business of player representation."

They've earned that trust—and express pride in it—because of their consistency and their longevity. As Escoto says, "They know that Alianza's coming back each year. They can expect high quality programs and opportunity. There are players who go to four or five cities every year to the tryouts until we tell them to stop going to the tryouts. There are people who don't give up, and of course, we encourage that."

The program is not just about finding players who might become pros, or who might find a place on the national team. They also annually take a team to the Surf Cup, a high-profile talent showcase for high school soccer players, attended by coaches and scouts from a number of soccer-playing universities in the United States.

"We're taking the best players with a really good GPA. But it takes over $30,000 to take a team. Not many Latino teams are going to be able to pay that. But we can take the best twenty players we have to San Diego and make them a team." From its competitions, Alianza handpicks a team of its talented players who fit a specific profile: "Low-income, high-level soccer players with great academics, so they can pretty much get a full ride."

In addition to helping universities find talented Latino players for their teams, Escoto is proud of the work Alianza has done to draw out players through Sueño who might not otherwise be able to connect with an academy or club.

"We started finding tons of good players who were not in a major metropolitan city," Escoto explains. "Even though we're only in eleven cities where we have tryouts, our players come from over 1,000 cities."

Sueño Alianza's most recognizable success story to date, the 2013 winner, is a player who came into his own with his club team during the ultimately fruitless US qualifying campaign in the fall of 2017, provided hope for American soccer fans in the uncertain post-Hex future, and then gave them cause for despair when he announced in January 2018 that he would instead pledge to Mexico in advance of a potential World Cup call-up: Jonathan González.

González, who had been involved with US youth teams since his early teens, was coached by US legend Hugo Pérez in his formative years. He looked like the type of player who could develop and flourish in an MLS academy—but he lived in Santa Rosa, an hour and a half (at best) from the South Bay, where the San Jose Earthquakes have their academy.

"He would have no chance to be in an academy system," Escoto says. "This country's too big, there are too many soccer players, and if you're lucky enough to be close to an academy, and you're a good player, you're probably going to get in for free, which is great. But if you're far from an academy, you're going to get lost."

While some MLS academies have remedied that by creating residencies, Escoto says, "It's different from Mexico. Pachuca can house over 400 players! Chivas can house fifty or 100. They can take players from the US and anywhere in Mexico, they can give them housing and develop those players. That's why Mexico's so successful in the youth level."

"There are so many players being left out," he says with concern. "The hard thing is when you find a player in the middle of nowhere, there aren't enough teams who can bring them in and pay their expenses. It's a different model in other countries. Here, you're investing all this money—housing, meals, school—but then you don't own the player. It's a different business than in Mexico where you can just take a player, provide housing, pay $200 or $300 and then you own the player. It's hard. It's moving the right direction, but I don't think it's enough."

González was among the best fifty-four players brought into the national showcase in 2013, and already had the chance to impress multiple scouts. Winning certainly did that. "He received offers from seventeen clubs—basically every team in Mexico wanted him," Escoto says. "He was very close to going to Chivas. They were very aggressive in pursuing him. But he went to Monterrey, because he wanted to play for the US, and the players for Chivas can't play for the US. That's just their politics. They only play with Mexican players, or if it's a Mexican American player, he has to play with the Mexican national team."

The decision to leave the US for a Mexican academy when he was still just fourteen wasn't an easy one. "My parents were really nervous," said González for Tom Marshall's August 2017 ESPN FC article. "I really wanted to go and they were between should we let him go, should we not. But we sat down, had a family talk and we thought it was probably the best for me."[3]

González started the 2017–18 season strong, emerging as a starter for Monterrey matches while still just eighteen, and helping them get to the two-leg Apertura finals in December against crosstown rivals Tigres. He played the entire first leg and eighty minutes of the second leg in the 3–2 aggregate loss, and distinguished himself enough to be named to the Liga MX Apertura Best XI—an honor that put him alongside some of the league's biggest stars.[4]

As Marshall remarked in his González feature, Monterrey had assembled one of the most expensive squads in North America and typically doesn't field youth players—making coach Antonio Mohamed's trust in González all the more remarkable. As the article noted, his performance with Monterrey placed him more squarely on the USMNT's radar. "The idea that United States head coach Bruce Arena would be asking for Monterrey midfielder Jonathan González's telephone number would've seemed almost inconceivable a couple of months ago," Marshall wrote. "But after the 18-year-old burst onto the Liga MX scene in some style early this 2017 Apertura, that's exactly what happened last week."[5]

But González's ascendency in Liga MX also inspired visions of González in an El Tri jersey. A September 2017 article in Mexican publication *Récord* revealed that Mohamed was urging Mexican coach Juan Carlos Osorio to steer González toward Mexico before González got his first senior cap with the US.[6]

In other words, González, developing as a potential future American World Cup starter, was showing real, tangible potential to crack Mexico's best twenty-three in 2018. And after October—with González continuing in his breakout season—Mexico had a distinct recruiting advantage over the US, as Mexico could offer a World Cup trip the US didn't have available.

González, part of the US's U-20 national team that won the CONCACAF Championship, was left off the U-20 World Cup roster, but was still clearly on a pathway to vie for the Olympics with the U-23s in 2020 and was projected to make his first World Cup as a twenty-three-year-old in 2022.

But he wasn't called up for the September or October qualifiers where he could have been cap-tied, and as *Soccer America*'s Mike Woitalla learned in an end of 2017 interview, US Soccer may have faltered in securing González's commitment to the red, white, and blue by not inviting him to a November 2017 camp and a subsequent friendly with Portugal.

"Personally, nobody came and talked to me and let me know about that friendly," González told Woitalla, "I just wasn't called in." In a follow-up question about Mexico's interest, he responded with a not-all-that-convincing, "I really haven't thought of it much," claiming focus on his season with Monterrey even as the US vs. Mexico questions swirled.[7]

Within days of that interview, on January 9, 2018, González officially announced he would make the FIFA-allowed one-time switch from US to Mexico, allowing him to be eligible for El Tri's 2018 World Cup and competitions to come—including Gold Cups and World Cup qualifiers where he will face down newly-formed American opponents. In a press release he tweeted, in both English and Spanish, González noted, "It is not easy to leave the country in which one is born; however, Mexico is also my home as it is the country in which my parents were born and, consequently, where my roots originate." Later in the release, he acknowledged that "I carry both nationalities in my heart very proudly," but he also characterized Mexico as "the country that opened the doors for me."[8]

American fans reacted with puzzlement and disappointment, with many looking to blame US Soccer for its failure to lock up González, while still others bristled at the suggestion that González was merely a player for the US to claim, rather than a person looking at his future with every right to choose between two options with distinct pros and cons.

Brad Rothenberg, in a *Soccer America* interview that came on the heels on González's announcement, said he was in contact with González as recently as New Year's Eve. At that time, according to Rothenberg, González was still undecided about his national team future, even though he was "bleeding red, white, and blue" when he first arrived as a Monterrey player.

Rothenberg castigated US Soccer for its handling of the González situation, declaring, "If anybody at US Soccer thinks they did enough to keep Jonathan, then they should resign before the new Federation president fires them. Our Federation lost Jonathan either by its own arrogance, apathy or incompetence. You pick it. We screwed up and I'm angry about it. I've grown tired of watching our Federation neglect this community. We didn't do enough, not nearly enough, to keep him. And the worst part is that it will continue if wholesale changes aren't made in the approach to finding talent in this community."[9]

On a personal level, Rothenberg is critical of US Soccer's unwillingness to scout tryouts for the Alianza platform he helped create. Perhaps in part because "Sueño MLS" looks to be a program of the past, MLS scouts are in attendance alongside the Liga MX scouts who are a regular presence at the tryouts. At the 2017 Sueño Alianza tryout in San Francisco, for example, scouts from the San Jose Earthquakes joined scouts from Liga MX teams Léon, Pachuca, and Querétaro, and each team offered an academy invitation to at least one player who came to the tryouts. Two weeks later, FC Dallas Academy U-18 coach Francisco Molina made the 650-mile journey from Frisco, Texas to El Paso to join multiple Mexican team representatives in scouting players, indicative of what Rothenberg labels as FC Dallas's longstanding support for Alianza's efforts.

But Rothenberg contended that US Soccer has been less than appreciative, contending that US Soccer Director of Talent Identification Tony Lepore "actually notified us in 2016 that they weren't interested in participating in Alianza since they haven't found any elite players." He added, "On more than one occasion, US Soccer scouts and coaches have secretly watched games hiding behind bleachers or our event inflatables but, when I asked, were unwilling to address our Alianza players directly for fear of endorsing an 'unsanctioned' event."[10]

"I love Alianza de Futbol," says Mexico-focused soccer journalist Maxi Rodriguez. "I think it's a wonderful program, and it provides opportunities to kids who wouldn't otherwise have a chance. That said, I think it's absurd that a program like this has to exist in the first place. We all know this issue of identification exists," adding that entities like the US Development Academy and the various MLS academies should be finding players before Alianza does.

The González saga, in particular, concerns him. "The fact that a young player has to win a contest in order to win a youth deal in another country is hugely problematic. Obviously the player is talented, so isn't it on MLS and [US Soccer] to devise ways to bring them into the system?" (And, it must be said now, to keep him in the system once he arrives.)

Escoto rightly says of González, "If he would have stayed in Santa Rosa, he would not be the player he is right now." But the irony, of course, is that the path that took him from Santa Rosa ultimately forked into an American path and a Mexican path, and González chose the latter. As I'll discuss at the end of this chapter, González is far from the last Mexican-American player who will face that choice.

While Escoto lauds MLS for the work it did in its Sueño MLS program, he notes, "I wish they'd do more programs for the Hispanic community, because when they did it, they did it at a really high level." He uses the past tense because he believes that they're no longer reaching out the Latino community in the way they could.

"There are millions and millions of Latino soccer players," he says. "To make it at the highest level is difficult. There are so many factors. But when you have a pay-to-play system, you're alienating not just Latinos, but the African American community. If you look at the NBA and the NFL, where their top players came from, they didn't come from high-income families."

"Americans need to believe in Americans," FC Dallas coach Oscar Pareja told Guardian writer Les Carpenter in a November 2015 feature on the FC Dallas Academy, which Escoto lauds as being most like the Liga MX academies where a number of young Mexican-American players go to develop. "We have talent here, we have players who can do it and there are many on the staff who say we are better than many other countries. Is it the future? For sure, but we have to believe that."[11]

Ultimately, the work that Escoto and his team are doing comes down to sharing that belief and wanting more success stories for Latino players who live in the United States. "All we're trying to do," he asserts, "is make a level playing field for the Latinos."

For nearly a decade now, Doug Andreassen has been on a personal crusade aimed at getting US Soccer to bring more Latino players into the youth national team ranks. The Diversity Task Force he's been involved with is still officially on the list of varied committees and task forces within US Soccer. Throughout 2017, though, its page on the US Soccer website was distressingly blank, despite other committees having full rosters listed. Andreassen wryly relates that the committee he is on has been placed in a "holding pattern."

Andreassen was featured in a June 2016 *Guardian* article, titled "'It's only working for the white kids': American soccer's diversity problem," spelling out a stark dichotomy in which children born into white American families with means obtain access to the Development Academy, while such access lies outside the grasp of less fortunate, non-white families. The article explores his concern of what he characterizes as a broken system, exemplified by this passage: "He sees well-to-do families spending thousands of dollars a year on soccer clubs that propel their children to the sport's highest levels, while thousands of gifted athletes in mostly African American and Latino neighborhoods get left behind. He worries about this inequity. Soccer is the world's great democratic game, whose best stars have come from the world's slums, ghettos and favelas. And yet in the US the path to the top is often determined by how many zeroes a parent can write in their checkbook."[12]

Andreassen, who has been involved as a youth soccer administrator for close to a quarter century, notes, "I've always had a passion for what I call the underserved population playing soccer in this country." He approached Sunil Gulati about the situation around 2009, and maintains that Gulati is cognizant of this issue and was committed to resolving it while at the helm of US Soccer.

When Andreassen first spoke with Gulati about the need to address the problem, Gulati put him on the Diversity Task Force, chaired by Nelson Rodríguez, now General Manager of the Chicago Fire.

Rodríguez has notably worked on diversity issues throughout his career in soccer. Lately, he has called into question whether MLS coaches have enough ethnic diversity. In an April 2017 *Guardian* article exploring the topic, Rodríguez said of American soccer, "I refuse to believe that the best people and best professionals are mostly white males. I would find that an incredible set of coincidences."[13] In August 2016, during a Chicago Fire home match billed as "Pride Night" to honor the LGBT community, Rodríguez took to the center circle with a microphone before the match to announce the club's intentions to shut down the "puto" chant[14]—seen by many as an anti-gay slur, employed whenever a visiting goalkeeper takes a goal kick—that's been virulent in a number of stadiums across the hemisphere.

Andreassen and Rodríguez worked on the committee for close to two years before Rodríguez left and tapped Andreassen to head it. The challenge they set upon in increasing diversity was to find a plan that would work for all of US Soccer, noting that the nation is so big and contains so many varied metropolitan areas that what works in one city very well may not work in another.

"They think they've got about 3.6 or 3.8 million kids playing organized soccer around the country," Andreassen said, "but we have come to believe that we think there's probably between eight and ten million kids who are playing in unorganized soccer." (By "unorganized soccer," he means kids playing soccer in the streets or in public parks, but he also means church leagues and other leagues outside of the assortment with which US Soccer has already established pipelines.)

Andreassen's goal, ultimately, is to identify more kids who would want to play organized soccer and eventually get into Development Academy affiliate clubs and academies by the time they reach the U-12 level, and clubs before that.

Part of the challenge in this, he admits, is in some established allegiances to other nations based on heritage and the soccer teams they grow up rooting for. Andreassen says if a boy grows up with parents from Mexico, for example, he'll likely grow up watching and being encouraged to root for the Mexican national team. By extension, he'll want to wear the Mexican national jersey, and he'll dream about—should he be good enough to play for a national team—playing for Mexico.

But Andreassen thinks that US Soccer is giving up on those players too easily, noting the work that Alianza de Futbol is doing—and how organized they've been—in reaching those players.

"If US Soccer said, 'We want to pick up these underserved kids, these Hispanic kids, and have US scouts looking for them,' they'd do it, but they don't do it for lots of reasons. They believe that they have all of the talent that's out there in the Hispanic community. They feel like those kids get identified."

He also faults the pay-to-play nature of the club system as a barrier, but points out that even when scholarships are utilized to bring certain players to clubs that will fast-track players to the Development Academy, it does so at the expense of the Latino community. He gives a hypothetical example of a Latino U-17 team: A Development Academy club comes calling, and the coach or the scout wants three specific players from that team. For those three players, it may work out well, but for the players and coaches that they leave behind, Andreassen has questions:

"The other boys on the team will say, wait a minute, the white coaches just want those three players. They don't care about the rest of us. Suddenly, that team may go from a winning record to a losing record. In Hispanic culture, by the way, winning is a big deal. What is the attitude of the other kids on the team towards the white coaches or the white scouts who came to have a look at them?"

What happens as a result, he says, is that the Latino community develops a distrust of the club teams, even though those teams may be well-intentioned in trying to elevate certain players. And while he does acknowledge that an occasional Latino player finds a path to success— he brings up Omar Gonzalez, the longtime USMNT defender who grew up in Dallas—he also notes a systematic disconnect that keeps a number of other potential Omar Gonzalezes from making it to the USMNT.

What concerns Andreassen, beyond losing the opportunity to cultivate American players, is losing the opportunity to cultivate American fans. He notes that while only a fraction of those who play soccer will make a national team, they all can be part of the audience to help grow and cultivate soccer. He worries that if those who play as children don't steer some of their attention to MLS or USL as adults, it could in turn impact their kids. This leads back to his hypothetical scenario, in which a young player who is US-eligible wants to play for Mexico if his family has Mexican relatives, or for Honduras if he has Honduran relatives, because he gravitates toward the teams he's learned to root for.

Andreassen is also concerned about equal access to fields for all who want to play, and this concern is central to his crusade. He notes that there might be linguistic or cultural barriers in the sign-up process, the awkwardness at best arising when police are called in to enforce an established, majority-white or fully-white team's claim to the field that evening, and the expense of insurance.

He also notes, while we're uncomfortably on the topic of expense, that games require paid referees. This means, in his estimation, that any time a team plans to travel to a tournament where scouts will be, it requires several hundred dollars that a family may not be able to spare in order to give the young player an opportunity to catch the attention of a scout.

"Club soccer fees come in on the average of $2,000 to $3,000 per year," Andreassen says. "Many times, these teams will travel to out of the region or even states for tournament play, thus escalating that fee by another $1,000 to $1,500 easily. These teams, by the way, will usually play at the premier level of the game." He even asserts that in some cases, the annual cost for a player can reach or even go beyond the $10,000 range.

And in this discussion of cost and underserved populations, he makes the point that underserved populations can also be white, perhaps in rural areas, though in their findings many of the potential players they see lacking equal access to the youth development soccer pyramid are Latino.

He also advocates for what he terms equity inclusion—a system by which underserved communities can get cost-free access to fields and other athletic facilities. The way Andreassen sees it, and what he's lobbied for in his Seattle hometown, equity inclusion will help young players in underserved communities get playing time in or near their own neighborhoods, versus taking the one- or two-hour bus rides that might be required in cities where the only option might be for a club located dauntingly far away.

In response to the objections which might be raised by club teams asked to participate in an equity inclusion program that would force them to curtail their own training schedules, Andreassen asks, "We're

This won't end well: The starting XI for the USMNT poses for the customary group photo before taking on Trinidad & Tobago at Ato Boldon Stadium in Couva on October 10, 2017, for its final match in the 2018 World Cup Qualification cycle. The Americans would lose 2–1, missing out on a World Cup spot for the first time in thirty-two years and creating a plethora of questions about the future of US Soccer.

FRONT ROW: Midfielder (6) Darlington Nagbe, defender (2) DeAndre Yedlin, midfielder (21) Paul Arriola, midfielder (10) Christian Pulisic, forward (9) Bobby Wood, and defender (15) Jorge Villafaña.

BACK ROW: Defender (3) Omar Gonzalez, goalkeeper (1) Tim Howard, midfielder (4) Michael Bradley, defender (5) Matt Besler, and forward (17) Jozy Altidore.

The team taking the field in the US's 2006 World Cup opener has so much promise—including key players from the 2002 team that came so close to toppling Germany and advancing to the semifinals—but they'd lose to the Czech Republic 3–0, starting an inglorious campaign that ended in the group stage.

FRONT ROW: Defender (6) Steve Cherundolo, midfielder (17) DaMarcus Beasley, midfielder (15) Bobby Convey, midfielder (21) Landon Donovan, defender (7) Eddie Lewis, and midfielder (10) Claudio Reyna.

BACK ROW: Defender (4) Pablo Mastroeni, defender (23) Eddie Pope, forward (20) Brian McBride, defender (22) Oguchi Onyewu, and goalkeeper (18) Kasey Keller.

(Credit: USA Today Sports © Ron Scheffler)

Landon Donovan and DaMarcus Beasley, arguably the two best players in
US Soccer's inaugural 1999 class of youth players at its residency program in
Bradenton, Florida, were a dynamic duo for the US for years. Here, Donovan
celebrates a second-half penalty goal with Beasley against Mexico in the 2007
CONCACAF Gold Cup Final at Chicago's Soldier Field. The US won 2–1.

(Credit: USA Today Sports © 2007 Tom Fluegge)

Perhaps the most famous, celebrated goal in US Soccer history, Landon Donovan's last-gasp game-winner against Algeria in the 2010 World Cup sent the US to the Round of 16—and set off celebrations across the US that galvanized American soccer fans and inspired a new wave to join them.

(Credit: USA Today Sports © Janet Sisco)

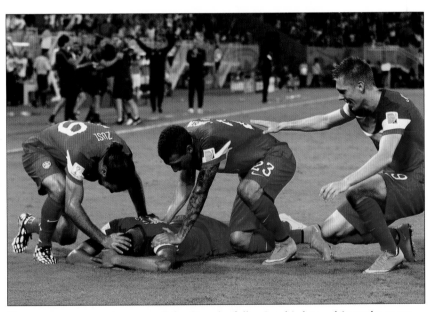

Teammates surround a prone John Brooks following his late, ultimately game-winning goal over Ghana in the US's opening game in the 2014 World Cup. Though the US would advance to the Round of 16 for a second straight World Cup, this would be their only win of the tournament.

(Credit: USA Today Sports © Mark J. Rebilas)

US head coach Jürgen Klinsmann comforts midfielder Alejandro Bedoya after he is subbed off in what would be the US's 2014 World Cup ouster. Despite holding Belgium to a scoreless draw in regulation, the US gave up a pair of goals in extra time and could only climb halfway back—on a goal scored by Bedoya's sub, Julian Green, within minutes of coming on—before the final whistle. *(Credit: USA Today Sports © Winslow Townson)*

Eighteen-year-old Christian Pulisic emerged as a key US player during the team's World Cup qualifying round in 2017; he's shown here battling Trinidad & Tobago midfielder Khaleem Hyland for the ball in the first half of the US's 2–0 win at Dick's Sporting Goods Park in Commerce City, Colorado. Pulisic scored both goals in the win; he would go on to score the lone US goal in the teams' rematch four months later—which the US infamously lost.

(Credit: USA Today Sports © Isaiah J. Downing)

LEFT: Derrick Jones, one of the best players to date coming out of the Philadelphia Union Academy, was discovered at age fifteen when his Junior Lone Star FC, a Philadelphia-based minor league soccer club, scrimmaged against a Union youth team. The Ghanaian-born Jones, who played for the Union's first team for parts of the 2017 season, represented the US at the U-20 level starting in 2016, and was part of the US's U-20 World Cup team in 2017. *(Photo courtesy of Philadelphia Union)*

RIGHT: Paul Arriola, shown training with DC United, was acquired by the MLS club from Liga MX club Tijuana in August 2017 in the team's most expensive deal to date. Arriola, emerging as a key young player for the USMNT, came to DC United to be at the center of that team's attempted resurgence. *(Photo courtesy of DC United)*

LEFT: Russell Canouse, a one-time New York Red Bull Academy member, became part of the trend of promising young American players moving to Germany with a 2011 move to Hoffenheim. By the summer of 2017, though—in large part to get more meaningful playing time—Canouse came back to MLS to play with DC United, the team he grew up rooting for. *(Photo courtesy of DC United)*

The Powerade® Sueño Alianza ("Dream Alliance") National Showcase draws hundreds of hopefuls to each of its stops. The August 30, 2017 tryout in San Francisco was no exception with Julian Varela, Cesar Medina, and Ali Radman standing out among about 540 youngsters. The three made it to the national finals while hoping to capture the eye of scouts from the San Jose Earthquakes and Liga MX teams Pachuca, León, and Querétaro. Eight aspiring players received one or more direct invitations from a Liga MX team as a result of their tryout; one player received an invitation from the MLS team as well.

(Photo courtesy of Alianza de Futbol)

here for the greater good of the game, right?" He believes—in part by seeing equity inclusion efforts in action—that if US Soccer put their endorsement behind such a move, it could affect changes that would, over time, bring more underserved players into the pool of potential youth national team players.

Other invested observers have their own theories. "I think it's largely due to a limitation on scouting resources when it comes to the US," says Maxi Rodriguez. "Especially when it comes to the Development Academy and the MLS academies, there's a massive area of the US that gets overlooked. Particularly when you consider the financial requirement to take part in club soccer, the end result is plenty of talented kids never having a chance to join the system. This affects all kids who struggle economically, but disproportionately hits Latinos."

Additionally, he forwards the theory he's heard from some that there's a "cultural divide when it comes to the [youth national team] coaches and the systems they try to implement." While he doesn't think it is as significant as others think it is, he believes it might come into play for those going between the Mexican system and the American system.

To be fair, those involved in the Development Academy are aware of these issues and welcoming of diversity. They do recognize some are critical of where and how they find players, but they also point out that the size of the country provides challenges that they're continually working to address.

"We're scouting predominately the Development Academy games, because that's the network we know and we've built," says DA Director Jared Micklos. "But it's a partnership with the clubs. So I think the root of the question is how we actually reach those communities. We would hope that through the club and the academy that we've gotten in the right markets, in the major markets." For what Micklos calls "inner city" players who might have difficulty physically getting to clubs or academies, they provide $400,000 annually in scholarships to help players offset travel costs or address other financial need.

"If a player is discovered or a player is desired by one of the teams, that's a need-based program that we would hope that's going to be another extension to pull players from any market into the academy,"

Micklos notes. Scholarships are typically in the $1,000 to $2,000 range, paid in several installments during the year. They also encourage clubs to adjust their prices down to help widen the pool of potential players available to review for the youth national teams.

Micklos does acknowledge the concern that a pay-to-play system represents, even as they're using scholarships to address those costs.

"I think it's a fair statement on the landscape overall, for sure, and not to say that we're not part of that landscape. There are some markets where it is it's expensive for a player, just based on the travel costs, so that is true." He maintains that the organization's "goal has always been to reduce any barrier for a player to play the sport. So via the clubs, and via us, we're hoping to offset that. I do think it is a challenge in our country for geography reasons, and for the way the structure makes the sport more expensive than it might be in another country that's a whole lot more condensed and has a lot more opportunities and a lot more players that are of the same quality in a closer area. They absolutely spread out when you get to some of our more remote states, our rural states." But he points out for MLS academies that are free of cost to players, "If they can get there, no matter what their demographic or their race of their ethnicity, they're there."

"There's not a set of criteria exclusive to what we're looking for," Micklos continues. "If you're looking for the best players, you're looking for them regardless of what any of their background and criteria are. And if players are so remote that they don't live in an academy market, then you're trying to get them to in an academy market. If they do live in an academy market and they can't get there, you're trying to figure out the logistics or the finances to get them." He says that focusing on one type of player or one style may be counterproductive. "I think what you actually want, you want diversity—not just diversity in the way the player is made up from race or ethnicity. You want diversity in the way the players play too. You don't want a team that's all the same style player."

Of course, some notable Latino players have found their way to the USMNT through various routes in recent years. The aforementioned Omar Gonzalez went the club soccer and college route—being picked for Bradenton along the way—before arriving at the Galaxy in 2009 via the

MLS SuperDraft to start his pro career, and parlaying his play there into his first senior team call-up in January 2010.[15]

Alejandro Bedoya, a Colombian American from New Jersey whose father and grandfather both played professionally in Colombia, played in college and then joined clubs in Sweden, Scotland, and France,[16] before returning to the US in 2016 to join the Union. Hérculez Gómez, who played for the USMNT between 2007 and 2013, describes himself as having a "self-made" development story, getting to professional play in both Mexico and the US outside of the conventional channels. His big break came in 2002, when his San Diego Gauchos played the LA Galaxy in a friendly match, and the Galaxy offered him a ten-day contract, which he then parlayed into an extended career.

"I wasn't recruited by colleges," he recounts. "I went out and took a chance, and my first go-around in Mexico didn't pay off. I came back, played [in the] USL, [and] got fortunate enough to be seen by the LA Galaxy in a time where it was still very much the norm to go to college and get drafted. I was 19, on the Galaxy, the youngest guy on the team. Three months later, we [won] MLS Cup and kind of things just went from there."

"I didn't play ODP; I couldn't afford it," Gómez said, referring to the Olympic Development Program. "I come from a very working class family, and we didn't do family dinners because my parents were working all the time. We didn't have $100 for a one-day mini-camp for ODP. It just didn't work like that."

Gómez grew up playing on a club soccer team in his native Las Vegas. He notes that every year, a teammate's wealthy father wrote out a $25,000 check to cover the team's annual tournament costs and travel expenses. "I was one of these Latinos who got helped out on a very Anglo team, and if not for that, I wouldn't have gotten hooked on the game and had that kind of energy going forward."

Despite acquiring what he describes as "intangibles that coaches like" in his unusual journey, Gómez noted that it had repercussions well into his career. "When I got back to Mexico [in 2010], what I noticed the most was how far behind I was in just the most practical football aspects. I needed to retrain myself."

While Gómez thinks the US is doing a better job finding the next generation of Latino soccer players, he remarks, "This is by default because the bar was set so low before. We're still losing players to Mexican teams, who are identifying these players through Alianza, or through tournaments in California, where underprivileged kids go out and have a showcase. [. . .] They go across the border at an early age, and for some of these kids, it pans out, and for others, it doesn't. But it's not a pay-to-play system down there," he notes. "They make an investment in you. We're still backwards. Our club soccer program here is you pay to play. They're not making an investment in you; you're making an investment in them."

Paul Arriola, who started his club career with Liga MX team Tijuana, found the situation to be "perfect for an American," as Gómez and other fellow Mexican-American players preceded him there. He now has a sizable fan base that crosses the border from San Diego to attend games.

"I'm from San Diego, so I was considered more of a homegrown player," he says. "I would be recognized on both sides of the border. And then especially in Mexico, I was one of the only white guys down there," he says with a laugh, "so I was obviously recognized more. I went to a private school where probably 70 percent of the kids spoke Spanish, and probably 50 percent of them lived in Tijuana and crossed the border every day to go to school. So I felt the rivalry between the United States and Mexico even there. When it was recess time, we'd go out and we start playing soccer, and it would be [the] Mexicans versus the Americans."

Though he describes himself as "pretty much full American," having a Mexican great-grandfather allowed him to obtain a Mexican passport to be on Tijuana's roster as a Mexican player under Liga MX's 10/8 rule limiting the number of foreign-born players than can sign with a club. When asked what he checks on the census box, he says, "It depends. Sometimes I put Hispanic, sometimes I put white. It depends on, like, 'I wonder what I'm feeling today.'"

Mexico's football federation did ask Tijuana about Arriola's potential interest in playing for its youth national team soon after he arrived, but as Arriola puts it, the club "shut that down"—in large part because billing him as a Mexican American was part of how they were marketing the team to fans north of the border.

Indeed, by the time the Mexican football federation expressed interest in Arriola, he was already well established in the US youth national team hierarchy, despite being a teenager. He started at the U-17 level, and he was most recently involved with the U-23 in efforts to get the US to the 2016 Olympics.

But Mexican interest in players like Arriola and González offer evidence to what soccer writer Leander Schaerlaeckens termed "the last great untapped well of soccer talent in the Western Hemisphere—and maybe beyond that: The Mexican American."

Writing for Bleacher Report in July 2017, Schaerlaeckens remarked, "These Mexican American teenagers are tugged back and forth between the two youth national team programs, negotiating their own preferences, those of their families, the clearest path toward a viable career in soccer and a conflicted patriotism for two nations."

He went on to explain:

At the root of the conflict is the Mexico federation's policy to actively recruit in the United States. With an extensive scouting apparatus for its youth national teams, the FMF [the Mexican football federation] collects multiple reports on potential additions. When three or four positive reports come in from different scouts or coaches, the player gets the call. And with scouts permanently based in Los Angeles and Texas, where much of the country's Mexican American population is concentrated, the FMF has a fertile field from which to choose new players.

"To us, it's not so [much] a concern where they're born," says Dennis te Kloese, director of Mexico's youth national teams. "If they have the Mexican nationality and are eligible to play for Mexico, they're candidates to represent our national teams. This is one of the unique situations in the world where so many people of one nationality live in another country. Of course, to the Mexican federation, this is an opportunity."[17]

It's entirely conceivable that future editions of El Tri could feature players who were born in the United States but commit to Mexico. As te Kloese said shortly after Jonathan González's switch, "The case of Jonathan won't be the last."[18]

But that's not to say the US will lose out in all future cases in which Mexican Americans experience dual national dilemmas. In fact, two of the highest-profile affiliation switches in all of world soccer during the summer of 2017—one for the men, one for the women—were from Mexico to the United States.

Jesse Gonzalez, the FC Dallas goalkeeper who came up through the team's academy, but played with Mexico's U-20 and U-23 national teams and seemed destined for its senior team, announced his one-time switch to the US to make the 2017 Gold Cup roster, and was called up to the January 2018 camp that effectively started the clock on 2022 World Cup qualification.

Sofia Huerta, a Boise-born player capped as a U-20 Mexican national player, but who played in college at Santa Clara and plays professionally in the US, saw her switch made official by FIFA in September 2017,[19] the day before she came on for her first USWNT cap. She subbed on in the second half of an international friendly against New Zealand and assisted on an Alex Morgan goal, doing her part to give American fans hope for the next Women's World Cup in 2019.

Remezcla writer Luis Paez-Pumar, musing on Jesse Gonzalez's situation as a potential heir apparent to the USMNT's aging trio of first-choice goalies, noted that he "could establish himself as the US #1 for the next decade with a few choice performances." He noted that the switch from El Tri to USMNT "seemed less about national pride—although he tried to spin it that way, saying 'the US has given me a lot. I'm grateful for what they have given me and the opportunity they have given me'—and more about potential playing time."[20]

Schaerlaeckens, in his article, noted that Gonzalez wasn't getting regular call-ups from Mexico prior to his switch—musing that "with Mexico managers historically slow to warm to new players active in MLS," Gonzalez might have seen a better opportunity to impress American coaches with his play for one of MLS's most consistent teams.

The 2017 edition of both the U-20 and U-23 rosters, it should be said, featured an appreciable level of diversity of the varied kinds Micklos discusses. For active proponents like Andreassen and Escoto, this is perhaps an encouraging sign not only for future national teams but for the entirety of youth soccer.

But how have the U-20 and U-23 teams performed? In many ways, they've performed like the senior team recently has, with the occasional disappointment but also with clear moments of hope—especially if this generation of American players performs to lofty expectations borne of anticipation to be one of the world's elite soccer nations.

CHAPTER 7

THE U-20s AND THE U-23s: FIRST TEAM PLAYERS-IN-WAITING

To glimpse the future of American soccer, you must look at the two rungs below the senior team. For players who are particularly talented and ready to make the leap to the senior team, the U-20 team is typically the last step in the journey before they leap into full-fledged international competition. The U-23 team can function as a finishing school or a place where young players who get senior team call-ups can get additional tournament experience.

The U-20s have their own World Cup, held every two years since 1977 and formerly known as the FIFA World Youth Championship.[1] The tournament has now grown to a twenty-four-team tournament involving all the federations under a different apportionment than the World Cup—notably, with Oceania getting two of the twenty-four slots, one going to New Zealand and one, amazingly, going to Vanuatu.[2] The 2017 edition, hosted by South Korea, treated American fans to late night and early morning start times reminiscent of the 2002 World Cup.

The U-23s have their own championship as well—it's woven into the Olympic Games. While teams going to the Olympics get to augment their rosters with three players of any age, qualification remains the realm of players twenty-three and younger. Even players who have senior team caps can play in U-23 competitions as long as they meet the age requirements, which is why the likes of Kellyn Acosta, Paul Arriola, and Jordan Morris, captained by Columbus Crew SC mainstay Wil Trapp, were part of the squad endeavoring to get the US into the 2016 Olympics.

If the future of the senior squad does indeed hinge in part on the per-formance of the youth national teams, the most recent performance on the world stage—from the U-20s—provided hope. For the first time ever, the US won the CONCACAF U-20 tournament, with captain Erik Palmer-Brown winning the award for the competition's best player. Jonathan Klinsmann—yes, the son of Jürgen—who started 2017 playing for the University of California and, by July, had signed on for Bundesliga team Hertha Berlin, was honored as the tournament's best goalkeeper.

Along the way, the US beat Mexico 1–0 in what was essentially a must-win match; Palmer-Brown headed in the match's only goal, dealing El Tri its first loss in the tournament since 2009. (MLS's Matt Doyle noted in a tweet that seven of the starting players hailed from MLS acad-emies, with an eighth, Paris-born Portland Timbers forward Jeremy Ebo-bisse, entering the league as a 2017 draft pick.[3])

By the time the Tab Ramos–coached U-20 team got to its final group stage match—a 6–0 romp over New Zealand—the squad certainly had a world-beating look about it. The scoring in that match started with seventeen-year-old Josh Sargent in the thirty-second minute, with five dif-ferent teammates scoring goals over the final half-hour of an eventually lopsided win.

In the quarterfinals, the US U-20s faced Venezuela and lost 2–1 in extra time, prompting Stars and Stripes FC's Rob Usry to say the loss "evoked the ghosts of USMNT past," in that it closely resembled the 2014 World Cup ouster to Belgium by the same score—an onslaught of saved chances, a muffed chance to win the match outright in second-half stoppage time, the ceding of two goals in extra time, a late US hope-giving goal providing a welcome answer (with Ebobisse playing the Julian Green role), but that hope ultimately extinguished with the final whistle.[4]

The difference here, though, was that had the US gotten past Venezuela—which was able to ascend all the way to the U-20 final, losing 1–0 to England—it very well could have found itself challenging England for the trophy. And judging from the retrospective quotes coming out of the US camp, they knew it.

Nine of the twenty-one players the US selected to the U-20 World Cup are affiliated with MLS clubs, many of them starting for those clubs at preternaturally young ages, with another four coming from MLS youth academies.[5]

Tyler Adams, for instance, became a regular contributor in the New York Red Bulls midfield and defensive line during the 2017 season and into the playoffs as an eighteen-year-old. Palmer-Brown was worked into the defensive rotation for Sporting Kansas City during the 2017 season, though it was announced soon after the U-20 World Cup that he was bound for Manchester City by the start of 2018.[6]

And then there's the remarkable youth movement at Real Salt Lake (RSL), where four of the players who went to the World Cup have worked their way into starting roles for the club.

Justen Glad started in club teams in Seattle and Tucson, and then, based on the recommendation of friends, tried out at fifteen for the RSL-Arizona Academy in Casa Grande, Arizona. (The club has since centralized its training facilities to a complex in Harriman, Utah, which includes dorms for out-of-state Academy members and, according to a spokesperson from RSL, cost nearly $75 million.[7] The Grande Sports Academy where RSL-Arizona was housed will become the Barça Academy, one of a handful of training centers FC Barcelona is opening in the US, but the first to align with the US Soccer Development Academy.[8] RSL will still maintain an Arizona presence though, via a partnership with two established soccer clubs in the state allowing RSL to train 7,000 youth players.[9]

"Going from a club to the RSL Academy was big time for me, obviously, in terms of development," Glad says. "It was five practices a day instead of two, better coaches, and then for most of our games we had US scouts who were watching. So, within six months of going to the Academy, I got invited to try out for residency [in Bradenton]. We went down there for a weekend, played a couple games, and then I ended up making that U-17 national team squad. And then once you're in the system, it's big time, because then they can keep an eye on you. I just kind of went through the ranks, U-17s, U-18s, U-20s, that was my path."

Glad actually started as an attacking player, but when he first got to the RSL Academy, coaches told the players to get into three groups: forwards, midfielders, and defenders. Glad sized up the groups: About thirty forwards, the same number going to the midfielders, and only about ten defenders. He laughs, "I just went to the defenders group because I figured my odds would be better."

Glad lauds the experience of the coaches there, including academy director Martin Vasquez, who served as an assistant coach with Jürgen Klinsmann at Bayern Munich as well as with the US team, and also had MLS experience with the Galaxy and Chivas USA.

"They're soccer guys through and through, whereas my coach for the club team, maybe that's a hobby or something he does on the side," he asserts. "The practices are more structured, each drill has a purpose, whether it's team shape, or passing patterns, there's more of an endgame for it. There's a reason behind it. And even on the individual level, they'll pull you aside and say, in this situation, this is what you've got to do, or this would be a smart thing to do."

Glad was slated to go to Stanford but signed a homegrown contract with Real Salt Lake instead as a seventeen-year-old in 2014.[10] He received his first start with the senior squad in 2015, and by 2016 he was named RSL's Defensive Player of the Year. The MLS website, naming Glad one of the league's top twenty-four players under twenty-four years old, lauded him for being "a cerebral center back comfortable with the ball at his feet," and declared him to have "one of the highest ceilings of any defender on the 24 Under 24 list."[11]

Brooks Lennon, like Glad, found his way to Casa Grande from the Arizona club soccer system, but after a year there, winning a U-16 national championship with his academy team (which also featured Glad) and getting U-17 looks from US Soccer, he got the opportunity to go to Liverpool—where he stayed for the next two-and-a-half years and continued moving up the ranks as Glad did.

Lennon says that Real Salt Lake and Liverpool have similar approaches to player development. RSL has a residential system that allows players to get immersed in the culture, as Lennon can attest, and he points to RSL's track record in bringing players from the academy to the first team as a sign of the academy's effectiveness. At Liverpool, Lennon lived with a host family and trained daily. He found that because "the league is a little bit more serious and a little higher level in England," (perhaps understating it a bit), playing there accelerated his development, especially when he got multiple individual call-ups to train with the first team.

"I think it helped me as a player just to realize how high the level is and how skilled the players are," Lennon says. "There are guys on Liverpool that are world class, so it was great for me to see that. It was really just the determination they have during training. They train as if it's a game. No one takes it personally, but everyone is going hard and everyone's fighting for our position to play on Saturday. So it's kind of a dog-eat-dog world. But that's kind of how it is. And that's what I liked most about it." (For the record, "going hard" meant Lennon endured his share of slide tackles.)

Though Lennon was still technically a Liverpool player in 2017, he was allowed to come back to Real Salt Lake, going on loan in February 2017 for the duration of the MLS season after playing in Liverpool's U-23 squad and working toward a first team call-up.[12]

Danilo Acosta, though born in Honduras, grew up in the Salt Lake City metro area, but also was part of the RSL-Arizona experience. Like Glad and Lennon, he found that the step up from club to academy play helped him develop and better prepared him for the youth national teams.

"From the club level to the academy level, it's a lot higher level, it's a lot faster, it's a lot more intense," he notes. "The way we train is the way the first team will train—it's really hard, it's all based on mentality. The mentality has to be there every day. We all have to push ourselves to do the little things. The academy helped me with that, to get to me to a pro level."

Of the twenty-one players who went to the U-20 World Cup, fifteen of them had been part of the team who had won the CONCACAF U-20 tournament. One of the newcomers was Josh Sargent, a seventeen-year-old high school player who has excelled with the U-17s and would score four goals in as many matches to get the team to the quarterfinals.

As U-20 coach Tab Ramos told the media in a teleconference just before the start of the tournament, the decision to bring Sargent to South Korea came out of discussions he had with U-17 coach John Hackworth—as he put it, "trying to provide better and more competitive opportunities for him from a national team standpoint." He even invoked Christian Pulisic when contemplating Sargent's situation and noted, "Some players sometimes outgrow their age group and they have to move on."[13]

The tournament started with Luca de la Torre scoring an opportunistic goal deep in stoppage time to salvage a draw against Ecuador, in a match where Sargent scored two goals. Then, Sargent scored the lone goal in the team's 1–0 win against Senegal to place them atop their group. In the final group match against Saudi Arabia, they drew 1–1, but still topped their group, and got to face New Zealand in the Round of 16. They looked indomitable against the Kiwis, before the Venezuela match saw them crash back to reality.

"We're always positive, and we don't expect anything but to win," said Palmer-Brown. "We went in there just having high expectations for ourselves." He said of the CONCACAF U-20s, "It was a long tournament, and so we learned to manage our bodies. In CONCACAF, you can kind of build into the tournament. And we knew that in the World Cup, you can't do that. Every game counts." He adds, "When we ended up winning CONCACAF, we had high expectations for ourselves going into it, and we had high expectations for ourselves going into the World Cup. Nothing really changed from our perspective when going into this tournament. Except that now it's on the world stage, instead of just regionally."

"We came in with a lot of confidence because we'd just won the CONCACAF U-20, which no American team had done before," Acosta said. "We thought we were champions and we felt that we could compete against anybody. And you could see it, in our going to the World Cup. I thought we played very well. Coach Ramos told us if you believe in yourself and you believe in this team, anything can happen. And the whole entire tournament was like that."

Acosta noted the team functioned well together. "If you don't have good chemistry as a team, once you have individual players who want to do their own thing you've never going to go nowhere," he said. "That's the one thing that we had on this U-20 group going to the World Cup. We were together no matter what. No one person thought he was the best person on this team."

But Venezuela proved to be too much for the Americans.

"When we went to play Venezuela," Acosta observed, "we knew it was going to be a tough team. We knew it was going to be hard, but we knew we were never going to give up."

"Venezuela was a really good team," Palmer-Brown added. "They had a lot of players who gave us a lot of problems. I don't think it was a fluke for them to win. I think they had good chances. But we also had our chances to put them away. I had a chance to win the game. I mean, that's football, that's how matches go. Both teams have chances to win the game, and you know every time you step out on the field, there's a chance to win or lose the game. And I think, that day," he concludes as simply as one could, "we weren't as good as the other team."

In the end, though, many of the players took encouragement out of how they did.

"I think getting the opportunity to play against the best guys in the world at your age was such an eye-opening experience," Lennon said. "I mean, some of the right- and left-backs I was playing against were guys you're going to see in a couple of years playing in the Premier League and some of the other top leagues in the world. So, to be able to see my abilities against theirs was really cool. And now I know that the US can play against anyone, and we can win games."

And, as Lennon's well aware, a team of nineteen- and twenty-year-olds in 2017—should they be able to keep the core together and developing—is a team of players that would be in their prime for a potentially US-cohosted 2026 World Cup.

"That's obviously something that we think about, especially me individually," Lennon notes. "My ultimate goal is to play for the full team. And that's how the U-20 is structured, it's a building block to kind of get you ready for the senior team. Going to the U-20 World Cup definitely helped in that aspect of it. Obviously, we would love to see a lot of the U-20 guys on that roster, as some of the core players in that group."

For Russell Canouse, who captained the 2015 U-20 squad during the CONCACAF qualifiers, the experience was different. He recounts how needing to win the last four matches in a row to get to the U-20 World Cup was a bonding experience for the team after an injury to Kellyn Acosta. En route to the finals, though, while training in Australia,

Canouse collided with another player—as luck would have it, Paul Arriola, his once and future teammate—and he was sidelined for the crucial month in which the U-20 World Cup was taking place.

While he laughs it off now, he also expresses disappointment at having to sit at home while his teammates advanced through to the quarterfinals, where they played Serbia to a scoreless draw, and missed three of their last four penalty kicks—just hours after Mali had dispatched tournament favorites Germany[14]—in a tournament the Serbians would go on to win.

Two straight quarterfinal exits for the U-20 World Cup, in which twenty-four teams play, does feel marginally better than the two straight Round of 16 exits in the World Cup, but given the level of optimism that accompanied both those teams, it registers as disappointment for those who follow US Soccer. But that's nothing compared to the disappointment that rides in a sidecar with the U-23 team, which failed to qualify for the Olympics in both 2012 and 2016. The last Americans to represent the US under an Olympic flame included longtime USMNT starters like Jozy Altidore, Brad Guzan, and Michael Bradley, and contributing players like Dax McCarty and Sacha Kljestan, but also included now-retired players like Charlie Davies, Robbie Rogers, and two players-turned-broadcasters, Stuart Holden and Brian McBride.

The team also included one of the most perplexing players in American soccer history. Freddy Adu, who was then with Portuguese team Benfica, had been touted as potentially the greatest American player ever. He was even dubbed "the next Pelé"[15] by ESPN when he debuted with DC United as a fourteen-year-old in 2003. But by the time the 2016 Olympics rolled around, he was with his thirteenth team—the NASL's Tampa Bay Rowdies—and will still be less than a year shy of his thirtieth birthday when the 2018 World Cup starts.[16]

Olympic men's soccer is a strange hybrid of a U-23 tournament and a modified World Cup, for a team must mostly be comprised of U-23 players, and three senior team players are allowed to join the squad at the Olympics regardless of age or senior team caps. In the 2016 edition of the Olympics, this most notably happened with burgeoning Ballon d'Or candidate Neymar. Rather than join the rest of Brazil's senior squad at the Copa America Centenario, Neymar opted to play with the youth squad in a quest for Olympic gold, when his club team Barcelona allegedly forced him into a choice between the two summer tournaments spaced more than a month apart.[17]

The Olympics has even emerged as a recent sore spot for the US women, who unlike the men, may field full senior teams and treat the tournament nearly on the same plane as the Women's World Cup. In fact, the USWNT took the core of their 2015 Women's World Cup–winning squad to Rio in an attempt to do what no other team had done prior: follow a World Cup win with an Olympics win the next year.

The USWNT won its third straight gold medal in the 2012 Olympics in London, beating Japan in the finals at Wembley Stadium—a win that came on the heels of a 4–3 extra-time semifinals match against Canada that I consider the greatest game in US Soccer history for its sheer emotional parabolas and to-the-death drama, as well as for its remarkable play from both teams. Those who followed the American women closely knew that despite several notable challengers—Germany and France, plus their final two 2012 foes—there was as much reason to be optimistic of victory.

Ultimately, the 2016 Olympians didn't even survive the quarterfinals, losing in penalty kicks to Sweden, coached by former US coach (but native Swede) Pia Sundhage after playing to a 1–1 draw.

But although the women's early exit from the tournament was a disappointment, the US men didn't even get that far. Trapp, one of the best-known Columbus Crew SC players, captained the U-23 team vying for a spot in the 2016 Summer Olympics. Trapp, like many on the U-23 squad, is a veteran of the U-20 squad, but his was the 2013 U-20 World Cup aspiring squad as opposed to the 2015 version many of his U-23 teammates hailed from. He describes the timing of his joining the U-23 squad as "an interesting little window of opportunity to step in," and says the challenge of captaining such a team is "combining multiple cycles for one team and trying to meld that group." Trapp was first called into the team in late 2015, but the team was playing warmup matches in England, Qatar, and Australia prior to the October 2015 CONCACAF tournament held at four MLS sites—Sporting Park in Kansas City, Kansas, the StubHub

Center in Carson, California, Dick's Sporting Goods Park in Commerce City, Colorado, and the finals-hosting Rio Tinto Stadium in Sandy, Utah.

Despite the US being the host nation, Trapp notes, "They're tougher games than a lot of people realize. It's an experience that puts you in the public eye, it puts you in situations that are difficult, against quality players."

"I think when you have less time to train together, and it's training and then play, the technical side maybe sometimes is a bit stretched," he says, noting that while the higher level of play is exciting, it also amounts to "being exposed to a new type of soccer and dealing with new challenges."

The US wasn't able to win one of the two automatic spots from CONCACAF in the October 2015 qualifying tournament—those went to Mexico and Honduras—but they did play their way into the third place game. They defeated Canada there, and in the first leg of an interfederation playoff against CONMEBOL representative Colombia, drew 1–1 in the South American nation on the strength of a Luis Gil goal.

Gil, though not as hyped as the young Freddy Adu, was lauded as "the future of American soccer" in a 2010 ESPN article that declared him "a technically gifted playmaker with uncommon vision." As the article noted, the then-sixteen-year-old was being courted by the likes of Arsenal, Manchester City, Real Madrid, and Sevilla.[18] At the time of the match, illustrating the unpredictability of a soccer career arc, Gil was in the midst of his first (and only) season for Mexican squad Querétaro after five full seasons at Real Salt Lake. He would go on to return to MLS via loans to Orlando City SC and the Colorado Rapids.

The 2–1 loss at Frisco's Toyota Stadium on March 29, 2016, four days after the draw in Colombia, led to a 3–2 aggregate loss in the series. For a second straight four-year cycle, the dream of American soccer players participating in the Olympics ended in disappointment. And the loss to Colombia, though not surprising given Colombia's talent, was still somewhat stunning given the confidence the team had going into the match, following the first leg's relative success.

The misfortunes of the American team were perhaps most personified by Gil. Gil came on as a sixty-seventh-minute sub shortly after what would be Roger Martínez's decisive goal, received a yellow card within five minutes, and then received a second yellow card five minutes later to put his teammates at a one-man disadvantage. Another of the more promising U-23s, defender Matt Miazga, received a straight red card in the ninetieth minute for denying an obvious goal scoring opportunity to further thwart the Americans' dimming chances to send the match into extra time.[19]

"We had some ups and downs during the tournament," understates Gil. "You know we put ourselves in a position where we had to play that play off against Colombia." He says, of the second leg match, with a wry laugh, "I let the frustration get to me, getting a red card playing only just about ten minutes. I feel like I could have been a little bit smarter. One call, I can say was my fault, I can put my hand up for that, but then the second yellow was just a terrible call, just a flop by another player, and he got me my second yellow card. But unfortunately, that's the way the game is. Sometimes the ref sees it, sometimes he doesn't, and he's going to dictate the game at the end of the day."

As a result, the US men's team would fail to make an Olympics for a second straight cycle—the first time that's happened in nearly half a century.

"I definitely took some lessons from it," Gil says. "You know, I always try and find a positive out of it, but I felt like it just really hurt me, because it was such an important game to me personally. I really wanted to be a part of that Olympic team. [. . .] To be a part of history, and being a part of an Olympic team, especially since in our last cycle we didn't qualify as well. I made it a little bit harder on myself. I might have been a little more tough on myself because I really wanted to make that happen."

Gil is still a confident player, but also one realistic about how many talented players exist in both the club and country arenas. He played in Mexico, where he notes, "Everyone's more technical there. From your goalkeepers to your forwards, everybody is good on the ball. I was basically another player there; I am a technical player, and I'm good on the ball, but every other player there is really good on the ball. Everybody has that confidence to want the ball."

And in MLS, where he says the discipline of players and the willingness to fight throughout a match characterize the league, he's had to play different roles with each of his teams. Colorado, while giving him more playing time, is asking him to do so in more of a defensive midfield role, which he describes as "getting into some tackles and recovering the ball for the team"—not quite the attacking midfield role he's more accustomed to playing. "I feel like this is making me more versatile," he says. "It's giving me more of an opportunity, and it can only be a positive thing for me."

He still hopes that he can break into the senior national team again, having debuted in 2014 in a friendly against South Korea and earning an additional cap as a sub in a 2015 match against Panama.[20]

"Obviously I feel like every player's dream is to be a part of a World Cup. You know there's something I strive for every day. And you know opportunities aren't always going to be there. So if that opportunity ever does come to make my case for that World Cup spot you know I will make the most of it." In moving from Liga MX to MLS, and particularly with the mid-2017 trade taking him from Orlando to Colorado, he sees the chance at increased playing team to, as he frankly assesses, "get my career back on track."

Trapp, like Gil, is a two-capped first-team player hoping to parlay the U-23 experience and his continued MLS play into more opportunities to move toward the 2022 or 2026 World Cups. And, like Gil, he's straightforward about the disappointment of missing out on the Olympics in the way that they did.

"We knew it was going to be difficult, but we made our bed, so we had to sleep in it," Trapp says. "If you don't take care of business in qualifying, that's the opportunity we presented ourselves with. To be honest, after the first leg in Colombia, we felt great. You go into an adverse environment and you grind out a result and, in a lot of ways, we probably could have won the game."

But he says, of the return leg in Frisco, "I don't think we prepared well enough mentally for how hard they were going to be coming and knowing the reality of the situation."

"The chances of playing in an Olympics are similar to a World Cup in terms of every four years, but with the age constraints, it's almost even less so," Trapp notes. "All of us were pretty disappointed in the fact that we weren't going to be able to represent the United States at the Olympics."

Still, though, Trapp is encouraged by what he sees in the U-23s, the U-20s, and the players who will make a run at getting back into the Olympics by 2020. "I think you're starting to see the youth movement come through and that's very exciting," Trapp says. He believes that the combination of talented younger players and experience means that, "in competing on the highest stage, I don't think we're far off."

"Anything can happen in a tournament scenario," he notes. "I mean, you look at 2002, you've got the right chemistry of players and you make it to the quarterfinal, and one handball away from a semifinal. So I really think it's just getting the right group of players, and then those players buying into whatever the coach has in store for them, and in a lot of that, it starts with just getting through the qualifying phase. When you step into a tournament, we've seen time and time again that that teams can make runs. It's execution at that stage."

And yet, some critics saw the U-23 team's falling short of an Olympic spot as a warning sign. Some took the result as a reflection (or, really, an indictment) of Jürgen Klinsmann's abilities as a technical director. At this point, critics were already heaping scorn upon him as a coach, and the U-23 coach for the qualifying cycle, Andi Herzog, has a long history with Klinsmann dating back to their days as Bayern Munich teammates in the mid-1990s.[21]

Sirius XM FC's Brian Dunseth expresses a widely-held frustration with the recent history of missed Olympics and the dearth of twenty-four- to twenty-eight-year-olds on the 2017 qualifying rosters, saying, "We have to figure out what's happening between twenty and twenty-three that we're seeing such a hiccup in these players' development."

ESPN's Noah Davis, for one, saw the US performance against Colombia trending toward a general malaise striking American soccer in recent months, including the U-23 CONCACAF qualifier in which Honduras vaulted themselves into the Olympics over the US several months prior, and the then-recent, still stinging USMNT qualifier loss to Guatemala, noting:

> Kellyn Acosta, who struggled in an unfamiliar full-back role in both matches, agreed. "We need to match their intensity," he said. "We came out kind of flat-footed, kind of slow. They kind of took the game to us. We need to battle. It was life or death, really. I think it shows. They outplayed us throughout the entire game."
>
> That's an honest, if brutal, assessment of the proceedings. It's also something we hear too often. The US comes out flat. It runs into trouble against physical opponents, whether it's Colombia in Barranquilla and Frisco, Honduras during Olympic qualifying in October or even the senior side against Guatemala on Friday.
>
> The coaches talk a good game about possession, patience and passing, but the words fail to manifest themselves into action and reality on the field. The American team fails to be more than the sum of its parts.
>
> And now we have another generation of US players missing the Olympics. Let's be clear: it's not the complete and utter disaster that failing to reach the World Cup would be [. . .] But the Olympics do represent a serious opportunity for younger players to experience high-quality matches in pressure situations. For a team like the US, which has a relatively easy road to World Cup qualification and whose continental championship lacks the rigors of the European Championship, three games or more at the Olympics create an excellent chance for players to develop and thrive.[22]

The Olympics did have a more diminished importance for American soccer fans in 2016 than it might have in past quadrennials, thanks to the Copa America Centenario providing the rare chance for the USMNT to face the hemisphere's best teams.

Also, success on the world stage in recent U-23 competitions doesn't automatically correlate to World Cup success, though winning squads from the last few Olympics have been strong contenders in future World Cup cycles where players on those gold medal-winning teams featured. Mexico won the 2012 Olympics and took nine players from that squad—including key U-23s like Giovani dos Santos, Héctor Herrera, Marco Fabián, and Javier Aquino—to the 2014 World Cup, and many of those champions are likely candidates to go to Russia in 2018.

Argentina won the two prior tournaments—the winning 2008 team in Seoul included U-23s who went on to be key members of the 2014 World Cup team that went to the final game, including Lionel Messi, Sergio Agüero, Ángel Di María, Ezequiel Lavezzi, Pablo Zabaleta, and Sergio Romero.[23] The 2004 squad included Javier Mascherano, who also played on the 2008 squad as one of the team's three senior players.

What does it really mean for the US that it missed out on the last two Olympics? Adnan Ilyas, in Stars and Stripes FC, argued that it might have contributed to the senior team's failure to reach the 2018 World Cup. Ilyas observed that the average age of the team called up for September 2017 qualifiers skewed on the older side: Its average age was close to twenty-nine, with twelve players thirty or older, and just six players under twenty-seven. As he noted:

> The U-23 players who fell short for the 2012 World Cup would be between 26 and 28 at this point. The players who fell short for the 2016 World Cup (and aged out) would be 24–25. And that just so nicely explains the relative gap for the age groupings for 24–28, with only seven players in there at all. Of that 2012 Olympic team, only Villafaña is on the full senior team at this point. The 2016 Olympic team is a bit younger, with more players with more senior experience, so there's a bit of hope there, yet. But the point still stands, the youth teams failed to provide a pipeline for senior talent.
>
> The high age for the national team further seems to demonstrate the idea that it takes longer for players to go through college, be identified, find a place where they are effective on the field at the professional level, and solidify themselves as full club (and then international) starters.[24]

Ilyas is quick to point out that this isn't as bleak as it may seem on its face. He notes that the median age does drop a year when taking out the three goalkeepers; Tim Howard and Nick Rimando were both thirty-eight and Brad Guzan was thirty-three when those September matches were played.

By comparison, though, he finds that nineteen members of the Costa Rican squad were between twenty-three and twenty-nine when those two teams faced, compared to nine for the US, and notes the Costa Rican squad average is a full two years younger than the USMNT's. He doesn't think that merits an alarm for the Americans' World Cup prospects going forward, noting the promising class of U-20s, as well a group of standout U-23s including Kellyn Acosta, Jordan Morris, Cristian Roldan, and DeAndre Yedlin (not to mention 2014 World Cup hero John Brooks) will each be under-thirty contributors to the USMNT in the 2022 and 2026 World Cup cycles.[25]

But the failure to qualify for a second straight Olympic cycle—with a roster including players who will certainly feature for the USMNT into the next decade—is an admitted worry for those who want to see the US succeed at all levels.

There is one player we haven't mentioned in this chapter yet who will be eligible to serve in both the U-20 and U-23 campaigns during the next World Cup cycle. But he probably won't even help with the Olympic efforts—because he's already definitively graduated to the first team.

Christian Pulisic should have featured in his first World Cup in 2018 as a nineteen-year-old, coming off playing Champions League games for a second straight season in 2017–18 for one of the highest-profile teams in Europe.

While American writers and fans have been eager to name an up-and-coming player the next greatest, Pulisic has the skills, the soccer IQ, and the countenance to transcend Donovan and Dempsey and the rest of the American soccer pantheon to date. And while a lot of it happens in red, white, and blue, a lot of it also happens in Borussia Dortmund's trademark yellow and black.

CHAPTER 8

AMERICANS ABROAD: WHEN YOUNG PLAYERS CHOOSE CLUBS IN OTHER COUNTRIES

WHEN WE LOOK BACK ON THE 2017–18 SOCCER SEASON—SPECIFICALLY, on how American players fared in top European leagues—the conversation won't solely be about Christian Pulisic. *Four Four Two*, on the eve of the season, published an article on players projected to make an impact.

Joshua Pérez, nephew of US Soccer legend Hugo Pérez, seems an obvious choice: He began his Serie A career in the 2016–17 season with Fiorentina, and signed a four-year contract with the club in February 2017, just past his nineteenth birthday. He was loaned to Serie C team Livorno several weeks into the season, which could give him the seasoning he needs before truly testing himself against the Italian league's best defenders on a weekly basis.

Desevio Payne, a right-back with Eredivisie's Excelsior, also makes their list. Thanks to a Trinidadian father and a Dutch mother, Payne could choose Trinidad & Tobago or the Netherlands over the US, though he was born in South Carolina and has already played for the US's U-20 and U-23 teams.

Weston McKennie, a Texan who grew up in the FC Dallas Academy, opted for German club Schalke over signing an FC Dallas homegrown contract at age seventeen, and made his first start in September 2017, going fifty-seven minutes against the fearsome Bayern Munich lineup. By Christmas, he'd appeared in thirteen league games and three additional DFB-Pokal games, with nine of those being starts, fairly cementing his place on the Schalke squad.

And Timothy Weah, the American son of Ballon d'Or winner George Weah, finds himself in an intriguing position. He signed a three-year contract with Paris Saint-Germain as a seventeen-year-old in July 2017, just a few months before showing immense promise in the U-17 World Cup, and started the 2017-18 season as part of PSG's B team in the UEFA Youth League.[1]

But the article's title was "In Pulisic's Wake," speaking to the idea that Pulisic is setting a trend that talented young American players are following in. Though many American players—of the teenaged and twenty-something variety—have gone to Europe seeking soccer success, Pulisic is already poised to become soccer's highest-profile American abroad ever.

He's even transcendent enough, at this stage, to be spotlighted beyond sports publications. A June 2017 feature in *The New Yorker*, written by Michael Luo, literally proclaimed him "American Soccer's Great Hope" in the headline, and praised some of his legend-making moments to date. However, Luo did focus on one dashed opportunity that might have propelled Pulisic beyond his current orbit—a second-half chance against Mexico, in Azteca, in a moment where the US could have finally bested its rivals in the most challenging of the Hex qualifiers. Luo set the stage poignantly, describing the "hammering of expectation in [his] chest"[2] as he set up for a shot that went just wide. Luo also drew from Michael Caley's typically trenchant analysis for *Five Thirty Eight* on how Pulisic has already emerged as one of the Bundesliga's best players.

"There have been roughly 100 million males born in America in the past 50 years," Caley noted, "Among that total, there appears to finally be *one* who can safely be called a legitimate international soccer star."

Caley points to a recent run of games in which Pulisic shone for the USMNT in 2017, starting with its 2–0 home win in Commerce City, Colorado over Trinidad & Tobago in June, which I witnessed from the press box. Pulisic broke a tense, scoreless tie in the fifty-second minute with great individual effort, and ten minutes later, practically teleported past defenders on his way to a second goal.

"This has become typical for the Americans," Caley noted. "Against Panama, Pulisic held off two defenders in the box to get free and feed

Clint Dempsey for the USMNT's lone goal. He scored one and assisted two in the 6–0 romp over Honduras. All told, over its crucial last three competitive matches, the US has scored nine goals and Pulisic has scored or assisted six of them."

Even that's not the whole story. As the footnote added, "Sebastian Lletget's goal against Honduras came from a rebound off a saved Pulisic attempt, and Dempsey scored a free kick after Pulisic won a foul, so you could count eight."[3]

Prior to the Trinidad & Tobago match in Colorado, Pulisic gathered in front of a throng of reporters as part of what is called, in soccer writing parlance, as a "mixed zone." Players are brought onto one side of a barrier, journalists gather across the barrier in front of the players they want to speak to, and a brief question-and-answer session takes place. If you scrutinize the stories that come after a match—and the stories after the Trinidad & Tobago match are as good a sample as any—you can see that those stories start with a very finite group of quotes that come from the coach's postgame press conference and the handful of mixed zone quotes that writers are able to glean from the players.

Three things struck me about Pulisic in the pre- and post-match interviews I was involved in. The first is that he's quieter than you'd expect him to be. He's not exactly soft-spoken, but he doesn't project with the same sort of overt directness of a Tim Howard or a Michael Bradley.

The second is that there's a confidence about him that is, in a word, pragmatic. There's something very reminiscent of Landon Donovan in his manner of answering questions. Pulisic could be dismissive or lean on clichés, and while that would be understandable and maybe even permissible, that's not quite where he is. Rather, he's no nonsense, as when he shrugged off a question about any special dispensation or consideration based on his age. His attitude is simply, refreshingly, that he is old enough and good enough to be on the senior team, so he should get the same treatment that everyone else on the team gets, be it praise, respect, or a bone-crunching slide tackle from an opposing defender.

The third is that for American journalists in the 2018 World Cup cycle, Pulisic was most definitely the story. In the post-match mixed zone, I was in the middle of asking Bradley a question—he is, after all, the team captain, an astute and honest observer of the team, and quotable—when Pulisic came out to the mixed zone for his interview. The entire assembled throng of press, including those journalists bunched around Bradley, moved over to Pulisic.

In the postgame mixed zone, Pulisic didn't say that much of import in front of the post-match throng to place his feats into context. The most remarkable postgame moment actually came in his Fox Sports telecast interview, where he promised a win over Mexico in what was, in retrospect, probably a more Arena-infused positive-assumptive pragmatism than the Namathian pre–Super Bowl III bravado we were all sort of hoping it was.

My favorite story from the US vs. Mexico match that followed, in part because of the audaciousness of that promise, came from *Howler*'s Brooks Peck. As he unfailingly does in opportune soccer moments, Peck channeled his inner *Onion* to comment poignantly on soccer expectations vs. soccer reality. In an article titled, "Christian Pulisic Shaves His Head, Scores Stunning Goal against Mexico," Peck takes the improbability of Michael Bradley's sixth-minute, forty-yard speculative shot that chipped keeper Guillermo Ochoa and attributes it to the player most likely to successfully attempt that.

"Christian Pulisic had either scored or set up Clint Dempsey for each of the US's last eight goals going into their World Cup qualifier at Mexico and just five and a half minutes into the match, he scored his best one yet, chipping the keeper from distance to put the US up 1–0," Peck hilariously and inaccurately reported. "Pulisic apparently shaved his head before the match and mistakenly put on Michael Bradley's kit, causing some confusion for the commentators, but his brilliant play was unmistakable."

And, as Peck concluded, acknowledging the rare result against Mexico at Azteca, despite Pulisic's relative lack of connection to said result, "Where would the US be without Pulisic and his magic right now?"[4]

Pulisic has been excelling for club as well as country. In the German Super Cup match to kick off the 2017–18 Bundesliga season, Pulisic scored the opening goal for his Borussia Dortmund, against Bayern Munich, in style. He stripped the ball from Javi Martínez, one of the best defensive midfielders in the world, went on a twenty-five-yard solo run, and coolly slotted the ball past substitute goalkeeper Sven Ulreich. Dortmund would lose the game in penalty kicks, but Pulisic certainly helped his legacy.

Then, in the season opener, he scored the opening goal and assisted on another as Dortmund beat Wolfsburg 3–0. And with Ousmane Dembélé moving from Dortmund to Barcelona in the 2017 transfer window, leaving them with one less attacker, Pulisic becomes even more vital to Dortmund, with the team's willingness to let Dembélé go (albeit for a significant transfer fee) readable as an endorsement of sorts for Pulisic.

Against Costa Rica in September, though—a 2–0 loss which sent the USMNT's 2018 World Cup hopes into some doubt—Pulisic was a primary target of Costa Rica's defensive 5–4–1 formation and physical play. The strategy to push Pulisic to the periphery of the field, even employing a double-team defense at points, largely neutralized him, although he did nearly have a game-tying goal in the second half expertly saved by Costa Rican (and, notably, Real Madrid) goalkeeper Keylor Navas.

"He had a tough, tough game today," US head coach Bruce Arena told the media after the game. "Obviously they paid a lot of attention to him. You could see early in the game, they sent a second player to him; I think he got a little frustrated."[5]

By the eve of the Honduras match three days later, Arena contended that the oft-fouled Pulisic was left vulnerable on the field thanks to "highly unpredictable" refereeing. Pulisic was fouled four times in the match against Costa Rica, though Arena alleged even more rough play, saying, "He's fouled just about every time he touches the ball. The referee hasn't protected him in a number of situations."[6]

Pulisic also struggled in the Honduras match, with the Catrachos employing much of the same aggressive defense that he encountered against the Ticos. But Pulisic did engineer, through guile and determination, a goal that could have been the most significant moment of the Hex. His run drew the foul that led to the crucial eighty-fifth-minute Kellyn Acosta free kick. Acosta's kick sent Honduras's keeper airborne to prevent it from crossing the line, and in the ensuing chaos, Bobby Wood chested down a loose ball and toe-poked it into the goal, allowing the US to escape with a crucial road point and place its World Cup qualifying destiny squarely back in its control. (For the time being, at least.)

Pulisic was literally born into a soccer family: Both his parents played college soccer at George Mason University, and his father Mark went on to play indoor soccer for the Harrisburg Heat of the National Professional Soccer League throughout the 1990s. The elder Pulisic, now an assistant coach with the Rochester Rhinos, recognized that Christian had talent early on, but initially tempered expectations and instead focused on whether Christian actually liked soccer.

"My wife and I were pretty realistic," he recalls. "We both played and had the experience, and understood that there's a lot of good players at young ages and you just got to make sure they're enjoying it, and make sure that they enjoy the game and play with an excitement and passion. So, basically that was our biggest goal, and when Christian was seven or eight years old, we saw him really enjoy the game. He was in his own zone."

Christian's mother was invited to go to England on a teaching exchange program when Christian was six and seven; that experience allowed Christian to learn more about the game on his own in a place where people were passionate about soccer.

"He really was engulfed in soccer from a daily standpoint," Mark Pulisic says. "It wasn't structured. It was a non-structured environment, which is very important to kids developing their game on their own. Not with coaches, and not with teams; just playing a game on their own and with friends and enjoying learning from the ball." Of course, European and South American children play at an early age, typically in informal, unstructured set-ups, and he sees that as an agreeable alternative to how the game is treated in the United States.

"You know we have a culture here in the US where it's very driven towards competition for postseason and winning," he noted. "And it's just how it is. The kids are pulled in so many different directions. They're not allowed to enjoy a game on their own and go outside. It's all about we're going to go over to this basketball tournament or this soccer tournament. We have to practice three days a week, and then we're going to do an extra training session this week. The poor kids are just being driven around all over the map and not really able to express how they want to enjoy the game. Maybe they just want to juggle or dribble and not pass the ball."

"There are a lot of coaches at young ages who are all about winning tournaments," he said, adding that Christian was playing competitively because he liked being on a team. But for Christian, the team wasn't his entire focus.

"He was also playing on his own," Christian's dad recalls. "If he had soccer practice at nine years old, it would only be two times a week. And we never really wanted him to play on multiple teams. We didn't want him in a structured environment at young ages. Even throughout his early teens he only played for one team. He played and trained with one team and then we would tell them if you want to play more, we're not going to be driving you around to all these tournaments. It's going to be more you enjoy the game on your own, you develop yourself, you know go out with the ball, if that's something that you truly want to do."

Pulitzer Prize-winning journalist George Dohrmann, in a June 2017 profile on Pulisic for Bleacher Report, got insight to his parents' approach from Steve Clark, who coached Pulisic at PA Classics, the club team where Pulisic developed. Clark believes there are two kinds of soccer parents: those who tell a player what he did wrong after a game and those who just take the kid to get ice cream. As Clark told Dohrmann, "Mark and Kelley are ice cream parents."[7]

From an early age, Christian attracted the attention of coaches—for whichever age group he was in and ones above it—who wanted him to moonlight on their teams for tournaments. His parents refused, guarding him against burnout, but were also looking for him to be challenged when he did play.

"We didn't want it to be easy but we wanted to make sure he found success," he said of Christian's time at PA Classics. "By playing two years up, he was challenged physically and he was he was still able to create and be one of the better players. At times he wasn't always the best player. So that was important, that he understood he would continue to work hard and fight and things wouldn't come easy."

Christian, as a fifteen-year-old, was on the US Soccer scouting radar.

He was also scouted in Turkey by Dortmund while he was there with the U-17 national team—the last youth team he'd play for before debuting with the senior team.

"He was ready to make this move that he wasn't really ready for beforehand," Mark Pulisic says. "And we decided it would only happen if I was with him because we knew he was still young, and the club supported that. Dortmund wanted me to come there and offered me a job [coaching in their academy]. And that's just kind of how it started."

"He just always wanted to challenge himself," he continues. "So he knew that going to Europe would be very challenging, not only from a sporting perspective, but from a life perspective. He wanted the challenge to step up to see if he could do it, to skip the college route. He wanted to go and dive into this headfirst and see if he could. And we supported him in that decision, but it was totally his decision. He wanted to do it. He knew that the level would be extremely high and he would have to fight day in and day out just to earn the respect of all the players on those teams."

"Going to Europe was [the right thing] for Christian," his dad reflects. "But it wasn't something that that he didn't want or that his parents were forcing on them. It was a calculated decision that we all made together for him and supported him on. But ultimately, it was his final call to make that move. And I think that's the only way you'll find success in these things, because if the player doesn't want to do it or is petrified of the move, then it'll never work out. A lot of things had to fall into place. [. . .] Christian's mature and he's smart. His confidence level had to be high. He was ready to go into that challenge."

Dohrmann noted in his article that US Soccer is creating a "Pulisic blueprint" to help prepare those overseeing player development to help players get the most out of potential short stints overseas. His article noted:

Video clips of Christian at various ages are shown to US Soccer's nine full-time technical advisors and some of its 150 part-time scouts. They are used to help scouts spot "the key predictors of future success," says Tony Lepore, a longtime US Soccer employee who in March took on the title of director of talent identification. "There is optimal technique and initiative, and an ability to analyze in a split second, make a decision and then execute." Scouts also show clips of Christian at 14, when a growth spurt threw off his timing, a point in his development "when we needed to show a lot of patience with Christian," Lepore says.[8]

Mark Pulisic feels that part of what's helped his son succeed at Dortmund is partially a function of playing beyond his age. "He's always been the youngest everywhere he's gone so he can never be anything other than humble and grounded. The most important thing is that when you're a new person coming in that you're respected by your teammates and your teammates like you. It's going to be difficult. He's a smart kid. So of course he's going to go in there and he's [. . .] going to carry the equipment bags. He knows he has to put in the time because he hasn't really proven anything yet."

And what if Dortmund hadn't work out? As he remembers:

We've always told him that you know you have a home and you have a family that will support you if things don't work out. But we also encouraged him to give it time, because you can't go there for a couple of weeks or a couple of months and then say I don't like this. If you're going to commit, we put a little bit of a timeframe on it, and said you've got to give at least a half a year and then we'll reevaluate the situation after that, but you need to commit to this and you know do the best you can.

   And he did that. There were tough times for sure. There were many tough times. The first month or two, he missed his mom and his sister, he missed home, he missed his friends, he missed his high school, he missed everything. Ultimately, he found a way to fight all those so-called demons and buckle down, in practice, in school, in German lessons. And when he got it done, he was rewarded.

After finding success with Dortmund's U-17 and U-19 teams, Pulisic was called up to the first team in January 2016. At first, he made appearances as a sub, but by April, was awarded his first start and marked the occasion by becoming the youngest non-German (and the fourth youngest player ever) to score in a Bundesliga game. He was a day shy of seventeen years and seven months.[9]

And he is doing the same sort of milestone setting for the US. An article on the US Soccer site simply titled "All the Things Christian Pulisic Did Faster Than Anyone" notes that Pulisic is the youngest player to appear in a World Cup qualifying match (at seventeen years, 193 days), to ever score for the USMNT (at seventeen years, 253 days), to score in a World Cup qualifier (at seventeen years, 349 days)—in a match where also became the youngest USMNT player to score two goals in a match—and the youngest USMNT player to start a World Cup qualifier (at seventeen years, 353 days).[10]

It was Jürgen Klinsmann who gave Pulisic his first starts for the USMNT, and though Bruce Arena certainly recognized what he had in Pulisic, any coaching change creates an air of uncertainty. Two changes in as many years can be hard on even veteran players. While the elder Pulisic feels Christian has been well equipped to deal with the changes on the national team, he also notes, "You're not automatically given anything. You have to now start again, which is not a bad thing. For young players, I think it's a great thing. You know that there's never a comfort level. You know whenever there's a comfort level, then you're never going to push yourself and pull out your fullest potential. You know that that only comes out when you're challenged and when you're put in situations where you have to be uncomfortable. Fortunately he's had a lot of those situations and he's come through."

Whereas Klinsmann typically would utilize Pulisic on the wing—where he also typically plays for Dortmund—Arena gravitated toward using him more centrally, in the attacking midfielder role. It's certainly an area of need for the US; some argue that the US hasn't had a true attacking midfielder since Claudio Reyna. Though Landon Donovan sometimes played that creative playmaker role, he was more typically a forward—certainly not in the mold of a classic "10" (a creative attacking midfielder so named for typically wearing a number 10 jersey) like Argentine legend Juan Roman Riquelme or, more recently, Germany's Mesut Özil or Brazil's Philippe Coutinho.

The elder Pulisic notes that for his son, "Any of the front positions is fine for the US national team. He's not competing against World Cup winners for positions." By contrast, with Dortmund, "He's on one of the top teams in Europe and he's competing for minutes against some of the top players in the world. So right now, he's not going to be playing predominantly central at a younger age."

"But for the US," he continues, "if there's a need for it, and they don't have players that can assume that role, and the coach decides to put him there, he can definitely play there. Good players can play many positions. Fortunately, he's done well in a central role for the US. But he's not quite there yet with his club team. Maybe he's going to end up being a flank player. At 18 years old, an attacking player who play different positions is not a bad thing."

Pulisic's relative three-game anonymity in the Hex, starting with the Azteca match and carrying over into the two September matches, created concern for American fans. Those fans, who'd developed an acute sensitivity to where Klinsmann placed his players in the lineup, were now giving Arena the same scrutiny.

ESPN's Jeff Carlisle, in his post-Honduras assessment of the USMNT's still perilous World Cup qualifying position, noted:

> The biggest issue for the US is attacking balance, or rather the lack of it. Much has been made of positioning Christian Pulisic on the wing, though he and the team would be better off playing more centrally. Arena has insisted Pulisic has license to go where he pleases and has used the Borussia Dortmund attacker in different positions.
>
> It's a debate reminiscent of the one that used to surround Landon Donovan, in terms of where he should line up. In the 2010 World Cup cycle, then-manager Bob Bradley opted to put Donovan out wide. The difference is that Bradley also had Clint Dempsey available to play on the opposite wing, which allowed for some variety in attack.

He also went on to argue that the team needed variety in offense, insisting that no one else on the team "has really provided the kind of attacking presence to make teams think twice about double-teaming—or even triple-teaming—Pulisic. Unless someone else starts shouldering some of the creative load, it won't matter where Pulisic lines up. The 18-year-old needs to do his bit as well and pass the ball quicker when opponents collapse on him and not try to dribble his way out of trouble, especially in the middle third."[11]

Arena had an additional, politically tinged theory about the team's struggles in CONCACAF. Prior to the match against Honduras in San Pedro Sula, he opined to reporters, "Our immigration policies are impacting people in Central America, right? And there's probably a little bit of anger over that. Then your national sport gets a chance to play the US. I'm sure that becomes very meaningful."[12]

In the October match against Panama, Pulisic was incredible. He scored the opener in the eighth minute, deftly reining in a pass from Altidore, making a marauding thirty-yard run to the goal, and getting past the keeper to finish from a tight angle. Eleven minutes later, he assisted on the Altidore goal that made it 2–0 and sent the team on its way to a 4–0 domination. Against Trinidad & Tobago, even though he scored the lone USMNT goal just after halftime, his efforts weren't enough to deliver his team to the World Cup, leaving those interested in watching Pulisic's progress largely having to settle for Fox broadcasts of Bundesliga matches.

Pulisic isn't the only young American who has recently journeyed to Germany. Indeed, Germany has been a proving ground for several generations of American players, dating back to Eric Wynalda, who played there in the early 1990s before coming home to join the first wave of MLS stars when the league started in 1996. Landon Donovan made a long-term commitment to Bayer Leverkusen in 1999 while still a teenager and, despite struggles in Germany and successes in England with Everton, played his best soccer and flourished in the MLS he helped take to new heights.

A December 2015 *Guardian* article, simply titled "Why German Soccer Wants American Players," focuses largely on Bundesliga club owners and officials eager to reach a burgeoning market of American soccer fans by having American players those fans can root for. The article pointed to

German clubs' increased social media efforts in the US, and in Bundesliga giants Bayern Munich opening a New York office as part of an audacious marketing expansion. But the article also argued, not so flatteringly, that a path to Americans making it in the Bundesliga was more viable than it was in other top European leagues.

Arguing that the Bundesliga "represents the best path to success for American players abroad," author Terrance F. Ross noted, "American players tend to lack the technical ability to make it in Spain, or the tactical ability to make it in Europe. Not to mention the different cultures require an assimilation on and off the pitch. They aren't as desired in England as there's no inherent need to focus on the American market. But in Germany, many of the factors align both on and off the pitch; it's why we've seen so many Americans thrive over the years. But there's certainly interest and now that German clubs have seen the impact a player can have in the American market they are finely tuned to any other opportunities."

Ross did also point out that the Bundesliga had found some resonance with certain American fans at the time the article was written, thanks to Mexican star Javier "Chicharito" Hernández flourishing at Leverkusen, reviving a career that had stalled somewhat at Manchester United and Real Madrid.[13]

Even those at the highest echelons of MLS notice when promising young players move from MLS academies to the Bundesliga. When McKennie opted for Schalke over FC Dallas, where he could have signed a homegrown contract and graduated to Pareja's first team, MLS commissioner Don Garber went on the record with his disappointment, saying, "That one hurt. We had a lot of forces that we were working against on signing that player, and that's the reality of how difficult it is with a player pool at the youth level that continues to attract the attention of very, very aggressive and well-funded international teams. [. . .]We did everything we could financially. The player had been in [FC Dallas's] system for nine years, so when you look at the investment that goes into supporting that development and then you lose him and get nothing, it makes you scratch your head and wonder, 'Why are we doing this?'"[14]

A September 2017 article on the Bundesliga's English-language website, touting McKennie as the "Bundesliga's Next American Star"—and

looking ahead to Schalke's late November match with Pulisic's Dortmund—emphasized that McKennie wanted to come to Germany to develop. A section of the article starts with this telling McKennie quote:

> "Playing soccer in Europe is like coming to America to play bas-
> ketball," he told ESPN. "I came over, and they showed me
> around the youth academy, the stadium. I talked to coach Nor-
> bert Elgert over the phone, because he was on holiday. And I
> kinda fell in love with the place."

McKennie joined the Schalke U19s in August 2016, excited
at the prospect of working at the famed Knappenschmiede academy with renowned youth coach Elgert—the man who has developed some of Schalke's biggest stars in recent years, including
four 2014 FIFA World Cup winners: Manuel Neuer, Benedikt
Höwedes, Mesut Özil and Julian Draxler.[15]

When McKennie signed with Schalke through 2022 that month, he
told the club's site, "It was an easy decision for me to make. I love the
club and everything here: my teammates, the head coach and the fans.
I'd love to stay here forever."[16]

McKennie did have another option beside Schalke and FC Dallas:
He'd made a verbal commitment to play soccer at the University of Virginia.
But as a November 2017 feature on the Bundesliga English-language site
underscored, McKennie sees Schalke as the best option for his development. In a quote that won't ease Garber's hurt any, he declared:

> "I made the right decision and I don't regret it at all. It wasn't
> easy for me to let go of FC Dallas. But you've got to think, will
> I look back in 10 years and wish I could've gone over to Europe?
> I feel like if you can make it there, you can come back over here
> and play at a high level. But if as a kid you go into MLS and then
> try to come over to Europe, you might not be ready."[17]

For all of the attention McKennie's drawing, he's actually one of a trio
of intriguing Americans currently in the Schalke organization. Haji Wright,

a tall attacking player who can play centrally or on the wing, is an LA Galaxy academy product and one-time New York Cosmos player. Nick Taitague, an attacking midfielder, trained at the FC Richmond soccer club and had a brief stint with the Carolina RailHawks before going to Germany.

One particularly promising young player who circumvented the MLS academy system altogether, Josh Sargent, is also hoping to develop in Germany.

Sargent, who starred as a striker for both the 2017 U-17 and U-20 World Cup teams as a seventeen-year-old, went the club route via the St. Louis Scott Gallagher Soccer Club in his stateside development, rather than training with the Sporting Kansas City academy to which he's zoned per the MLS map. But he also trained with PSV Eindhoven and Schalke en route to deciding, in September 2017, to join longstanding Bundesliga club Werder Bremen, a decision which became official upon his eighteenth birthday the following February.

ESPN's Taylor Twellman reported on his Twitter account that Sargent turned down the higher-profile Bayern Munich and Borussia Dortmund to join the team.[18] Presumably Sargent could find a more regular place in the Werder Bremen lineup than he could with either of the German super clubs. (Given that Werder Bremen was sixteenth of eighteen teams as of the mid-season winter break, his new team was in a relegation battle with Bobby Wood's Hamburger SV immediately upon his arrival.)

Werder Bremen recently opened its doors to another USMNT player, the Alabama-born, Icelandic American player Aron Jóhannsson, who came via Eredivisie club AZ Alkmaar in 2015, but it hadn't worked out as he'd hoped. The 2016–17 ended with the club hinting that they'd be open to moving Jóhannsson to MLS via the league's allocation process[19] (for select US national team players not in MLS and other players worthy of the designation[20]), and the 2017–18 season started with Jóhannsson being passed over for playing time even in domestic cup games, and subsequently telling local media, "As things stand I am no longer wanted here. It disappoints me and makes me sad."[21]

Despite Jóhannsson seemingly not working out for Werder Bremen, the club went into Sargent's signing with a good deal of confidence in their latest American prospect.

"We have been keeping tabs on Joshua for a long time and so it isn't a great surprise to us that his brilliant performances have attracted attention on an international scale," said Werder Bremen head of squad planning and scouting Tim Steidten in the club's official press statement. "Therefore we are extremely happy that despite the numerous offers from other top clubs in Europe, he was convinced by our philosophy at SV Werder and that we can now oversee his development as a player and support him along the way. He has a great understanding of the game and he is one of the most promising talents of his age in the world."

The club's plan, according to the release, is to have Sargent train with the U-23s through the end of the 2017–18 season, and then get him into the first team when the new season resumes after the World Cup.[22]

While Germany is an enticing destination for a growing number of young American-born players, it's not necessarily where those players will stay. In one notable recent case, the road for a promising young American player who spent his late teenage years in the Bundesliga led back to the United States and MLS.

In 2011, then fifteen-year-old Russell Canouse joined the youth academy for ascendant Bundesliga club Hoffenheim. He saw an opportunity to develop and improve in Germany that was, if not better, at least different. He initially trained with the Red Bulls Academy via a winter program when he was twelve, and then a year later joined the Academy and played with the likes of Matt Miazga (now in the Chelsea organization) and Alex Muyl (now with the Red Bulls' first team) in what he describes as a "very professional organization" before getting the opportunity to do the US Soccer residency at Bradenton.

In part because Canouse's dad worked for SAP, Hoffenheim's corporate sponsor, Canouse landed a trial at Hoffenheim halfway into his yearlong residency at Bradenton and liked what he saw. "I saw the quality there and the possibility to grow as a player," he says. "Hoffenheim made an offer; they said if I came back in the next six months, I wouldn't need to come back and try out again."

"It wasn't easy, though," he notes. "The Red Bulls were very accepting. I was a young player; I ended up going to Germany when I turned fifteen. It was a big risk, but it seemed like the right thing to do at the time, and I'm glad I did it."

Canouse thinks of it as an excellent learning experience for him. "It's a different environment, there are different tactics, there's different stuff involved with the game over there. Not even including the soccer, but the whole experience itself, just being over there by yourself, having to do school over there, with your whole family still in the US. That makes you grow up as a player really, really quick. Even though you're not considered a professional over there, technically, you're a professional, which makes you grow as a player and challenges you at an early age."

Canouse went on loan to VfL Bochum in the 2016–17 season, placing him just twenty minutes from Dortmund. This allowed him to compare notes with Pulisic. Both hail from the same Pennsylvania region, and they both played club soccer at PA Classics—in fact, Canouse's younger brother played on PA Classics teams with Pulisic.

"We both really had a similar storyline in our past," he notes. "And being away from family in Germany, we were both in the same situation. It's nice to have someone like that by your side where you can just chill and converse about those things. It's tough over there as an American. What Christian's doing is very special. Not very many people from anywhere in the world, not even the German youth national team players, get to do that."

Though Canouse had played in the Red Bulls Academy and grew up just eighty miles from where the Philadelphia Union would eventually play, DC United was his first MLS love. As a kid, he made the two-hour trek to RFK with his dad to games. So when the organization reached out about bringing him back to the US, his childhood connections to the team, the opportunity to make an impact on the team's fortunes (in the same way it had appealed to Arriola), and even the construction of the new Audi Field (slated to come online by the summer of 2018) all combined to make it an enticing choice.

Since joining DC United in the summer of 2017, Canouse has become a staple in the team's midfield. He sat out the first game he was eligible to play, but then played each minute of every subsequent game until the final match of the season. In that season-ending match, he started but

was subbed off in the fifty-eighth minute for Ian Harkes—the son of MLS
and USMNT legend John Harkes, in a move that may have been more a
celebration of the team's last day at RFK Stadium then an actual strategic
necessity.

Of course, Germany is not the only road for American players aspiring to greatness. England has long been a favorite destination. First-team
goalkeepers for the USMNT in particular have a somewhat established
pathway to playing with English clubs in their prime.

Brad Friedel, who began his pro career with the USMNT preparing
for the 1994 World Cup in the between-leagues era, played in England
between 1997 and 2015, first with Liverpool, then with Blackburn
Rovers, Aston Villa, and Tottenham Hotspur. Kasey Keller featured for
Millwall, Leicester City, Tottenham, Southampton, and Fulham during
a twenty-year professional career that wrapped up with three years in
Seattle from 2009 to 2011. Tim Howard, in his third decade of professional
soccer, spent most of his career with Manchester United and Everton,
though he started his pro career in MLS with the MetroStars and is closing it out with the Colorado Rapids.

Brad Guzan is the latest example of a goalkeeper who's taken this
pathway. Like Howard, he began in MLS (with Chivas USA), spent the
bulk of his career in England (with Aston Villa and Middlesbrough), and
with his move to Atlanta United FC in 2017 looks poised to finish his
career in MLS.

Guzan experienced the ultimate ignominy for a Premier League goalkeeper: relegation, twice over. Villa went down in 2016, and though
Guzan remained in the Premier League by moving to the newly promoted
Middlesbrough for the 2016–17 season, that team was relegated the following season thanks to an anemic, league-low twenty-seven goals
scored.[23] Guzan's goalkeeping stats were more toward the middle of the
pack (fifty-three goals conceded[24]), though in the match that sealed Middlesbrough's relegation—a 3–0 loss to Chelsea which all but clinched the
league title for them—Guzan let in all three goals between his legs, an
unfortunate fact not lost on a number of pundits and online commenters.

Of the few American players who started the 2017–18 season in the
Premier League—including capped USMNT World Cup players Geoff

Cameron and DeAndre Yedlin—none are goalkeepers, perhaps signaling that American soccer might have arrived at end of an era.

"I think it's eye-opening and a good thing for US keepers to see there is no divine right to play in the Premier League," Howard told the *Telegraph*'s Bob Williams for a July 2016 article on his move to Colorado. "People have mistakenly thrown that rhetoric around, 'What are you going to do—play in England?' Well it's not that easy."[25]

Perhaps the most touted and most intriguing of the young American players in England was born and raised there. Cameron Carter-Vickers is the son of Howard Carter, a former first-round NBA draft pick who spent a year in the NBA before playing the bulk of his career in France and Greece. Carter-Vickers grew up playing soccer and trained in the Tottenham Hotspur academy, but he has played for the US rather than the English youth national team so far.

As Carter-Vickers told *VICE* in a June 2015 interview about his decision to play for the US youth nationals, "England never called me up, so I haven't had the choice of playing for them or not."[26] Carter-Vickers, who has most recently played for the US at the U-23 level, did reportedly attract interest from England the following year.[27] Several months after, he received his first call-up to the senior squad for the November 2016 matches against Mexico and Costa Rica, though he didn't get the opportunity to get capped in either match.[28]

In the fall of 2017, Carter-Vickers moved on a loan from Tottenham Hotspur to Sheffield United, after playing in just two FA Cup matches for the 2016–17 season. According to coach Mauricio Pochettino, the move allows Carter-Vickers—who Pochettino admitted wouldn't have much opportunity to see regular first-team action with Spurs—to get playing time and develop in the hopes that he can return a more seasoned player.[29] Because Sheffield United—and Ipswich Town, where Spurs moved him in January 2018—are both in England's second-tier league, he'll test himself against teams that aren't quite on the level of Premier League teams.

Another of the touted young American players who found his way to England, Emerson Hyndman, went a similar route to Bundesliga counterparts like McKennie and Canouse. He moved from club soccer to the FC Dallas Academy in 2010—in the midst of his grandfather Schellas Hyndman's tenure as FC Dallas head coach—but moved to Fulham's academy in London in 2011. He eventually graduated to Fulham's first team in 2014 and made his way to Premier League club Bournemouth in 2016.

Hyndman spent the latter half of the 2016–17 season, which included his twenty-first birthday, on loan from Bournemouth to legendary Scottish club Rangers. Will Parchman, writing on Hyndman's future in June 2017, noted that his season at Rangers "was perhaps his most individually rewarding as a pro, even if accomplished under the cloak of the Scottish Premier League. Rangers has been something of a salve for American players over the years, a warming beacon in the midst of the gray buffeting winds of the UK's more difficult league, but it has not been an automatic thing."

Now, Hyndman is with one of the more fun and promising Premier League squads, who could legitimately threaten for a Europa League spot under the guidance of highly regarded up-and-coming-coach Eddie Howe. But Parchman noted that fun might not be in Hyndman's ken, as "the Premier League is nothing if not a series of escalating arms races, and it is not particularly kind to its youth."[30]

Hyndman was also recovering from a stress fracture in his foot suffered at the tail end of his time at Rangers, causing him to miss out on the 2017 Gold Cup, which would have been an ideal place for him to test his mettle. With a breakout Premier League season, his skills in central midfield could be of use in the next two World Cup cycles, if he can shine beyond Scotland.

Danny Williams, a German-born veteran midfielder with over twenty US senior caps dating back to 2011, is the player perhaps most bandied about by American soccer fans looking for a secret weapon to improve the current iteration of the team. Williams, a dual citizen of Germany and the United States, was actually the first player to get his first cap under Klinsmann.

Williams, like Hyndman, made it to the Premier League for the 2017–18 season in a circuitous way. He tried to play his way into the Premier League in the 2016–17 season with second-tier club Reading by helping them reach the playoffs for a single Premier League spot. Reading got to the finals, where they lost to Huddersfield Town in a penalty shootout, but Williams still made it to the Premier League the following season by joining his Huddersfield Town opponents. The move was appropriately announced on the Fourth of July.

"It seems like Williams has been on the bubble for the USMNT for a long time," wrote Rob Usry in Stars and Stripes FC, on Williams' exclusion from the 2016 Copa America squad. "Klinsmann has given him chances to prove his worth and it's been a mixed bag of results. His form with the national team would likely need to be described as erratic. He has some very good performances and then can follow up them up with ones that make you question how he received a call up in the first place."[31] Williams will be thirty-three when the 2022 World Cup commences.

It's impossible to conclusively say if it's better for a promising sixteen-year-old player to develop in Germany or England (or Mexico, for that matter) rather than in an MLS academy in the United States or Canada. Each individual player learns differently and develops differently, and adjusting to new cultures and new languages can be exhilarating for some and disorienting for others.

The increased American appetite for soccer in Europe—as evinced by NBC's coverage of the Premier League, Fox's coverage of the Bundesliga, and beIN Sports' coverage of La Liga and Ligue 1—bodes well for young American players who want to test themselves overseas as well as the fans who are increasingly in tune with the heir apparent to the senior team. McKennie's first (and second) Bundesliga starts in September 2017, for example, were available to American TV viewers and were roundly discussed on Twitter before he took the field. Jason Foster (on Twitter as @jogabonitousa) provided heat maps, pass completion statistics, and other facts and figures that wouldn't be readily available in prior eras. Certainly, it's a different world for American soccer fans compared to when the US last hosted the World Cup in 1994, when coverage was filtered through traditional media outlets that didn't exactly specialize in soccer.

And a return of the World Cup to the United States is looking more and more likely. Alexi Lalas, speculating on the prospects of a US-hosted World Cup in 2026, exclaims, "Oh my God, it'll be a '94 on steroids! It'll be the most successful World Cup in history, not just because it makes ridiculous amounts of money for FIFA, but for what it does for soccer and for coming back into a country and a culture that is so vastly different than 1994." He notes that there are now "multiple generations of people who identify as 'soccer people,'" and credits supporters' culture—which he calls "much more educated when it comes to the global game than any supporters' culture out there"—as reason to be excited for the home-field advantage the Americans would provide.

And thanks to recent developments in an ever-evolving American fandom, which we'll explore in the next chapter, what has been hewn largely in 20,000-seat soccer stadiums has now crossed over to 60,000-plus football-first stadiums—for better *and* for worse.

CHAPTER 9

HOME-FIELD ADVANTAGE (AND HOW TO CREATE SOCCER-SPECIFIC SUPPORT IN AMERICAN FOOTBALL STADIUMS)

Six of the eight nations who have won a World Cup—between the first tournament in 1930 and the latest in 2014—have done so at least once on home soil. Uruguay won the debut tournament in Montevideo and its second in neighboring Brazil twenty years later. Italy won the first time it hosted in 1934, and while it didn't win in its second go-around as a host in 1990 (despite being one of the tournament favorites), it did win an all-European World Cup finals match against France in 2006 when Germany hosted. Germany's second of four championships (back when it was West Germany) came in 1974 in Munich. England won the only time it hosted, in 1966. France has hosted twice, winning in 1998, 60 years after the tournament was first there. And Argentina, winners of the 1978 and 1986 World Cups, did it first in Buenos Aires before triumphing again before the largest-ever finals crowd in Mexico City.[1]

It's not required to be the home team to win, of course: Spain won its sole World Cup in Johannesburg, South Africa, whereas Brazil has won its titles in far-flung locales like Solna, Sweden; Yokohama, Japan; and Pasadena, California. When Brazil had the opportunity to finally win a World Cup at home—specifically, a record sixth title in 2014 in front of loyal fans—it suffered a crushing 7–1 semifinal loss to eventual champions Germany—a defeat that Brazilian center-back Dante described as "very, very painful" to CNN even three years removed from Brazilian soccer's day of infamy.[2]

But it's not just speculation to say that it certainly helps to have familiar stadiums and passionate, patriotic fans filling them, which brings us to the prospect of a US-hosted tournament—or more accurately, thanks to recent developments, a World Cup jointly hosted by the US, Canada, and Mexico in 2026.

On June 13, 2018—on the eve of the 2018 World Cup—FIFA is set to determine, through a "fast-tracked" process, where the 2026 World Cup will be hosted.[3] A joint bid from the United States, Mexico, and Canada—with the vast majority of the matches to be staged in the US—initially appeared likely to win FIFA's election, though Morocco is making its fifth bid for the games and could build a coalition to challenge the favored North American bid.[4]

A December 2017 article by *The Washington Post*'s Steven Goff hints that the North American joint bid may not be the slam-dunk that Americans first thought it would be. He noted that "a precipitous decline in U.S. popularity around the world and, to a smaller extent, the fact that the American judicial system took the lead in prosecuting FIFA scandals" may help sway votes to Morocco. As he explained:

> The four involved countries are ineligible to cast ballots, leaving the bids seeking to secure 104 of the 207 votes. Before FIFA's reforms, the 24-member executive committee decided the winner by secret ballot. New guidelines mandate an open vote.
>
> Morocco presumably would receive backing from most, if not all, of the other 53 African countries. The North American bid would likely claim 32 from CONCACAF and, it hopes, 10 from South America. That leaves Europe (55), Asia (46) and Oceania (11) up for grabs.[5]

A US-hosted tournament was actually supposed to happen in 2022, if a number of those behind the American bid for that edition of the games are to be believed. The tournament was instead awarded to the tiny, oil-rich nation of Qatar. Any initial feel-good narratives of the first-ever World Cup on the Arabian Peninsula were soon obliterated with widespread allegations of corruption in the bidding process (leading, circuitously, to the less-than-dignified exit of longtime FIFA head Sepp Blatter) and widespread allegations of human rights violations (including the deaths of workers) in the construction of the stadiums that Qatar needs built in the run-up to 2022. A smaller but certainly not insignificant issue is the proposed rescheduling of the games from late summer to late autumn due to summer temperatures that can be inhospitable for not only high-stakes soccer but for human existence itself.

The United States, even without the other North American nations, has stadiums at the ready and an infrastructure to match. A press release put out by US Soccer in August 2017 cited 44 cities in the three proposed host nations they would invite to "declare their interest to serve as Official Host Cities." By early September, forty-one cities officially declared their intentions, with only Calgary, San Diego, and Green Bay, Wisconsin, passing on the opportunity, ending the unlikely but fun possibility of a World Cup match at historic Lambeau Field.

Thirty-four of the forty-four invited cities were in the United States. Stadiums ranged in capacity from Salt Lake City's Rice-Eccles Stadium at 45,807 to Arlington, Texas's AT&T Stadium at 105,000.[6] They also spanned nearly a century in age, as if to flaunt the US's longtime readiness to host the games, from the completed-in-1922 Rose Bowl[7] (listed at just 87,527, despite holding more than 94,000 for the 1994 World Cup Final[8]) to Atlanta's fresh-out-of-the-box Mercedes-Benz Stadium, which was several weeks from hosting its first-ever soccer match upon the announcement.

Assuming the North American bid emerges triumphant, the US will host a second World Cup in thirty-two years, equal to what Germany experienced in 1974 and 2006. Mexico, which hosted in 1970 and 1986, will host matches for the third time in just over a half-century. And though the US-hosted 1994 World Cup still boasts the best average attendance of all World Cups, it's conceivable that the 2026 World Cup could surpass that.

That would make for an incredible home-field advantage. Should the US-hosted World Cup become a reality in 2026, the American Outlaws will be ready to lead. The group officially formed in 2007, but its origin story goes back to the 2006 World Cup, when Korey Donahoo and eight other American soccer fans travelled to Germany. They made a cramped one-bedroom apartment in Köln their home base—Donahoo slept in the kitchen because he's a snorer—and eagerly awaited the chance to connect with members of Sam's Army, the most notable and active supporters' group of that era, for the pregame tailgate they assumed would be happening in Gelsenkirchen that day.

Because this was 2006, Donahoo trekked to an Internet café on the morning of the match, and navigated over to the Sam's Army website. But rather than the when-and-where information he was expecting, there was just a message on the page where the info should have been that said, "Check back later for details."

"And the game was that day," he recalls, "so we were really kind of disappointed." But they nevertheless took the train into Gelsenkirchen, found American fans congregated in the city center, and had the experience he'd hoped for—a self-described "rise of intensity" that left him hooked on the US soccer experience even though his beloved team was about to play, as he now reflects, "a horrible game; we got destroyed by the Czech Republic."

Fast forward several months later, and Donahoo was determined to go to the next US match he could. He traveled with friends to a match at the Home Depot Center in Carson, California, and arrived early for what he expected would be a Sam's Army tailgate in full swing. "We got there and sat in the parking lot and didn't really see anything organized to unite the fans who came from all over. And so we sat there and talked amongst ourselves and said there should be somebody doing this a little more consistently."

Together, they pondered how they could harness the power of the Internet to organize fans and create a centralized place to find tickets. When US Soccer announced a match against Brazil on September 9, 2007, just eight hours from their Lincoln, Nebraska, hometown, they devised a plan to charter a bus with their own money, fill it with fans, and travel en masse to the match.

Ten years after American Outlaws was founded, it's now approaching the 200-chapter mark: The first is in Lincoln, the second one was created in Kansas City, and the 150th was the American Outlaws' first non-US chapter, created in London for ex-pats in England. Other chapters are located in a broad array of big cities, mid-sized cities, and college towns. Each local chapter partners with a soccer-friendly bar to host watch parties. Some American Outlaws are so proud of their local chapter affiliations that rather than rep their favorite players, they customize their jerseys to feature their local AO chapters and chapter numbers. They've even created a chapter where you might least expect one: Mexico City, AO Chapter 192, with watch parties hosted at the perfectly-named-for-its-situation Pinche Gringo BBQ Warehouse.

While the watch parties are central to the American Outlaws experience, the organization started with travel, and they've since taken on the ultimate challenge in soccer tourism: World Cup expeditions to South Africa in 2010 and Brazil in 2014, chartering flights to bring American fans onto a literal global stage. Their mission also includes support for the US Women's National Team, and that manifested in what was essentially a massive road trip to neighboring Canada for the 2015 Women's World Cup.

It's in part due to their travel packages that their membership numbers swelled to above the 34,000 mark prior to the 2014 World Cup; registrations today are $25 for a year and membership kits include an AO-themed T-shirt and bandana.[9] Based on the spike in interest they've gauged in the last few World Cups—either from those seeking to be eligible for travel packages, those who wanted to be in the American Outlaws section for the World Cup qualifiers, or who just wanted to become more involved and publicly declare their fandom—Donahoo and company were eyeing the 50,000-member threshold as an achievable milestone by the opening of the 2018 World Cup. (The USMNT's failure to qualify promptly derailed those plans.)

Though Donahoo knew that AO was reaching like-minded fans in its first few years, he began to grasp the impact of the organization during the 2010 World Cup. He was in South Africa with a select group of members, but it was seeing what was happening back home half a world away that really caught his attention.

"When Donovan scored against Algeria and you saw all the reaction videos on YouTube from all the bars and all the parties and all the celebrations and get-togethers around the country, that really blew my mind, how much of a unifier this was around the country, how many people actually cared about it. In South Africa, I didn't have very good Internet access, but as it slowly trickled in on videos on YouTube at the end of the night, I was just blown away by that."

The party at the organization's original home base, Captain Jack's Bar in Lincoln, is featured in what Donahoo calls the most famous of the compilation videos. The videos showed American soccer fans how joyful the watch parties could be, but the next qualifying cycle, in 2013, showed how that ebullience was blossoming in the stands.

"You know we've got ninety minutes in this one town to put on the best show that we can, like a traveling circus or a rock concert," Dan Wiersema, American Outlaws Director of Communications and one of its principal logistics experts, says of the organization's approach to managing the in-game stadium atmosphere. "We're going to do our piece, we're going to put on a great show, hopefully get the win and move on from there."

The show reached new heights in 2013. The Snow Clasico in Denver, kicking off the home 2014 World Cup qualifying cycle, showed a resilient group of fans caught up in the bizarre history of the moment. In another home qualifier, an August 2013 match against Panama in CenturyLink Field, more than 40,000 packed into the stadium to create boisterous, raucous, and sometimes harrowing-to-the-opponents support. And when the Americans clinched their spot in the 2014 World Cup, it was against Mexico in Columbus, Ohio, in front of a capacity crowd of nearly 25,000, with American Outlaws leading the chants.

The American Outlaws were propelled further into national awareness when ESPN released a minute-long commercial in April 2014 featuring stirring scenes of AO members marching to a stadium for qualifying matches, hoisting scarves aloft with both hands and then gathering in the stadium to stand and chant. The shots of the Outlaws were interspersed with game action clips and slow-motion shots of individual players, and the commercial ended on the soccer-as-patriotism note, "Every Four Years, The Banner Yet Waves." It featured what was becoming a go-to chant for the group: "I Believe," a call and response starting with a simple intoned, "I," followed by "I believe," then, "I believe that," before shifting into an in-unison, repeated, "I believe that we will win."

"It definitely got the word out about us," Donahoo said. "ESPN played it so often, and during all kinds of programming. It wasn't just on during halftime of soccer games; it was on during *SportsCenter*. It let the average sports fan know, first of all, that the World Cup was coming. It showed them that the US had these kinds of fans and this kind of culture."

Justin Brunken, who cofounded American Outlaws with Donahoo and remains one of its leaders, says that they coordinated with ESPN to produce the commercial and advocated for "I Believe" to be featured. "They understood that it's not just about [. . .] featuring the players before the World Cup, but also the people that are watching the players and what they World Cup means to them," he emphasizes. "They featured the fans building the hype for the World Cup, and it got a lot of people excited, showing a community of fans as well as the players and what they do on the field."

Brunken claims, with a hint of apology, "I'm partially to blame for 'I Believe,'" but he also marvels at how effective the commercial was in moving the chant from their circles to the American mainstream. As he observes, "It was really cool to see something from US Soccer get into pop culture."

Though American Outlaws was originally created to organize fans and provide the structure to make American fans a single, unified group, the commercial also highlighted an identity that was, even with the 2014 World Cup on the horizon, only just beginning to coalesce. According to Wiersema, it's an identity that's still a work in progress.

American fans have certainly seized upon what Wiersema labels the "fun nationalism" of most soccer-mad European nations, though for American fans, it has gone beyond wearing red, white, and blue clothing and face paint into some fans breaking out tricorn hats and other Revolutionary War–era garb. There's even one fan, Chicago's Mike D'Amico, who became a sensation in Brazil by parlaying his resemblance to President Theodore Roosevelt into a costumed character named, awesomely, Teddy Goalsevelt.

"We can't ever be modeled after one nation because we are an amalgamation of so many different groups," Wiersema notes. "You see that in supporters' culture throughout the United States. Ultimately, American soccer is as much a melting pot as the country itself. And so you know we can't say, well, we want to be like a *barra brava*, we want to be like hooligans, or we want to be like Italian fans. We have to embrace all styles and I think that kind of mishmash of soccer support becomes the American style."

Because that can be perceived as "chaotic and messy," Wiersema added, "I think some people would say we do lack an identity, but the team itself is a mishmash of immigrant stories and diversity and homegrown players and dual nationals. So I think through all of that kind of sausage making of soccer support, something will emerge." He continued:

I think what was solidified in Brazil, and then followed up in Canada for the Women's World Cup is that right now, much like the team itself, the United States is underestimated. When you show up in huge numbers marching through the streets of Natal like we did in Brazil, or in Vancouver for the [Women's World Cup] final, people go, "Holy smokes, I'm impressed." You know and it's that kind of bigotry of low expectations that by exceeding those and exceeding them quite regularly and way beyond anybody's expectations is kind of punching above our weight. Whether with the [Men's National] Team or as fans, I think this is kind of our signature thing right now: That we're able to be underestimated and surprise the world on the field and off the field.

The first step is to parlay those numbers into visible and audible support during matches, gathering several thousand fans into one end of a stadium for a World Cup qualifier or a Gold Cup match or another match of some import to the USMNT. The second step is to harness that potential support through what is known in supporters' culture as capos.

Capos are functionally cheerleaders, but in the literal sense of leading cheers, akin to the yell leaders who amp up the throngs of fans at Texas A&M football games. With bullhorns, and sometimes with microphones and PA systems, but also sometimes just with hand signals and their own voices, they lead the American Outlaws into selected chants from its playbook. The hope, ultimately, is for other fans around the stadium to join in, but AO members, as coordinated by capos, are resolute to be an impactful embodiment of fandom no matter how much the rest of the stadium may or may not be participating.

Donald Wine II began his capo career as a DC United fan who joined the field team for the Screaming Eagles, one of the team's three primary supporters' groups, in 2010. In 2012, Wine worked his first USMNT match, relaying chant directions to his section from a capo in front of the other Outlaws—sometimes necessary when a stadium's acoustics make it hard to hear a single capo beyond the first few rows of stadium seats.

Wine is currently the group's in-stadium chair, organizing the capos and drummers that work each match, making sure experienced capos are at the front of the throng, while working in new capos who are increasingly invested and want to step up their involvement in the organization.

Wine notes that the biggest, most obvious challenge in creative cohesive support is that the team moves to different cities in each qualifying cycle or tournament. For DC United, Wine has a crew of dedicated fans on the field team who work each home match, and they've had literally years of experience to navigate RFK Stadium's peculiarities. As Wine notes, "When I deal with DC United, it's the same thing every single week. You have relationships with those people, you're working with people you know are going to be there on a regular basis."

But because US Soccer wants to maximize its reach to fans from sea to shining sea, the USMNT and USWNT play in a variety of stadiums, and the American Outlaws have to adapt.

Wiersema characterizes the typical calendar year for the group as accounting for "twenty cities, twenty stadiums, twenty sets of rules, twenty different crowds, and all sorts of different authorities all the time." He then asks a rhetorical question striking at the heart of the work his organization strives to do: "How do you standardize support or create the maximum possible in in every sort of unique situation?

"I wouldn't say that we're reinventing the wheel every single time," Wiersema says, "but we certainly have a lot of different wheels that we have to use over and over and over again, and the wheel that is StubHub Center, versus the wheel that is Levi's Stadium, are two very different things."

During the Hex leading up to the 2018 World Cup, Wine was charged with staffing capos and drummers for MAPFRE Stadium in Columbus, Ayava Stadium in San Jose, Dick's Sporting Goods Park in Commerce City, Colorado, Red Bull Arena in Harrison, New Jersey, and Orlando City Stadium in Orlando. As with the 2014 World Cup qualifying cycle, US Soccer scheduled all five home matches in soccer-specific stadiums primarily occupied by MLS teams, meaning that Wine could tap experienced capos who know the stadiums. Some of those fans already serve as capos with their MLS teams. Those fans can help answer some of the most fundamental questions capos face when preparing to enter an unfamiliar stadium—such as where in the stadium capos can stand, where they can best be seen, and where they can best be heard. As a veteran capo at the oft-used-by-US Soccer RFK Stadium, for example, Wine's been on the other end of the equation, as part of a team of DC fans advising AO on best practices.

With US Soccer beginning to anchor to stadiums like DSG Park and StubHub Center (and, of course, MAPFRE Stadium) for USMNT matches in multiple cycles, American Outlaws can create a more consistent in-game experience. As Wine notes, "It's easier for us to walk in knowing what to expect from security, what to expect from the stadium as a whole, and where to point your voice where it's most effective and it's not being lost in the space."

In some stadiums, American Outlaws are able to create tifo—the term soccer supporters use to describe large, fan-created art, sometimes spanning the entirety of the section behind goal where the American Outlaws stand. Tifo is typically painted on a patchwork of sewn-together bedsheets over a period of days, using an image drawn by an in-house artist and then projected onto the sheets so AO members can trace and paint them. A tifo display is unveiled in the seconds between the pregame singing of the National Anthem and the kickoff. As with many other elements of organizing fan support, different stadiums have different policies and different logistical possibilities for tifo, and it's up to AO to navigate those.

While American Outlaws leaders do meet with US Soccer officials periodically to discuss ticketing and logistics issues, they don't have any say in where matches are staged. Wine said that, in an ideal world, they'd rotate between three or four stadiums that they're intimately familiar with—including RFK Stadium, which has been a de facto national stadium despite its age. But that wouldn't readily bring the fans experiencing the magic of a qualifier for the first time, which is both a blessing (as American Outlaws get new, energized fans making the pilgrimage to see the US play) and a curse (in that it complicates the project of delivering cohesive support for ninety minutes).

"The big challenge is that most everyone in our section is new; ninety to ninety-five percent of AO has five or fewer caps," Wine says, borrowing the National Teams' terminology for how many matches an AO member has "played in."

"For the most part, for every single match," he continues, "we have a section largely filled with people where it might be their first or second time attending. That means we have to start from scratch every single time."

Capos do provide a chant sheet to fans in the American Outlaws section prior to the match. While some question the need for it—concerned that it projects an image of inexperience that some fan groups are derided for—Wine sees it as a necessity precisely because the fans in any given match *are* inexperienced. "We have people that may not know our chants," he explains. "If they want to be in the section, we want to make sure they're part of the section, and that they feel included, they feel welcome, they know what's going on."

"We release them a few days ahead of time, we let people know what's going on through email, so when they come to a match, they're prepared to sing the songs that we normally sing."

"I Believe" isn't even included on the chant sheet anymore, as it's an easy call-and-response chant that's just that well known by fans. In the past few years, some AO capos have been specifically using it at the start of matches—as Wiersema notes, to express an appropriate optimism. Wiersema claims to someday want to write an impassioned defense of "I Believe." He likens it to the Top 40 hit that got played too much on the radio, but still makes you tap your toe when it gets played.

"I feel like [it] has been really kind of dragged through the mud," he said, noting that even though it's now lost some of its novelty, it allows American Outlaws to reliably unite a stadium. "We finally got every city, every section in every stadium to sing one song that had more than three letters, U-S-A. And that's not easy to do. And it fit a moment and it fit a wave. For once, in the only time in our great soccer history, everybody knows the words to one chant. So rather than saying that song is simple and overplayed, why can't we look back and say: We all did it. We made soccer punch through."

To Wiersema, the chant represents a moment in the cultural zeitgeist, in the weeks leading up to and during the 2014 World Cup, where soccer finally reached the American masses. He recalls the pregame party for the US's last group match against Germany in Recife during the tournament as a special moment for the chant. "You know, CBS, NBC, and ABC were all covering the Germany match, live within 12 feet of each other. And they all wanted us to do 'I Believe' because they knew it would resonate with their audiences. We should appreciate that moment."

In this latest World Cup cycle, American fandom has intersected more and more with popular culture. At the June 2017 World Cup qualifier against Trinidad & Tobago in Colorado, fans protested a referee's call by chanting "Shame, shame, shame," while pretending to ring a bell—taken from a memorable scene in HBO's popular *Game of Thrones* series. (Wiersema notes the chant actually started when AO members in Phoenix used it on an online message board to criticize the frowned-upon practice of selling coveted AO section tickets on third-party websites, where neutrals or even opposing fans can buy them, rather than putting them on the AO ticket exchange where they can be sold "within the family.")

A quite notable recent example of soccer and pop culture crossover came via tifo: Before the World Cup qualifier in March 2017 against Honduras, fans in San Jose unfurled a massive 67.5-foot-by-45-foot banner reading "Not Throwing Away Our Shot," inspired by the popular musical *Hamilton*. The tifo captured the attention of *Hamilton* creator Lin-Manuel Miranda, who tweeted out his appreciation for the nod to his more than 1.5 million followers.

Wiersema expects even more popular culture will work its way into future chants and tifos. "You're going to see that because that makes the sport relatable to a whole different audience. Your goal is to support the team to win, but if a *Hamilton* tifo gets retweeted by Lin-Manuel Miranda, you just hit a whole other level of integration of the sport."

Pop culture can occasionally backfire, though. AO's tifo before the USMNT's July 2017 Gold Cup opener against Panama in Nashville referenced Van Halen's "Panama"—specifically the line, "Don't you know she's coming home with me?"—with a painting of the Gold Cup laid over a banner suggesting guitarist Eddie Van Halen's distinctive guitar design. The tifo designers changed "me" to "us," to reference the whole US team, but didn't change "she" to "it" to refer to the Gold Cup. Some found this problematic, including *VICE*'s Liam Daniel Pierce, who chided, "You shouldn't refer to an inanimate object that men compete over as a woman."[10]

Despite that initial misstep, the 2017 Gold Cup gave American Outlaws—and indeed, US Soccer—a chance to preview what a 2026 World Cup hosted in North America would be like. The Gold Cup tournament, like the US-hosted 2016 Copa America Centenario before it, showcased a number of the 50,000-to-80,000-seat NFL stadiums that are on US Soccer's big list of potential host stadiums.

While those football-first stadiums have the capacity to house an international swell of World Cup fans, and give the potential North American 2026 host nations the chance to break the US's still-standing 1994 records for average World Cup attendance, the size and design of those stadiums provide significant challenges for AO capos.

Even though American Outlaws would love the chance to host a World Cup—Donahoo simply says, "We daydream about what it would be like"—they're aware that those stadiums present a higher degree of difficulty in all they set out to do.

"When we're in an NFL stadium, those aren't built for soccer acoustics," Wine explains. "They're built more for creating general noise, but not coordinat[ing] chants. There are no sightlines for capos. You have to adjust for every single match. You have to adjust to the people who are there. You have to adjust to whether it's assigned seating versus general admission. With general admission, you're able to surround the section with veterans, who have been to a lot of matches and will help carry your sound. Whereas, with assigned seating, you may be next to someone for who it's their first match, someone who's not an AO member who has no idea you're showing up."

The USMNT's opening match in the 2016 Copa America Centenario tournament and the 2017 Gold Cup Final were both staged at San Francisco's Levi's Stadium, a football-first stadium opened in 2014. Despite the attraction that soccer governing bodies seem to have to it, AO San Jose president Crystal Cuadra-Cutler—lead capo for that Gold Cup final—flatly states, "Levi's Stadium does not understand soccer."

She first experienced frustrations with the stadium configuration during the Copa America Centenario, in which "the drums had to lead, ultimately, since communication between capos and drums was minimal."

The Gold Cup Final was even more logistically challenging, in part because Levi's Stadium didn't allow capos to use megaphones. "Not having megaphones is also really rough on the capo voices," she notes. "I started to lose my voice in the third minute of the game, but managed to somehow rally and get through the whole game." But they were able to rally together to rally the fans, in part due to an innovation inspired in part from American football. She says, "We utilized a quarterback play calling system, in which the capos each use a quarterback sleeve with songs listed with a number combination next to them. This system allows capos to communicate what song we plan to sing, and for all capos to know what the song is, rather than just waiting for the sound to travel to them."

The lessons they took from the previous tournament at Levi's also mitigated their Gold Cup Final experience. "Copa America Centenario was great to have under our belts before having to organize the Gold Cup Final on just a few days' notice," she observes. "The drum corps and tifo crew learned that they needed to upgrade the way they transport their goods to the stadium. [. . .] The tailgate crew learned the most efficient, and quick, way to set up and organize our area. Once in the stadium, we knew exactly what seats not to ask for. We also knew to plan on how to communicate in a stadium where the sound dissipates quickly."

But there's still a stark difference between Levi's Stadium and Avaya Stadium in San Jose, where Cuadra-Cutler also served as capo for the March 2017 match against Honduras. Her duties included keeping the Hamilton tifo in the trunk of her car for the first two weeks of its creation. "Avaya Stadium is very accommodating," she notes. "It's more intimate, and the roof really pushes the sound downward, so the capos and drummers are heard so much better." She also finds that working with stadium officials in a soccer-specific stadium, not put off by requests to bring in drums, megaphones, flags with poles, and tifo, make for a smoother experience.

Houston's NRG Stadium, the site of the USMNT's 2016 Copa America Centenario semifinal match against Argentina, and another prime candidate for World Cup hosting, presented its own challenges for capos. Wine notes that its immense height, and an absence of overhangs or close-in roof structures to angle a voice off of, results in individual voices being effectively swallowed by the stadium.

"It's just a tall stadium, so if I scream my heart out, I may be really loud," Wine notes. "But someone in the fourth deck can't hear what I'm saying, just because they're 200 feet above me, and that's just a lot of space for a voice to travel in a concentrated form, in something that can be heard and repeated back."

Cuadra-Cutler notes that stadiums sized to host NFL, Gold Cup, and World Cup games *can* be made as formidable to opponents and inspiring to American players as the soccer-specific stadiums where they excel, but American Outlaws have to work with stadium staff, not in spite of them.

"If stadiums such as Levi's Stadium are to be a regular host to US games, I would like to see them embrace supporter culture more," she said. She notes that Seattle's CenturyLink Field, the nation's only active NFL/MLS dual stadium before Atlanta United hosted its first match in Mercedes-Benz Stadium in September 2017, could serve as a model for how big stadiums can help AO. Her advice to staff and those stadiums is simple: "Be more supporter friendly; allow megaphones, allow flags and tifo, allow some type of temporary capo stand to be erected."

She notes that during Copa America Centenario, the Century Link staff sided with American Outlaws in a dispute with tournament officials over the microphone-and-speaker set up, along with capo stands, that Sounders supporters' groups typically employ.

"CenturyLink Field understands the value that items such as the microphone bring to the organization of supporters and the game day experience," she says. "Perhaps with time, and developing a level of trust between the stadiums, US Soccer, and AO, we will eventually be allowed the tools to be more successful. A capo that cannot be seen or heard is an ineffective capo by default. If we cannot eventually have these tools by the time of 2026 World Cup, you can bet that we will still have a stadium that does no better than chanting U-S-A."

Yet capos in big stadiums, without all their usual tools at their disposal, sometimes keep it simple (and catchy) to involve fans. One option—popularized by Iceland fans at the 2016 Euros, but a staple in MLS stadiums since 2008 (thanks to Toronto FC and later Seattle Sounders FC)—is the "Viking Clap" or "Icelandic Clap." (Sounders fans know it as "Boom Boom Clap.") It's a slowly building cheer in which fans start with a single clap. In the Icelandic version, the clap is accompanied with a guttural grunt, whereas in the American version, fans offer up the "U" in "U-S-A" and spell the other two letters with subsequent claps. It then grows faster and faster, until it eventually works into very emphatic applause.

"We do the U-S-A Clap a lot in big stadiums," says Wine, cognizant of the importance of visual cues. "The fans may not hear what we're saying, but when they see the clap going, they know what's going on and they're able to join in. We've seen a lot of those chants take off quite quickly. One, it's very simple—we use 'U-S-A' in every sport known to man. They can see what beat we're on and join in, even from the opposite end of the field. That makes them feel like part of the action."

That's not as easy as it sounds. As Wine explains, many of the US fans attending games don't come in with the same commitment to fervor that AO members have. "They're not going to be standing and singing and jumping up and down for ninety minutes. They're going to pick and choose their moments. When they hear the U-S-A chant, they don't even need to stand up to do that. They can clap in their seats. They can clap standing up. It's one of those things that's so natural to any American sports fan that they all have their ways of following on. If it's as simple as their sitting in their seat and clapping along with us, we're still helping create that atmosphere and spreading it along to the next section so that everyone's involved."

"We always joke about how, in theory, the plan for American Outlaws is to be obsolete," Wiersema laughs. "You shouldn't need a supporters' group necessarily. If you become a full-fledged soccer nation, if it's just a whole American Outlaws stadium, then it's just called a really awesome stadium."

But until then, expect more U-S-A Claps and more "I Believe."

"People ask why we do these rudimentary chants all the time—it's because we want to get these people involved," Wine says. "It's not about AO creating all of the atmosphere. We are creating the atmosphere that we want everyone to participate in. We want everyone to feel involved and feel [like] part of the success of the team and the success of that experience. In getting some of these chants started, if you're two years old or 100 years old, we want you to be able to join it."

But are the fans really making a difference for the players? Does a group of several thousand American fans, congregating at one end of the stadium, going to tried-and-true chants that unite a stadium in voice, mixed with chants that unite just that one section in voice, inspire the players to leave it all out on the field?

Wine says, in a word, yes: The American players note that the American Outlaws are there, and see and hear that they're active in the stands. They've been able to highlight endorsements from current and former players on their website and in promotional videos mining the same emotional vein that the ESPN "I Believe" commercial tapped.

"They hear it," Wine said of the support. "They absolutely hear it. They're not paying us lip service or just saying that we're doing really well. When that atmosphere is there, it really spurs them on."

"100 percent it's motivating," says Paul Arriola about playing in front of the American Outlaws. "It's a great feeling to hear them chant all the time, to chant players' names. The understanding that they have of the game, and the recognition of players throughout the United States [. . .] It's a great thing. It's great for soccer, it's great for the fans, and it's great for the players."

"When these guys hear us on the field, when they walk out and see a wall of support, they're motivated to play," Wine says. "We love them, and they love us, and that camaraderie between us makes this great." He notes that at the 2017 Gold Cup trophy ceremony, a good number of the players were wearing AO scarves they'd been gifted from fans. Though players don't always get that up close and personal with fans, they do customarily walk over to the AO section after matches—win, lose, or draw—and applaud the fans for their effort.

(Imagine NFL or NBA players doing that, realize the incongruity in conjuring that up, and you have some sense of what makes soccer special among American sports for featuring this element.)

"It's a small thing for them to come out and walk over to our section and clap after a game, but to some people, it's everything," Wine notes. That's what motivates people to keep coming out to matches and showing the same support—because they know it's making a difference."

On September 9, 2017, American Outlaws celebrated its tenth anniversary, with members taking to social media to share memories of favorite games and celebrate friendships initiated by taking part. The organization also shared a compilation video of well-wishers; the impressive list includes USWNT players like Carli Lloyd, Heather O'Reilly, Christen Press, and Meghan Klingenberg, former USMNT Coach Bruce Arena, and past and present USMNT players including Kyle Beckerman, Landon Donovan, and Jozy Altidore. Jimmy Conrad, a former USMNT player and effusive friend of the American Outlaws, lauded them as "creating a positive force for good, who organize and mobilize Americans from all backgrounds and cultures and beliefs, and molds them into one living, breathing, kickass mass of people that do everything that they possibly can to help our national teams be successful on the field."[11]

Wine sees a growing sense of the US soccer teams as an "outlet" for

people who might not be fans of soccer, but want a team to place its patriotic feelings behind:

> There are a lot of people who say, 'I wish the Olympics was year-
> round.' Well, here you go. Here are teams that play year-round and
> represent their country every single time. We're getting a lot of those
> fans out. With our exposure, and with our growth, people can walk
> into the stadium and know what to expect from us. They know
> we're going to bring it, they know we're going to have a great time,
> and we're going to provide a positive fan experience for our mem-
> bers. I think that's what they want to be a part of. Our sections
> have grown because people have come to matches and said, oh,
> those people are pretty cool. They come to matches and they want
> to be in our section. I think that is a wonderful thing for us.

The American Outlaws had plans for the 2018 World Cup. Brunken
says that the morning after the team's anticipated qualification, AO had
initial travel packages ready to offer on their website.

Yet fans had expressed uncertainty during the 2017 qualifying campaign about making the trek to Russia, even as they assumed the USMNT
would be there. By contrast, Wine notes, "For Brazil, there were people
planning three years in advance." There were a whole host of reasons
for concern. Wine, who is African American, had been planning to skip
the Russia trip, not wanting to experience the country's racism, and instead had sought to visit AO-hosted watch parties around the nation.
Wiersema, loath to take his two-and-a-half-year-old son on a fifteen hour
flight or on the marathon bus rides they'd endure in traveling from match
to match, also had planned to stay stateside.

Though some of them had personal reservations about Russia and
its recent, awkward relationship with the rest of the world, they'd come
too far as a trusted, reliable resource not to take on the responsibility.

The 2014 World Cup in Brazil had provided considerable obstacles
for the AO trip planners, including the second group stage match assigned
to Manaus, an outpost in the middle of the Amazon primarily accessible
by boat or plane.

"We had a hell of a time in Brazil, and it took every ounce of our energy to get people around that country safely," Wiersema said.

Brunken adds, "Telling you the story of what all happened, every little thing, could take literally three hours. I think there could be a whole book of what happened behind the scenes." But as he proudly notes, "We were able to get every person [who bought an AO travel package] to every game and there and back safe. I think it's the most accomplished we've ever felt."

Wiersema points out that before the US was eliminated, AO's philosophy about Russia 2018 was, "Whoever wants to take on the adventure, they can do that. And those who don't want to go for political reasons or safety reasons or distance reasons [. . .] everybody's got their own barometer of what's tolerable and what is not."

They do have concern that subdued enthusiasm for the host nation could indeed repeat itself in 2022 with Qatar. "There are a lot of people saying they won't go in 2022 and are really secretly hoping that it gets moved somewhere else," Wine notes. "When you consider what's being done over there to get that World Cup ready, on the backs on some less fortunate people, that is what people are weighing. It's a moral dilemma of whether they can even support a World Cup in that country."

On the other hand, the organization provides support for all US Soccer teams, and an enticing Women's World Cup in France awaits in 2019.

"We've always been focused on the next two summers, and that focus hasn't changed," Wine said. "We will do all of the events we possibly can surrounding the women as they first seek to qualify next fall and then the Women's World Cup"—not taking anything for granted anymore—"should they make it." With only international friendlies on the horizon for the USMNT until the 2019 Gold Cup, they'll have more time to focus on a tournament which, being in France, will be easier to plan than what they were facing with Russia.

The USMNT's failure to qualify for the 2018 World Cup also brought forth another change for the American Outlaws: For the first time in its history, the organization weighed in on the only US Soccer president it has ever known—though, Brunken points out, he has never once met with him or the group's other leaders. The day after the US was knocked out of the World Cup, AO posted a statement on its website, which began:

> There are hardly any words that can do justice to the feelings of disappointment, anger, and dumbfoundedness that come from watching your men's national team fail to make the World Cup. Our gut wrenches for our #AOFamily that is hurting today. Our USMNT will not be in the World Cup and this is something that hits home with all of us.
>
> Dramatic changes must be made at many levels, but it all starts at the top. In no uncertain terms, the President of the United States Soccer Federation, Sunil Gulati, must go. Despite past successes he has presided over an unmitigated disaster and the Federation needs fresh leadership and ideas from top to bottom. Bruce Arena was brought in with the singular mission of getting us to the World Cup. He has failed and should step down as well. The buck stops with them and we call on them to accept the responsibility of this outcome.[12]

The statement went on to express support for the players, requesting that when they return to competition, that they "individually and collectively play with a renewed sense of urgency as we reinvigorate the fan base and begin to build towards qualification for the 2022 World Cup."[13]

"We felt a statement was necessary after taking the pulse of the membership and how they were feeling about everything," Wine says. "We went back and forth over whether we should take a stand on asking for their resignations, but in the end it was a near consensus from members that this was what needed to happen. I'm proud of our statement calling for change."

And certainly, with Gulati's eventual decision to not seek reelection, their wish for a "dramatic change" came true, and they didn't sit idly by. Prior to the elections, they hosted a series of online candidate forums that allowed rank-and-file members the chance to ask questions of the potential new presidents, branded with the hashtag #TimeForChangeUSSF.[14]

The ultimate wish for American Outlaws, of course, is to be in the

stands of a World Cup final, and that happening in an American stadium—even of the large and challenging variety. Though many American
Outlaws have favorite club teams and watch far more soccer than the
average fan, it's still uncertain how they'll take to the 2018 World Cup,
if any of them will travel to Russia, or if chapters will even host weekend
watch parties.

In 2014, Donahoo and Brunken didn't stay in Brazil once the US was
knocked out of the tournament. They watched the final surrounded by
locals in Lincoln at their beloved Captain Jack's, as fans of the game,
while still wondering how long they would have been able to keep the
party going had Wondolowski not missed on the winning goal opportunity against Belgium.

This year's World Cup will cruelly continue without the US, leaving
the American Outlaws to mourn alongside fans of other nations who
have surprisingly missed the cut. For some participants, the 2018 World
Cup provides them the chance to finish a multi-generational quest to win
the tournament, though previous winners, hungry for more glory, stand
in the way.

Though the allure is unfortunately diminished for American fans who
wanted to root for the red, white, and blue, it will still be a fascinating
tournament worth following—if for nothing else, to see how far the US
will need to go once it does get to another World Cup.

CHAPTER 10

HOW THE REST OF THE WORLD WILL WEIGH IN ON AMERICA'S WORLD CUP ASPIRATIONS, AND HOW WE MIGHT RESPOND

FOR MUCH OF THIS BOOK, WE'VE DISCUSSED THE USMNT'S PATH TO DEVELoping and eventually amassing the talent necessary to win a World Cup, and the need for a coaching staff that can effectively direct a sufficiently talented team toward that goal. It's tempting to view the team's future with a certain myopia, built around the presumption that we are Americans, and Americans find ways to win, regardless of what the rest of the world might want.

And yet, world soccer is fiercely competitive; this most recent World Cup had 211 nations vying for thirty-two spots. Even the expected expansion of the pool to forty-eight teams in 2026 means that four of five soccer-playing nations will be excluded from each quadrennial tournament, as compared to the five of six denied admission now. The tournament's new format may make luck a greater part of the World Cup–winning equation, but talent, player development, and team cohesion will remain the predominant factors for success, regardless of how many teams are entered.

As a new generation of US fans have learned acutely and painfully, it's never a given to get into the World Cup. The only team to appear in all twenty World Cups prior to 2018 is Brazil, who easily made it twenty-one in an otherwise-wild qualification round-robin in CONMEBOL. Other nations have long strings of success in getting to a World Cup: In

2018, Germany will be in its seventeenth straight tourney, Argentina and Spain in eleven straight, and South Korea—from the haves-and-have-nots that make up the Asian Football Confederation—will be in its ninth straight. (Italy, had it survived its November playoff with Sweden, would have been in its fifteenth straight World Cup; the United States would have been in its eighth straight, having been to eleven World Cups overall.)

For some nations, though, just getting to the World Cup is a generational triumph. In 2018, Peru is making its first appearance since 1982, having survived the fiercely competitive CONMEBOL qualifiers *and* an intercontinental playoff against New Zealand. Egypt is returning to the World Cup for the first time since 1990.

But a number of teams have realistic designs on winning the tournament outright. As 2018 began, various oddsmakers, as reflected on the betting website aggregator Oddschecker, had two clear favorites in the 9–2 to 5–1 range: Germany, who could become the first back-to-back World Cup winner since Brazil did it in 1958 and 1962, and Brazil, looking to rebound from its disappointing (by Brazil's standards) fourth-place finish.

France, Spain, and Argentina nudged just under those two favorites; France is most commonly listed at 11–2, with Spain at 7–1 and Argentina split fairly evenly between 8–1 and 9–1. The first CONCACAF team appearing in the odds, Mexico, is no better than 66–1.[1]

Those same oddsmakers had the US team on par with where Mexico is now. The US was listed anywhere from 50–1 to 100–1 to win the 2018 World Cup during the summer of 2017. Then, after the team's September swoon, those odds expanded a bit from 66–1 to, in at least one dismissive estimation, 150–1. That positioned the US anywhere from fifteenth and twentieth for a tournament that has just thirty-two teams—before they disappeared from the board altogether—and that's now where CONCACAF's best hope going into 2018 sits relative to the other participants.[2]

A US team in the 2018 World Cup, as currently constituted, certainly would have played under the weight of questions about their fortitude, talent, and cohesion, assuming a late last-gasp goal for the draw against Trinidad & Tobago. Had they been drawn into Group G, where the third-place CONCACAF team landed, they would have been in a group with a very familiar English team, the Belgian team that knocked them out of the 2014 World Cup, and a Tunisian team that is all but certain not to advance into the Round of 16. A third-straight Round of 16 appearance would have required the Americans to dispatch one of two European contenders in the group stage—just as they did in 2014 when drawn into a group with both Germany and Portugal.

So how does the whole of the international field look today? To start, consider the 2017 Confederations Cup—not only to marvel at the strength of co-favorites Germany, but also to marvel at how rapidly a team's fortunes can change in a year.

The Chilean team that faced Germany in the World Cup warm-up tournament's final match won't even be present in Russia for a World Cup they could have conceivably won. After all, Chile won two recent major tournaments after a respectable showing at the last World Cup— it beat Argentina in both the 2015 Copa America finals on its home turf and the 2016 Copa America Centenario finals in the United States. Chile boasts three veteran anchor players in Alexis Sánchez, Arturo Vidal, and Gary Medel, and the team has one of the most distinct identities of any team in the world, blending tenacious defense with creative attacking. In recent years, it has vacillated between being the fourth and the seventh best team in the world.

But in the 2017 Confederations Cup finals, Chile lost 1–0 to a German team that sent what many considered a B- or even a C-level roster into competition. German Julian Draxler, the then-twenty-three-year-old Paris Saint-Germain winger, led the team's dynamic attack after being a peripheral player for the World Cup–winning team three years prior. Timo Werner, who began to make a name for himself at RB Leipzig in the 2016-17 season, became a presence during the tournament despite just having turned twenty-one four months prior to the tournament.

Rory Smith, discussing the German team's victory in *The New York Times*, wrote:

> What is significant, then, about Germany's success over the last few weeks, in both Russia and Poland, is that it has come without the majority of its most illustrious names, that the likes of Özil, Kroos, and Müller could only enjoy those twin triumphs vicariously.

That German soccer's strength is more than skin-deep indicates that there is, indeed, a program that has been put in place, a system that has been fine-tuned, a grand plan enacted. That can be gauged not by those players whose gifts are so lavish that they would have succeeded regardless of their education, but by the broad standard of those behind them.

Dietrich Weise, the man who helped shape the transformation of German soccer in the early 2000s, never believed the country lacked talent. As he told the journalist Raphael Honigstein in *Das Reboot*, Honigstein's book on the revival of German soccer, the issue was that too much of it was being overlooked in the search for a star. Germany's revolution was to ensure nobody was left behind.

That is what enabled Germany to win in Russia over the past two weeks—and in Poland, too—without so many of its best and brightest: not the brilliance of its outstanding individuals, but the quality of its rank and file, the depth and breadth of its talent. That is what makes it such a fearsome prospect for next summer, too, whatever happens: the idea that, whoever makes it into [German national team coach Joachim] Löw's squad, there will be dozens more who might have been there, condemned by the country's success to watch on from home.[3]

As formidable as Germany looks, they're not the only European team with a credible claim as World Cup favorites. France may not be capitalizing on a system of player development like the one Germany has in place, but it shares one similar advantage: a naturally deep talent pool. Though France, like all other World Cup nations, is limited to sending a twenty-three-player squad to the tournament, a team comprised of its twenty-fourth through forty-sixth choices could quite conceivably emerge from the group stages as one of the World Cup's best sixteen teams. If star power and value is indicated by the transfer fees that players can command—even in a market that seems more and more madcap each year—France has amassed euros upon euros worth of star power. For evidence, consider the premiums that top international club teams have been willing to pay for French players of late.

In August 2016, Manchester United—who did not correctly consult their crystal ball when they shipped nineteen-year-old French national Paul Pogba to Juventus in 2012—bought twenty-three-year-old Paul Pogba back for a then-world-record £105 million (approximately $116.4 million). A year later, Paris Saint-Germain picked up Monaco striker Kylian Mbappé, a young French rising star, for £155 million, which would have set a transfer fee record if not for the same club's budget-busting £222 million acquisition of Brazilian star Neymar—arguably the third-best player on the planet—earlier that summer.[4]

Barcelona, flush with Neymar money to spend, invested in the twenty-year-old Ousmane Dembélé—who only first appeared for the French senior team in September 2016—for £105m from Borussia Dortmund. And earlier in the summer, Alexandre Lacazette—who scored at least twenty goals a season in each of his final three seasons with Ligue 1 side Lyon—was signed by Arsenal for a team record £53 million—though he'll likely be the sub on the French national team behind now-former Gunner Olivier Giroud.

Look up and down the current French depth chart—some soccer writers have projected five-deep rosters for each position, because they can—and you'll see many of the names recognizable from Champions League play and Europe's top domestic leagues. (You'll also see André-Pierre Gignac, who has found a welcoming home in Liga MX playing and excelling for the Monterrey-based Tigres.)

France has weathered some internal strife for the past few cycles. In November 2009, in a playoff home-and-away series between France and Ireland to see which team would advance to the 2010 World Cup, legendary French striker Thierry Henry infamously touched the ball with his hand in the build-up to what was teammate William Gallas's game-deciding goal. Though Henry apologized after the match, the incident snowballed into notoriety from its onset; Ireland made the bold request to be admitted to the World Cup as its thirty-third team to make up for the injustice of losing the playoff as the result of a handball—which then-FIFA president Sepp Blatter appeared to entertain in that he publicly let it be known they'd made the ask.[5]

Once France arrived at the 2010 World Cup under a cloud of controversy, the team made the wrong kind of headlines. They openly re-volted against coach Raymond Domenech after he sent striker Nicolas Anelka home following an R-rated confrontation during halftime of France's group stage loss to Mexico. After signing autographs for fans prior to what was supposed to be an open practice, the team withdrew to its bus, closed the curtains, and sent out a statement for Domenech to read, articulating their unanimous opposition to his decision to exclude Anelka. *The Guardian*'s David Hytner assessed, "Domenech suffered the ultimate humiliation at the hands of his players as strikes, rows, resignations and recriminations left the French in disarray on one of the darkest days in the country's football history."[6]

In a 2014 article I wrote, perhaps prematurely declaring France "done with failing at the World Cup," I included details of the cathartic move Adidas made just before that year's World Cup with the Fédération Française de Football's blessing: Crushing the infamous 2010 team bus with a giant crane-and-claw contraption.[7] With this specter of the past behind them, the team had a definitively better outing in 2014, advancing to the quarterfinals where they were edged by eventual champion Germany. They've since been without two of the starters from that World Cup—forward Karim Benzema and midfielder Mathieu Valbuena—due to their embroilment in a scandal in which Benzema allegedly worked with blackmailers who approached Valbuena over a sex tape they threatened to make public. Neither player has featured for France since the case came to light in October 2015, even though Benzema continued to be a reliable goal scorer for Real Madrid through the 2016–17 season. (The 2017–18 season, however, started with just two goals between August and December for the now-thirty-year-old striker.)

But even with this recent history of turmoil, there's no denying France's talent, or its potential to celebrate the twentieth anniversary of its first World Cup win with a second.

The first team from Europe to actually qualify for the 2018 World Cup (not counting, of course, the Russian hosts) was Belgium. Though Belgium is an immensely talented team—recall the barrage of shots that Tim Howard faced in the 2014 World Cup Round of 16 match that knocked out the Americans—they've also struggled to coalesce as a functioning unit compared to other top European teams.

Three of the key Belgian players are also key players for top Premier League sides: Kevin De Bruyne earned a lofty #4 ranking in the 2017 edition of the Guardian's "Best 100 footballers in the world" annual feature as he found his next level at Manchester City,[8] Romelu Lukaku started the 2017–18 season on a literal goal-a-game clip for Manchester United, and Eden Hazard has been a perennial Player of the Year candidate for Chelsea since arriving there in 2012. Hazard's Chelsea teammate, Thibaut Courtois, is one of the world's best goalkeepers, and another Chelsea teammate, Michy Batshuayi, is Belgium's heir apparent as striker (though Lukaku is only five months older).

Premier League fans might recognize the trio of Belgian players contributing to Tottenham Hotspur's first-team: defenders Toby Alderweireld and Jan Vertonghen, and midfielder Mousa Dembélé (not to be confused with France/Celtic striker Moussa Dembélé or France/Barcelona midfielder Ousmane Dembélé).

Other Belgians bolstering top European teams include Yannick Carrasco at Atlético Madrid, Dries Mertens at Napoli, and Divock Origi at Wolfsburg.

Roberto Martínez, known to American audiences tuning into the 2014 World Cup as the dapper, intelligent Everton manager providing valuable studio analysis, has been leading the team since 2016. If the team can find cohesion—a big if—it has the talent (not to mention the staggering, cumulative Champions League experience) to challenge the top teams in the world.

It's tempting to call France, Germany, and Belgium the three favorites from Europe, but what of the reigning European champions? Portugal has Cristiano Ronaldo, who has been dueling with Lionel Messi (for most of the last decade now) for recognition as the world's best player, starting with their competition over the Best FIFA Men's Player award, the not-so-imaginatively named honor replacing the Ballon d'Or as the talisman of individual soccer supremacy. Portugal beat France at home in the 2016 Euro finals, a match in which an injured Ronaldo had to be carried off the pitch midway through the first half with a knee injury. The team was able to rally and play in the grinding, stultifying manner that character-ized much of their tournament run, finding the game's lone goal in the second half of extra time.

After the match, Ronaldo's sister, Katia Aveiro, ill-advisedly took to Instagram and said, "These tears I cried for my wounded brother were like daggers to the heart, and we all cried with him for the awful pain we had together. But God is great and just as our savior Jesus Christ suf-fered on the cross for a better world for us, Cristiano cried in the pain of not being able to help his teammates and his beloved people." She went on to state that, because "God is just," Portugal "deservedly lifted the trophy."[9]

In the 2014 World Cup, Portugal couldn't get past Germany and the United States in the tournament's most difficult group; its opening 4–0 loss to Germany proved too deep a hole for them to dig out from, despite a comeback draw against the US and a win over Ghana to close out the tournament. There's a new rising generation of intriguing Portuguese players featuring in top European leagues, including Renato Sanches, André Silva, Bernardo Silva, and Bruma, but ultimately, as captain Ronaldo goes, so goes Portugal.

The expectation to win a World Cup hasn't been placed on Cristiano Ronaldo the way it has on his inextricably linked counterpart. Messi, who will be turning thirty-one during World Cup 2018, may be looking at his last best chance to lead Argentina to a World Cup win—albeit with a squad that has struggled just to qualify out of an increasingly compet-itive CONMEBOL. Argentina went through three coaches in a single qualifying season, eventually settling on Jorge Sampaoli, who coached Chile to a Copa America title (over Argentina) in 2015 and Sevilla to a Champions League qualification in the 2016–17 season.

Though there are some talented younger players on the squad, notably forwards Paulo Dybala and Mauro Icardi, the national team leans heavily on players in their early-to-mid thirties. Argentina could potentially fea-ture some combination of a thirty-year-old Sergio Agüero, thirty-year-old Ángel Di María, thirty-two-year-old Lucas Biglia, and a thirty-year-old Gonzalo Higuaín to complement Messi in the team's attack, with thirty-year-old defenders and defensive midfielders in Nicolás

Otamendi, Federico Fazio, and Ever Banega, and an even older one in Javier Mascherano, who will turn thirty-four before what he's said will be his final World Cup.

Argentina's implacable rival, Brazil, was the first to qualify for the 2018 World Cup, and in switching out one single-named former player for another in the head coaching post, seems to have seized on success. Tite, who formerly managed Brazil club giants Corinthians, led the team to a staggering nine-win run since taking over for Dunga, with Neymar and Co. outscoring opponents 25–2 in that stretch.[10] A key player for Brazil in the 2018 World Cup tournament will be Philippe Coutinho, who started the 2017-18 season as the centerpiece of a Champions League–level Liverpool squad, even though he was openly courted by Barcelona before the season started. As the January 2018 transfer window opened, Liverpool added to the will-he-or-won't-he saga by setting a price of £130 million for Coutinho's potential move to Spain, setting him up to be the second most expensive transfer ever.[11] Liverpool eventually acceded to Barcelona's wishes for £142 million; manager Jürgen Klopp characterized the move as "an easy decision . . . once it became clear Liverpool had 'no chance' of keeping the Brazilian committed for the remainder of the season."[12]

Looking for an unconventional dark horse? Consider Iran. Though Asia's federation isn't as strong as Europe's or South America's, Iran looked dominant in their qualification run. They were the second nation to qualify for the 2018 World Cup, after Brazil, and they were ranked above the Gold Cup–winning Americans in the world standings throughout the summer of 2017. Though Team Melli didn't make it past the group stages in 2014's edition of the global games, it did memorably push Argentina to its limits in a 1–0 group stage match settled by a late Messi goal. The squad heading to Russia has several key players playing professionally in the Eredivisie and the Russian Premier League. And its manager has a curious American connection—Carlos Queiroz, manager of Iran's national team since 2011, authored the Q-Report created as part of US Soccer's forward-looking Project 2010.

Iran certainly believes they are destined for greatness beyond just getting into the tournament. "My goal and dream is to get to the knockout stage at the 2018 World Cup," said Queiroz. "I am fighting against this satisfaction disease. We should not be satisfied with the first round. We need to be ambitious. We need to think big. We will not go to Russia as tourists."[13]

CONCACAF's first two qualifying teams, Mexico and Costa Rica, had the chance to meet each other in the 2014 World Cup quarterfinals. From that match, the newly crowned king of CONCACAF would have advanced to the World Cup semifinals—which would have been the first such appearance for a CONCACAF nation since the American presence in 1930. As it turns out, the Netherlands was the undoing of both nations, though Costa Rica pushed its quarterfinals match all the way to penalty kicks.

The oddsmakers don't seem to like any CONCACAF team's chances—Mexico finished the qualifying season more or less alongside the US, whereas Costa Rica was ranked in the 200-to-1 to 500-to-1 range. The 2018 version of Costa Rica is arguably better than the 2014 team that was two saved penalty kicks away from the tournament's final four. Keylor Navas is the one of the best goalkeepers in the world, minding Real Madrid's net as his day job, and as we've noted in what has not been a terribly-fun-to-recount recent history for American fans, the team in front of Navas played well in the run-up to the World Cup.

Mexico looks especially ready to make a deeper tournament run than it did in 2014, though the team's opening match will be against Germany in a tricky group that also includes South Korea and Sweden. Experienced players like Andrés Guardado, Javier "Chicharito" Hernández, and Oribe Peralta will likely play prominent roles in whatever level of success Mexico is able to achieve. Rising star Hirving Lozano, who will be just twenty-two when the tournament kicks off, is poised to be one of the breakout players of the tournament. Though he started the year with top Dutch team PSV Eindhoven, after featuring with Liga MX side Pachuca the previous three seasons, he very well could finish 2018 (or even enter the World Cup) playing his club soccer with a top Premier League team.

Though the African federation has an unusual group of representatives for the 2018 World Cup—consider that not even one of the familiar Algeria, Ghana, and Ivory Coast trio of teams is the mix—two Liverpool teammates will lead their respective national teams to what could be surprising runs into the knockout stages of the tournament. Reds forward Sadio Mané features on a Senegal squad that also includes towering defender Kalidou Koulibaly (with Napoli), team captain Cheikhou Kouyaté (with West Ham), and veteran forward Moussa Sow (now with Shabab Al-Ahli, though he's featured for the likes of Lille and Fenerbahçe), while Mohamed Salah, enjoying a breakout season pleasing the Kop faithful, stars for an Egypt team that also includes Arsenal midfielder Mohamed Elneny, veteran defender Ahmed Elmohamady (whose latest stop in seven years of English club football is Aston Villa), and Omar Gaber (who has moved from Swiss power Basel to MLS's newest team, LAFC). Senegal will start its World Cup in a confounding-the-experts group that also includes Poland, Colombia, and Japan, while Egypt is a group with the Russian hosts, Uruguay, and a Saudi Arabian team that possesses the lowest FIFA world ranking of any team in the tournament. (The hosts, incidentally, have the second-lowest ranking.)

On July 15, 2018—a few months after the release of this book—a World Cup final match will be played, a narrative (sadly, without the United States playing a role) will conclude, one team will be heartbroken, one team will be momentarily satiated, and the countdown to the next World Cup will begin anew. Odds are that the number of World Cup–winning nations will remain the same. If a new champion does manage to get past all the favored, previously-crowned teams, it will add a novel element to the history of soccer's greatest tournament, but it will do little to fundamentally transform the motivations of those vying for a World Cup title in 2022.

Especially for those nations who felt they should have been there in 2018.

Even before the 2018 World Cup field finalized, there was talk of a consolation tournament to be staged in the summer of 2018, for those notable teams who missed out on the World Cup, in the way that the

NIT (National Invitation Tournament) functions for those teams who don't qualify for the annual NCAA men's basketball tournament.

Shortly after the World Cup field was set, with the United States excluded from play, US Soccer and Soccer United Marketing reportedly investigated how a US-hosted tournament might be staged. Some lauded the idea as a welcome chance to see the Americans play respectable international competition in a World Cup year, rather than just languishing at home or serving as an opponent for World Cup-bound teams' send-off matches. Others derided it as an arrogant plan, inadvertently highlighting the US team's failure to gain entry to an international tournament on its own merits. In his November 2017 coverage for *Sports Illustrated*, Avi Creditor noted, "plenty would have to fall into place" before the tournament could take place *and* before it would "carry any clout" with the international soccer community.[14]

The very contemplation of an NIT-style tournament illustrates just how much American fans will miss a World Cup without the United States in it. The USMNT last missed a World Cup over three decades ago, in 1986, and for a generation who doesn't remember a time before the 1993 advent of MLS, and who weren't cognizant of or even alive for the US-hosted 1994 World Cup, there's uncertainty as to what a World Cup without the United States looks like or feels like.

There's certainly a concern among those invested in growing soccer in the United States that the casual fan who would tune in to the World Cup out of a sense of patriotism rather than an innate love of soccer simply won't tune in. Given that 21.6 million Americans watched the USMNT's final 2014 World Cup match against Belgium,[15] nearly 25 million tuned in for the group stage match between the US and Portugal (leading *The New York Times* to trumpet "Bigger Than Baseball" in its headline),[16] and more than 27 million watched the Germany-Argentina final,[17] there's a valid concern that a US-less World Cup will result in a lower ceiling for viewership numbers.

The American soccer audience has grown to the point that the World Cup will have an audience, of course; it just may not be as large or as collectively, emotionally tied to the results as it would have been with a USMNT presence. As Americans, we're all a little poorer without the opportunity to see how the 2018 World Cup could piggy-back on the "I Believe" wave that crested four years prior.

Christian Pulisic let his feelings be known in an essay he wrote for *The Players' Tribune* website several weeks after the US ouster. Titled "1,834 Days" (for the wait between the article's publication date and the start of the Qatar-hosted World Cup on November 21, 2022), it captured his reaction to the crushing disappointment of the Hex finale, discussing his childhood dreams of scoring a winning goal in a World Cup final, the camaraderie felt among friends and family in watching the 2014 World Cup together, and thoughts about what it will take for the US to make the next World Cup—which, in his view, involves more talented American sixteen-year-olds being allowed to compete for European club teams, as he was able to with Dortmund.

Building on a moment he referenced earlier in the essay—Clint Dempsey's goal less than thirty seconds into the USMNT's 2014 World Cup opener against Ghana—he wrote:

> Soccer . . . it's just this way of life in other countries. It's part of the fabric of who they are, and of what they do. There's this sense of identity that I think is baked into global soccer — that touches everyone, and connects everyone together. If your city's club team is having success, or if your national team is having success, there's just this amazing sense of personal pride that comes with it. I saw a spark of that with Clint's goal in 2014—it almost felt like that one moment changed the mood of the entire country. And it's hard to put into words how powerful that is.
>
> Which is why I feel so crushed that we won't be giving people that feeling this summer.
>
> Something that I think is important to point out, though, is that—even with us coming off of this terrible loss, and even with everyone wanting to talk about what's wrong with American soccer —our soccer culture in the U.S. is getting better all the time. MLS has made great strides as a league, over the last few years, and there are so many incredible American soccer markets that have emerged. You look at what they've built in cities like Portland and Seattle,

and what they're building in places like Atlanta and Cincinnati, and what's happening with the movement to try to save soccer in Columbus—and it's inspiring. And I mean, the atmosphere that we had going on that field in Orlando, in that stadium, for our qualifier against Panama . . . it was unlike anything that I'd ever experienced in the U.S. before. Those fans were unreal — and I was so proud to be a part of that match. It really felt like we were all working together that night to make something special happen.[18]

He ended the essay with the hope that the US's growing soccer culture can withstand the team's absence from one World Cup, along with the pledge that the US will return to the World Cup in 2022. He contends that the fact that younger players were deployed for the team's first post-World Cup qualifying match, an international friendly against Portugal in November 2017, already shows a motivation on US Soccer's part to build a team that will be focused on qualifying for 2022.

Then-USMNT Coach Bruce Arena opined about the rigors of CONCACAF qualifying prior to the fateful October 2017 match in Couva—he called it "survival of the fittest," suggested it was worthy of a *Survivor*-like reality show, and even bellowed, "I would love to see one of these hot-shot teams from Europe come here and play in our CONCACAF qualifying and really get a taste of this and see what that's about."[19] While the quote itself is part of the unfortunate lore of the failed campaign, it reflects a respect of very real challenges from CONCACAF teams, which I predict will bear out in a more purposeful approach to the 2022 campaign.

Qualifying for the World Cup is one thing, but winning it altogether—the fundamental question that initiated this book—is another. But perhaps the question to be asking, with the American team at least five years from its next World Cup appearance, is when it will become elite enough to need that final, essential piece of luck that separates a World Cup–winning squad from those squads who are the last to fall.

"That's a really hard question," says current USMNT player Benny Feilhaber of when the US might win the World Cup. "I think the easier question is when we can get to the semifinals. At that point, you have a team that's potentially good enough to win the World Cup. And I think we'll do that in the next twenty to thirty years." While he echoes his former Sporting Kansas City teammate Graham Zusi in acknowledging that the US can beat any team in the world in a one-off when the stars align, he notes that winning a World Cup at this juncture would require winning several matches against teams above our level.

Feilhaber is, in a way, an embodiment of the hope and disillusionment has marked this decade of US soccer history. He was part of the 2010 World Cup squad that inspired American soccer fans, was sparingly utilized during the Klinsmann era despite consistently strong showings for Sporting Kansas City (to the point where some soccer journalists characterized it as an "exile"). He was brought back into the squad for the crucial October 2017 matchups after showing some spark in friendly matches tied to the prior Arena-led January camp. And he was the last substitute to take the field in the heartbreaking loss to Trinidad & Tobago, brought on to offer creativity in the team's last, desperate moments.

In coming to the 2017 edition of camp, Feilhaber found a team with a similar identity to the one he knew in 2010. He says:

> Team is number one, just first and foremost. Everybody's success is based on the success of the team. We have to know what we're good at is being organized, being a team that's tough to score on, even if it's a team that's more technically gifted than us. We're organized and we're athletic enough to provide cover defensively. And we're a team that is opportunistic on the attack, whether it be on the counter, on set pieces, or what have you.

Feilhaber notes it's the defense-first, counter-attacking style that propelled the US to its touted 2009 Confederations Cup semifinal win over Spain. In the 2010 World Cup, they played a little more freely in the group stages, against teams they felt they matched better with in terms of talent—though, as we know, almost to their peril.

Feilhaber gave some valuable insight to Leander Schaerlaeckens, in an article for Bleacher Report that ran shortly after the US's World Cup ouster, on the contrast between the team he expected to be part of versus the team that actually showed up:

"The whole time, my point of view was, 'We're not playing well, we're playing poorly. We're not doing the things that we used to be good at that made us a tough team to play against. But [. . .] there's no way we're missing the World Cup.' My mentality was, 'We're going to get it done. We're better than the Panamas of the world, the Hondurases.' It's almost embarrassing the way we were getting it done in the first place, but we were going to get it done in the end. I think that was the mentality of everyone on the team."[20]

The 2018 World Cup will undoubtedly be bittersweet for American fans. But I believe the pain of missing it will motivate all invested in the USMNT's success to not experience that heartbreak again. Though Feilhaber's conception of a team that can make the semifinals isn't as glowingly positive as a team that wins it all, it reflects what I believe we as American fans all ultimately want: To see the US listed alongside the top European and South American teams as contenders in any given World Cup, to propel ourselves from the ranks of hopefuls to dark horses to a select coterie of favorites. His prediction of twenty to thirty years to get to the level of contention isn't so far away.

I expect whoever takes the coaching helm for 2022 qualification will help the team both articulate an identity and play with a purpose it didn't consistently find in this last qualifying cycle. I expect some of the promising U-20s and U-23s we've met here will be taking their places on the first team. I expect the infusion of what's been learned in MLS academies, in an MLS featuring exciting young players from throughout CONCACAF and CONMEBOL, and in an increasingly integral Bundesliga, to take hold. I also expect the influence of the Development Academy to take shape on the squads we send to future iterations of the World Cup, and I'm hopeful that American-born and American-eligible Latino players, whether they train in Mexico or the United States, fulfill the *sueño* of representing the United States on the highest stage (though some may choose the *sueño* of playing for Mexico, which will only add to the keen rivalry between the USMNT and El Tri). I believe that American-eligible players from any place, who want to contribute, should be embraced in order to create a national team as wonderfully diverse as the nation it represents.

And I believe, even though all of this adds up to a steady progression that will place the USMNT at the level of perennial World Cup contenders in two or three decades, we have a unique and special opportunity to jump the line in 2026 and see Americans hoist a World Cup trophy in an American stadium. As an optimist who thinks we're due for the grace of the soccer gods—especially given the complicated jumble of feelings we've experienced since October 10, 2017—I believe that we can win, and you might catch me in a stadium that summer chanting a belief that we will.

WORLD CUP HOSTS, WINNERS, AND RUNNERS-UP

Year	Host Country	Winner	Runner-Up
1930	Uruguay	Uruguay	Argentina
1934	Italy	Italy	Czechoslovakia
1938	France	Italy	Hungary
1950	Brazil	Uruguay	Brazil
1954	Switzerland	West Germany	Hungary
1958	Sweden	Brazil	Sweden
1962	Chile	Brazil	Czechoslovakia
1966	England	England	West Germany
1970	Mexico	Brazil	Italy
1974	West Germany	West Germany	Netherlands
1978	Argentina	Argentina	Netherlands
1982	Spain	Italy	West Germany
1986	Mexico	Argentina	West Germany
1990	Italy	West Germany	Argentina
1994	United States	Brazil	Italy
1998	France	France	Brazil
2002	South Korea/Japan	Brazil	Germany
2006	Germany	Italy	France
2010	South Africa	Spain	Netherlands
2014	Brazil	Germany	Argentina
2018	Russia	TBD	TBD

SOURCES

Introduction: How American Soccer Got Its Own Day of Infamy

1. CONCACAF, "History." http://www.concacaf.com/concacaf/history.

2. "Soccer Power Index Explained," ESPN, June 11, 2014, http://www.espn.com/soccer/news/story/_/id/1873765.

3. Paul Carr (@PCarrESPN), "CONCACAF standings and SPI projections after last night. #USMNT is in great shape, but still with a bit of work to do," Twitter, October 7, 2017.

4. FIFA, *Fifa World Cup™ Teams Statistics*, http://www.fifa.com/fifa-tournaments/statistics-and-records/worldcup/teams..

5. Jeff Carlisle, "U.S. World Cup Woe: Time Up for Gulati and Arena; Help Needed for Pulisic." ESPN.com, October 11, 2017, http://www.espnfc.com/team/united-states/660/blog/post/3226631.

6. Ibid.

7. Christian Araos, "Claudio Reyna: Culture of Arrogance in American Soccer." Empire of Soccer, October 17, 2017, http://www.empireofsoccer.com/claudio-reyna-culture-of-arrogance-within-american-soccer-66217/.

8. Michael Lewis, "Revisiting Project 2010." US Soccer Players, January 27, 2010, https://ussoccerplayers.com/2010/01/revisiting-project-2010.html.

9. Ibid.

10. Matt Doyle, "What Is American Soccer?" *Howler*, Fall 2012, p. 96-102.

11. "FIFA/Coca-Cola World Ranking: USA." FIFA, last modified 2017, http://www.fifa.com/fifa-world-ranking/associations/association=usa/men/index.html.

12. "Unanimous Decision Expands FIFA World Cup™ to 48 Teams from 2026." FIFA, January 10, 2017, http://www.fifa.com/about-fifa/news/y=2017/m=1/news=fifa-council-unanimously-decides-on-expansion-of-the-fifa-world-cuptm—2863100.html.

13. Simon Kuper and Stefan Szymanski, *Soccernomics*, Nation Books, 2002.

Chapter 1: How Americans Became Worthy of the World Stage

1. "1938 FIFA World Cup France," FIFA, last modified 2017, http://www.fifa.com/worldcup/archive/france1938/index.html.

2. Ed Farnsworth, "The World Cup Drought, US Soccer 1950-1990," The Philly Soccer Page, April 10, 2014, http://www.phillysoccerpage.net/2014/04/10/the-drought-us-soccer-1950-1990/.

3. "World Cup Qualifying – About," CONCACAF, last modified 2017, http://www.concacaf.com/category/world-cup-qualifying-men/about.

4. Michael Janofsky, "U.S. Awarded '94 World Cup Tourney in Soccer," *The New York Times*, July 5, 1988, http://www.nytimes.com/1988/07/05/sports/us-awarded-94-world-cup-tourney-in-soccer.html.

5. Ed Farnsworth, "The US and the 1990 World Cup," The Philly Soccer Page, April 17, 2014, http://www.phillysoccerpage.net/2014/04/17/the-us-and-the-1990-world-cup/

6. Jeff Crandall, "The Other Side of the Coin," U.S. Soccer, November 16, 2015, http://www.ussoccer.com/stories/2015/11/16/19/00/151116-mnt-trinidad-keeper-michael-maurice-recalls-paul-caliguri-1989-wcq-goal.

7. John Bolster, "The Unheralded Heroes of American Soccer at the 1990 World Cup," MLSsoccer.com, June 5, 2014, https://www.mlssoccer.com/post/2014/06/05/unheralded-heroes-american-soccer-1990-world-cup-word.

8. Ibid.

9. Prior Beharry and Nicholas Casey, "'Revenge Was Sweet': Trinidad and Tobago Exults in Soccer Victory over U.S.," *The New York Times*, October 11, 2017, https://www.nytimes.com/2017/10/11/world/americas/usmnt-trinidad-world-cup.html.

10. John Bolster, "The Unheralded Heroes of American Soccer at the 1990 World Cup," MLSsoccer.com, June 5, 2014, https://www.mlssoccer.com/post/2014/06/05/unheralded-heroes-american-soccer-1990-world-cup-word.

11. Mike Downey, "World Cup '90: It Will Get Worse for U.S.," *Los Angeles Times*, June 11, 1990, http://articles.latimes.com/1990-06-11/sports/sp-193_1_world-cup.

12. Ibid.

13. Ed Farnsworth, "The U.S. Soccer Team at the 1990 World Cup," Philly.com, April 22, 2014, http://www.philly.com/philly/sports/soccer/worldcup/The_US_soccer_team_at_the_1990_World_Cup.html.

14. Ibid.

15. Ed Farnsworth, "The US and the 1994 World Cup," The Philly Soccer Page, April 25, 2014, http://www.phillysoccerpage.net/2014/04/25/the-us -and-the-1994-world-cup.

16. Gary Mihoces, "US Team 'Proved It Could Play,'" *USA Today*, July 5, 1994, 1C.

17. "1998 FIFA World Cup France," FIFA, last modified 2017, http://www .fifa.com/worldcup/archive/france1998/matches/preliminaries/nccamerica/index .html#1003.

18. Bonnie DeSimone, "Controversial Sampson Resigns after World Cup Debacle," *Chicago Tribune*, June 30, 1998, http://articles.chicagotribune .com/1998-06-30/sports/9806300138_1_soccer-president-alan-rothenberg -alexi-lalas-world-cup-debacle.

19. Simon Borg, "USA Greatest World Cup Moments, No. 5," MLSsoccer .com, June 3, 2014, https://www.mlssoccer.com/post/2014/06/03/usa-greatest -world-cup-moments-no-5-torsten-frings-handball-may-have-cost-semifinal.

20. Michael A. Lev, "U.S. Wins Respect in Cup Defeat," *Chicago Tribune*, June 22, 2002, http://articles.chicagotribune.com/2002-06-22/news /0206220067 _1_soccer-teams-bruce-arena-world-cups.

21. "U.S. Top Mexico 2–0, Clinch Berth in 2006 World Cup," U.S. Soccer, September 4, 2005. http://www.ussoccer.com/stories/2014/03/17/12/43 /u-s-top-mexico-2-0-clinch-berth-in-2006-world-cup.

22. Ed Farnsworth, "The US and the 2006 World Cup," The Philly Soccer Page, May 16, 2014, http://www.phillysoccerpage.net/2014/05/16/the-us-and -the-2006-world-cup/.

23. "U.S. Draws Italy 1–1, Still Alive in FIFA 2006 World Cup," U.S. Soccer, June 17, 2006, http://www.ussoccer.com/stories/2014/03/17/11/35 /u-s-draws-italy-1-1-still-alive-in-2006-fifa-world-cup.

24. Jason Davis, "Ghana Memories a History Lesson for U.S.," ESPN .com, June 15, 2014, http://www.espnfc.us/team/united-states/660/blog/post /1881386/davis-history-unkind-to-us-vs-ghana.

25. Brian Trusdell, "Bruce Arena Out as U.S. Soccer Coach," *USA Today*, July 14, 2006, http://usatoday30.usatoday.com/sports/soccer/national/2006 -07-14-arena-contract_x.htm.

26. Roger Cohen and George Vecsey, "Not This Year," *The New York Times*, June 22, 2006, https://www.nytimes.com/video/sports/soccer /1194817093185 /not-this-year.html.

27. "2010 FIFA World Cup Schedule Results," U.S. Soccer, last modified 2017, https://www.ussoccer.com/mens-national-team/tournaments/2010-fifa -world-cup-qualifying-final-round#tab-2.

28. George Vecsey, "Reason to Believe but Also to Be Cautious," *The New York Times*, December 4, 2009, https://nyti.ms/2Fra2Es.

29. Jeré Longman, "U.S. a Winner, Brazil a Loser in World Cup Draw," *The New York Times*, December 4, 2009, http://www.nytimes.com /2009/12 /05/sports/soccer/05draw.html.

30. "USA-Ghana Match Draws Highest US Soccer Audience Ever," Nielsen, June 28, 2010, http://www.nielsen.com/us/en/insights/news/2010 /usa-ghana-match-draws-highest-u-s-soccer-audience-ever.html.

Chapter 2: Klinsmann and the Dual National Debate

1. "Quote Sheet: Jürgen Klinsmann Introduced as Head Coach of U.S. Men's National Team," U.S. Soccer, August 1, 2011, http://www.ussoccer .com/stories/2014/03/17/13/25/quote-sheet-klinsmann-introduction.

2. Cameron Abadi, "Jürgen Klinsmann's Soccer Mandate," *The New Yorker*, June 3, 2014, http://www.newyorker.com/news/sporting-scene/jrgen -klinsmanns-soccer-mandate.

3. Ibid.

4. Frank Isola, "U.S. Soccer Coach Jürgen Klinsmann Urges His Players to Get Nasty after Watching His Team Get Schooled by Brazil," *New York Daily News*, May 31, 2012, http://www.nydailynews.com/sports/more -sports/u-s-soccer-coach-jurgen-klinsmann-urges-players-nasty-watching -team-schooled-brazil-article-1.1087524.

5. Brian Phillips, "U.S. Men's National Team: Baby Steps to the Elevator," *Grantland*, June 1, 2012, http://grantland.com/features/is-us-men-national -soccer-team-making-progress-new-coach-jurgen-klinsmann/.

6. Ryan Rosenblatt, "Jurgen Klinsmann Introduced as New United States National Team Coach," SB Nation, August 1, 2011, https://www. sbnation.com/soccer/2011/8/1/2310116/jurgen-klinsmann-hired-united -states-coach-manager-usmnt-usa-soccer-press-conference.

7. Ryan O'Hanlon, "Playing Soccer with a Plastic Bag on Your Head," *Outside*, August 16, 2012, https://www.outsideonline.com/1903076/playing -soccer-plastic-bag-your-head.

8. Jason Longshore, "The History of Dos a Cero," Stars and Stripes FC, November 9, 2016, https://www.starsandstripesfc.com/2016/11/9/13524068 /the-history-of-dos-a-cero.

9. Sam Borden, "U.S. Is Hosting Mexico Again? Road Trip to Columbus!" *The New York Times*, November 7, 2016, https://www.nytimes.com/2016 /11/08/sports/soccer/us-is-hosting-mexico-again-road-trip-to-columbus.html.

10. Grant Wahl, "Mexico Conquers Columbus," *Sports Illustrated*, November 11, 2016. https://www.si.com/planet-futbol/2016/11/11/usa-mexico -columbus-world-cup-qualifying-rafa-marquez-klinsmann-layun-wood.

11. Paul Carr (@PCarrESPN) "#USMNT's 30-game home unbeaten streak in World Cup qualifying is snapped." Twitter, November 11, 2016, https://twitter.com/PCarrESPN/status/797272710980206592.

12. "2002 Fifa World Cup Qualifying Round," U.S. Soccer, accessed January 2018, https://www.ussoccer.com/mens-national-team/tournaments /2002-fifa-world-cup-qualifying-final-round#tab-2.

13. Noah Davis, "How a Chinese-Funded Costa Rican Soccer Stadium Explains the World," *Pacific Standard*, September 4, 2013, https://psmag.com /economics/chinese-funded-costa-rican-soccer-stadium-explains-world-65667.

14. "USA Suffers 4–0 World Cup Qualifying Defeat Away to Costa Rica," U.S. Soccer, November 15, 2016, http://www.ussoccer.com/stories /2016/11/16/02/00/161115-usa-suffers-4-0-world-cup-qualifying-defeat -away-to-costa-rica.

15. Graham Parker, "USA Slump to 4–0 Defeat in Costa Rica as pressure builds on Jürgen Klinsmann," *The Guardian*, November 15, 2016, https:/ /www.theguardian.com/football/2016/nov/15/usa-slump-defeat-costa-rica -jurgen-klinsmann.

16. Billy Witz, "Fast Start by Guatemala Keeps United States Off Balance," *The New York Times*, March 26, 2016, https://www.nytimes.com /2016 /03/27/sports/soccer/united-states-is-unable-to-find-its-footing-after-a- fast-start-by-guatemala.html.

17. Roderick MacNeil, "Guatemala vs. USA, World Cup Qualifying: What We Learned," Stars and Stripes FC, March 26, 2016, https://www .starsandstripesfc.com/2016/3/26/11308878/usa-vs-guatemala-2018-world -cup-qualifying-recap-player-ratings.

18. Doug McIntyre, "Michael Bradley on Klinsmann Firing: 'Nobody Takes

That Harder Than Me,'" ESPN.com, November 23, 2016, http://www.espnfc
.us/united-states/story/3002829/michael-bradley-on-jurgen-klinsmann-firing
-players-have-to-look-at-ourselves-in-the-mirror.

19. Brian Straus, "Friendly Fire: US Coach Jürgen Klinsmann's Methods,
Leadership, Acumen in Question." *Sporting News*, March 19, 2013.

20. "Brian Straus; Sports Illustrated," an episode from the podcast
Planet Fútbol with Grant Wahl produced by the *Sports Illustrated* podcast
network, released November 28, 2016.

21. Ibid.

22. Ibid.

23. "Mexican Television Announcers Lose Their Minds as USMNT Win
Sends El Tri into Playoff," MLSsoccer.com, October 16, 2013, https://www
.mlssoccer.com/post/2013/10/16/mexican-television-announcers-lose-their
-minds-usmnt-win-sends-el-tri-playoff.

24. "Brian Straus; Sports Illustrated," an episode from the podcast
Planet Fútbol with Grant Wahl produced by the *Sports Illustrated* podcast
network, released November 28, 2016.

25. Ibid.

26. SportsCenter (@SportsCenter), "USA's future is bright. Julian
Green (19 yrs, 25 days) is youngest to score at World Cup since Lionel Messi
in 2006." Twitter, July 1, 2014, https://twitter.com/SportsCenter/status
/484107087258333184.

27. "Brian Straus; Sports Illustrated," an episode from the podcast
Planet Fútbol with Grant Wahl produced by the *Sports Illustrated* podcast
network, released November 28, 2016.

28. David Rudin, "US Soccer Needs to be Honest about Dual Nationals
in the Bruce Arena Era," *The Guardian*, January 27, 2017, https://www
.theguardian.com/football/2017/jan/27/us-soccer-mens-national-team-dual
-nationals.

29. Jürgen Klinsmann (@J_Klinsmann), "'We are absolutely thrilled
that Julian Green has chosen to be a part of the U.S. National Team Programs!'" Twitter, March 18, 2014, https://twitter.com/J_Klinsmann/status
/446035584792805376.

30. Nate Scott and Jesse Yomtov, "18-year-old Julian Green Choosing
America over Germany is Big News for US Soccer Fans," USA Today, March

18, 2014, http://ftw.usatoday.com/2014/03/julian-green-usmnt-bayern-munich
-germany-usa-world-cup.

31. Doug McIntyre, "Julian Green Takes His Chance as US Stumbles in Draw versus New Zealand," ESPN.com, October 11, 2016, http://www .espnfc.us/blog/the-match/60/post/2966854/julian-green-taking-his-chances -as-us-stumbles-in-draw-vs-new-zealand.

32. Charles D. Dunst, "The Miseducation of Julian Green," Stars and Stripes FC, May 3, 2017, https://www.starsandstripesfc.com/2017/5/3 /15513936/julian-green-usmnt-jurgen-klinsmann-stuttgart-hype.

33. Jeremy Stahl, "World Cup Jerk Watch: Is U.S. Coach Jürgen Klinsmann Maybe a Little Jerky?" *Slate*, June 30, 2014, http://www.slate.com /blogs/the_spot/2014/06/30/jurgen_klinsmann_at_the_world_cup_is_the_u_s _coach_maybe_a_little_bit_of.html.

34. Jack Kerr, "USMNT: Does Jürgen Klinsmann Pick Too Many German American Players?" *The Guardian*, December 18, 2015, https://www .theguardian.com/football/blog/2015/dec/18/usmnt-jurgen-klinsmann -german-american-players.

35. Mix Diskerud (@mixdiskerud), "Wow Abby," Instagram, December 17, 2015, https://www.instagram.com/p/_Z4ChQk1t0/.

36. Sam Borden, "Abby Wambach, Retired U.S. Soccer Star, Reflects on Her Addiction," *The New York Times*, October 10, 2016, https://www.ny-times.com/2016/10/11/sports/soccer/abby-wambach-addiction-alcohol-painkillers.html.

37. "Landon Donovan, Mix Diskerud Take Sides on Abby Wambach's Remark About 'foreign' US National Team Players," MLSsoccer.com, December 17, 2015, https://www.mlssoccer.com/post/2015/12/17/landon-donovan -mix-diskerud-take-sides-abby-wambachs-remark-about-foreign-us.

38. Grant Wahl, "Klinsmann's Donovan Omission Caps Rocky Relationship, Puts Pressure on Bold Coach," *Sports Illustrated*, May 22, 2014, https://www.si.com/soccer/planet-futbol/2014/05/22/landon-donovan-jurgen -klinsmann-world-cup-usa-roster-gamble.

39. Jeremiah Oshan, "Jurgen Klinsmann Is Actually Making the USMNT More American," SB Nation, June 6, 2014, https://www.sbnation.com/soccer /2014/6/6/5766076/us-soccer-german-americans-jurgen-klinsmann.

40. "Brian Straus; Sports Illustrated," an episode from the podcast

Planet Fútbol with Grant Wahl produced by the *Sports Illustrated* podcast network, released November 28, 2016.

41. Jeff Carlisle, "Playing for United States 'Much Bigger' than Playing for Israel – Kenny Saief," ESPN.com, June 30, 2017, http://www.espnfc.com /united-states/story/3151381/playing-for-united-states-much-bigger-than -playing-for-israel-kenny-saief.

42. "FIFA Approves Change of Association Request for Goalkeeper Jesse Gonzalez," U.S. Soccer, June 29, 2017, http://www.ussoccer.com/stories /2017/06/29/15/08/20170629-news-mnt-fifa-approves-change-of-association -request-for-goalkeeper-jesse-gonzalez.

43. "Dom Dwyer," MLSsoccer.com, last modified 2017, https://www .mlssoccer.com/players/dom-dwyer.

44. "Watch: Dwyer, Acosta Score, Guzan Saves PK in USA's Gold Cup Tune-up Win vs. Ghana," *Sports Illustrated*, July 1, 2017, https://www.si .com/planet-futbol/2017/07/01/usa-ghana-friendly-usmnt-arena-dwyer-morris -gyan-accam-goals-video.

45. Elliott Turner, "Julian Green and the Ongoing Saga of US Soccer's Immigration Policies," *The Guardian*, March 26, 2014, https://www. theguardian.com/football/2014/mar/26/julian-green-ongoing-saga-us-soccers -immigration-policies.

Chapter 3: How MLS was Created, Saved, and Nurtured to Respectability

1. William N. Wallace, "Improvisation Lies at the Heart of Arena Football," *New York Times*, May 9, 1998, http://www.nytimes.com/1988/05 /09/sports/improvisation-lies-at-the-heart-of-arena-football.html.

2. Grahame L. Jones, "McBride Is Chosen First in No-Name Soccer Draft," *Los Angeles Times*, February 7, 1996, http://articles.latimes.com /1996-02-07/sports/sp-33227_1_brian-mcbride.

3. Tim Froh, "A League Is Born: An Oral History of the Inaugural MLS Match," MLSsoccer.com, April 6, 2016, https://www.mlssoccer.com/post /2016/04/06/league-born-oral-history-inaugural-mls-match.

4, Grant Wahl and Brian Straus, "The Birth of a League," *Sports Illustrated*, 2015, https://www.si.com/longform/2015/mls/index.html.

5. Phil West, *The United States of Soccer: MLS and the Rise of American Soccer Fandom* (New York: The Overlook Press, 2016), 37.

6. Ibid, 37-38.

7. Alicia Rodriguez, "From Guzan to Bradley to Cubo: 10 Memorable Moments in Chivas USA History," MLSsoccer.com, October 28, 2014, https://www mlssoccer.com/post/2014/10/28/guzan-bradley-cubo-10-memorable-moments-chivas-usa-history.

8. Jon Carter, "Beckham Agrees Galaxy Move," ESPN.com, January 13, 2012, http://www.espnfc.us/story/1004691/rewind-to-2007-beckham-agrees-galaxy-move.

9. Ibid.

10. Paul O'Hehir, "US Soccer is No Doddle," *Daily Mirror* (Ireland edition), November 23, 2013, 59.

11. Steve Brisendine, "Sounders Midfielder Nicolas Lodeiro Named 2016 MLS Newcomer of the Year," MLSsoccer.com, November 21, 2016, https://www.mlssoccer.com/post/2016/11/21/sounders-midfielder-nicolas-lodeiro-named-2016-mls-newcomer-year.

12. Charles Boehm, "Best of 2013: Clint Dempsey's Return to MLS Is the Story of the Year," MLSsoccer.com, December 30, 2013, https://www.mlssoccer.com/post/2013/12/30/best-2013-clint-dempseys-return-mls-story-year.

13. Jeff Bradley, "Clint Dempsey's Return Is the Biggest Shock Move in MLS History," MLSsoccer.com, August 4, 2013, https://www.mlssoccer.com/post/2013/08/04/jeff-bradley-clint-dempseys-return-biggest-shock-move-mls-history.

14. Matthew Futterman, "Mediocrity Will Not Be Tolerated," *Wall Street Journal*, January 23, 2013.

15. Ibid.

16. Graham Ruthven, "Klinsmann Speaks to ASN in Bosnia," American Soccer Now, August 13, 2013, http://americansoccernow.com/articles/asn-exclusive-klinsmann-speaks-to-asn-in-bosnia.

17. Jeremiah Oshan, "Jurgen Klinsmann Has a Bit More to Say about Clint Dempsey's Decision," Sounder at Heart, August 13, 2013, https://www.sounderatheart.com/2013/8/13/4618204/jurgen-klinsmann-clint-dempsey-decision-mls.

18. Jeff Bradley, "Clint Dempsey's Return Is the Biggest Shock Move in MLS History," MLSsoccer.com, August 4, 2013, https://www.mlssoccer.com

/post/2013/08/04/jeff-bradley-clint-dempseys-return-biggest-shock-move -mls-history.

19. "Sebastian Giovinco," MLSsoccer.com, last modified 2017, https://www .mlssoccer.com/players/sebastian-giovinco.

20. "Antonio Conte: Italians Who Move to MLS Must 'Pay the Conse-quences,'" *The Guardian*, May 24, 2016, https://www.theguardian.com /football/2016/may/24/antonio-conte-italians-mls-consequences.

21. "Sebastian Giovinco not picked for Italy because 'MLS doesn't matter much,'" *The Guardian*, November 7, 2016, https://www.theguardian.com/foot-ball/2016/nov/07/sebastian-giovinco-italy-giampiero-ventura-mls.

22. Sam Stejskal, "Giovinco's Agent Fires Back at Italy Manager after Roster Exclusion," MLSsoccer.com, November 9, 2016, https://www.mlssoccer .com/post/2016 /11/09/giovincos-agent-fires-back-italy-manager-after-roster-exclusion.

23. Dylan Butler, "David Villa 'in a Dream' after Receiving Call-Up to Spain National Team," MLSsoccer.com, August 25, 2017, https://www .mlssoccer.com/post/2017/08/25/david-villa-dream-after-receiving-call-spain -national-team.

24. "MLS Player Poll: Salary Concerns, Promotion & Relegation, Prem Chances," ESPN.com, March 22, 2016, http://www.espnfc.com/major -league-soccer/19/blog/post/2826676/2016-mls-anonymous-player-poll.

25. Michael Caley, "Real Madrid, Arsenal, LA Galaxy, Boca Juniors— In One Giant Power Ranking," FiveThirtyEight, August 22, 2017, https:/ /fivethirtyeight.com/features/real-madrid-arsenal-la-galaxy-boca-juniors-in -one-giant-power-ranking/.

26. Ibid.

27. "About the Scotiabank CONCACAF Champions League," CON-CACAF, last modified 2017, http://www.concacaf.com/category/champions -league/about.

28. Michael Caley, "Real Madrid, Arsenal, LA Galaxy, Boca Juniors— In One Giant Power Ranking," FiveThirtyEight, August 22, 2017, https://fivethirtyeight.com/features/real-madrid-arsenal-la-galaxy-boca -juniors-in-one-giant-power-ranking/.

29. Steven Goff, "DC United Signs Paul Arriola in Most Expensive Deal in Club History," *The Washington Post*, August 9, 2017, https://www

.washingtonpost.com/news/soccer-insider/wp/2017/08/09/d-c-united-on
-brink-of-signing-paul-arriola.

30. "MLS Confidential: Players Polled on Pro/Rel, Beckham Miami
Team, Salaries, Donovan Return, Giovinco Snub, More," ESPN.com, March
7, 2017, http://www.espnfc.com/major-league-soccer/19/blog/post/3073497
/2017-mls-anonymous-player-survey.

31. "Red Bulls Coach Jesse Marsch Calls for Promotion and Relegation
in MLS," ESPN.com, August 25, 2017, http://www.espnfc.com/major-league
-soccer/story/3188731/red-bulls-coach-jesse-marsch-calls-for-promotion
-and-relegation-in-mls.

32. Chris Smith, "Major League Soccer, Adidas, Agree to $700 Million Ex-
tension," *Forbes*, August 2, 2017, https://www.forbes.com/sites/chrissmith
/2017/08/02/major-league-soccer-adidas-agree-to-700-million-extension
/#d4050674d891.

Chapter 4: MLS Academies: The New Tip of the Spear

1. "What Is the Development Academy Program?" U.S. Soccer Development Academy," last modified 2017, http://www.ussoccerda.com/overview
-what-is-da.

2. Charles Boehm, "MLS Clubs Feature as US Soccer Unveils Development Academy Expansion," MLSsoccer.com, February 6, 2017, https://www
.mlssoccer.com/post/2017/02/06/mls-clubs-feature-us-soccer-unveils
-development-academy-expansion.

3. Sam Stejskal, "MLS Announces 2017 Generation Adidas Class and
Senior Signings," MLSsoccer.com, January 4, 2017, https://www.mlssoccer
.com/post/2017/01/04/mls-announces-2017-generation-adidas-class-and
-senior-signings.

4. Ibid.

5. "MLS Homegrown Players," MLSsoccer.com, last modified January
1, 2017, https://www.mlssoccer.com/glossary/homegrown-player.

6. Brian Lewis, "Red Bulls Prospect Matt Miazga in $5M Transfer to
Chelsea," *New York Post*, January 27, 2016, http://nypost.com/2016/01/27
/red-bulls-prospect-matt-miazga-in-5m-transfer-to-chelsea/.

7. Jeff Rueter, "MLS' Focus on Development Academy Has League's
Next Stars Shining Brightly," ESPN.com, July 31, 2007, http://www.espn.com

/soccer/major-league-soccer/19/blog/post/3168239/mls-focus-on-development
-academy-has-leagues-next-stars-shining-brightly.

8. Scott Sidway, "How FC Dallas Became Home to the Best Academy in the United States," MLSsoccer.com, September 23, 2016, https://ww.mlssoccer .com/post/2016/09/23/how-fc-dallas-became-home-best-academy-united -states.

9. Benjamin Baer, "FC Dallas Score Huge Win Against Real Madrid in Generation Adidas Cup," MLSsoccer.com, April 11, 2017, https://www .mlssoccer.com/post/2017/04/11/fc-dallas-score-huge-win-against-real -madrid-generation-adidas-cup.

10. "Academy Youth Model," Philadelphia Union, last modified 2017, https://www.philadelphiaunion.com/academy/about.

11. Charles Boehm, "24 under 24: The Philadelphia Union Academy Project That Could Transform North American Youth Soccer," MLSsoccer .com, September 29, 2015, https://www.mlssoccer.com/post/2015/09/29/24 -under-24-philadelphia-union-academy-project-could-transform-north -american-youth.

12. "Programs," YSC Academy, last modified 2017, https://www .yscacademy.com/athletics/programs/.

13. Will Parchman, "Nine MLS Clubs Told Grant Wahl How Much They Spend on Their Academies," TopDrawerSoccer.com, March 3, 2017, http://www.topdrawersoccer.com/the91stminute/2017/03/nine-mls-clubs -told-grant-wahl-how-much-they-spend-on-their-academies/.

14. Jacob Born, "Derrick Jones Becomes First Player to Go from Union Academy to Starting for the Union," Philadelphia Union, March 7, 2017, https://www.philadelphiaunion.com/post/2017/03/07/derrick-jones-becomes -first-player-go-union-academy-starting-union.

15. Matt Ralph, "Go Pro or Go to College?" Brotherly Game, March 24, 2017, https://www.brotherlygame.com/2017/3/24/15012534/mls-usl-col- lege -soccer-academy-player-decisions.

16. "RGVFC Awarded the USL's Newest Franchise," Houston Dynamo, July 15, 2015, https://www.houstondynamo.com/post/2015/07/15/rgvfc-awarded -usls-newest-franchise.

17. Rob Usry, "Red Bulls Suffering from US Soccer Shortcomings in Youth Retention," Once A Metro, July 24, 2015, https://www.onceametro

.com/2015/7/24/9023629/mls-has-a-youth-retention-problem-and-the-red
-bulls-are-suffering.

18. "MLS Roster Rules and Regulations," MLSsoccer.com, February 1;
2017, https://www.mlssoccer.com/league/official-rules/mls-roster-rules-and
-regulations.

Chapter 5: Beyond Bradenton: The Development Academy Reinvents Itself

1. "U.S. Soccer Residency Program Set to Complete Final Semester after
18 Years," U.S. Soccer, March 17, 2017, http://www.ussoccer.com/stories
/2017/03/17/19/22/20170317-news-u17mnt-after-fulfilling-mission-us-soccer
-residency-program-to-complete-final-semester.

2. "John Ellinger, Jozy Altidore, and Kyle Beckerman Reflect on the History of U-17 Residency Program," U.S. Soccer, March 17, 2017, http://www
.ussoccer.com/stories/2017/03/17/13/20/20170317-feat-u17mnt-john
-ellinger-jozy-altidore-kyle-beckerman-history-of-u17-residency-program.

3. "U.S. Soccer Residency Program Set to Complete Final Semester after
18 Years," U.S. Soccer, March 17, 2017, http://www.ussoccer.com/stories
/2017/03/17/19/22/20170317-news-u17mnt-after-fulfilling-mission-us-soccer
-residency-program-to-complete-final-semester.

4. "Five Things to Know: How Small-Sided Standards Will Change
Youth Soccer," U.S. Soccer, August 1, 2017, https://www.ussoccer.com
/stories/2017/08/01/18/15/20170801-feat-coaching-ed-five-things-to-know
-how-small-sided-standards-will-change-youth-soccer.

5. Jacob Bogage, "Youth Sports Study: Declining Participation, Rising
Costs, and Unqualified Coaches," *The Washington Post*, September 6, 2017,
https://www.washingtonpost.com/news/recruiting-insider/wp/2017/09/06
/youth-sports-study-declining-participation-rising-costs-and-unqualified
-coaches.

6. Sean Gregory, "How Kids' Sports Became a $15 Billion Industry,"
Time, August 24, 2017, http://time.com/magazine/us/4913681/september
-4th-2017-vol-190-no-9-u-s/.

7. "U.S. Soccer President Sunil Gulati Addresses State of MNT After
2018 World Cup Qualifying," U.S. Soccer, October 13, 2017, https://www
.ussoccer.com/stories/2017/10/13/21/21/20171013-news-us-soccer-sunil-
gulati-conference-call-bruce-arena-future-2018-world-cup-qualifying

8. Will Parchman, "What's Wrong with American Youth Soccer Development," *Howler*, March 30, 2016, http: //www.whatahowler.com/http-swhatahowler-com201603whats-wrong-with-american-youth-soccer-development-html/.

9. Ibid.

10. "Academy Homestay," Seattle Sounders FC, last modified 2017, https://www.soundersfc.com/academy/homestay.

11. Noah Sobel-Pressman ("Noah.Sp"), "US Soccer Scouting Ignoring Some Key Population Centers," Stars and Stripes FC, October 20, 2017, https://www.starsandstripesfc.com/usmnt-youth/2017/10/20/16501882/usa-usmnt-us-soccer-scouting-lacking.

12. "Coaching License Pathway," U.S. Soccer, last modified 2017, http://www.ussoccer.com/coaching-education/licenses.

13. Will Parchman, "The High Cost of American Coaching," TopDrawerSoccer.com, July 1, 2016, http://www.topdrawersoccer.com/the91stminute/2016/07 /the-high-cost-of-american-coaching.

14. "U.S. U-15 Boys National Team Advances to CONCACAF Championship Final," SoccerWire.com, August 18, 2017, http://www.soccerwire.com/news/nt/international-men/u-s-u-15-boys-national-team-advances-to-concacaf-championship-final/.

15. Stephen Uersfeld, "U.S. Youngster McKinze Gaines Leaves Wolfsburg to Join Darmstadt," ESPN.com, June 22, 2017, http://www.espnfc.com/story/3147091/us-youngster-mckinze-gaines-leaves-wolfsburg-to-join-darmstadt.

16. "Development Academy Alumni – U.S. Men's National Team," U.S. Soccer Development Academy, last modified 2017, http://www.ussoccerda.com/da-alumni-mnt-production.

17. Jeff Carlisle, "New England Revolution's Kelyn Rowe Out 6-8 Weeks with Knee Sprain," ESPN.com, August 24, 2017, http://www.espnfc.com/new-england-revolution/story/3187877/new-england-revolutions-kelyn-rowe-out-6-8-weeks-with-knee-sprain.

Chapter 6: *Bienvenido al Futuro*: On Finding and Developing Latino Players

1. Steve Brisendine, "Timbers Ex, Sueno MLS star, Jorge Villafana Waits for His Chance with US," MLSsoccer.com, June 22, 2016, https://www.mlssoccer

.com/post/2016/06/22/timbers-ex-sueno-mls-star-jorge-villafana-waits-his-chance-us.

2. "Oregon Product Alan Gaytán wins Sueño MLS 2016," MLSsoccer.com, May 22, 2016, https://www.mlssoccer.com/post/2016/05/22 /oregon-product-alan-gaytan-wins-mls-sueno-2016.

3. Tom Marshall, "U.S. Youth International Jonathan Gonzalez Making Strides at Monterrey," ESPN.com, August 22, 2017, http://www.espnfc.com/club/monterrey/220/blog/post/3185741/us-youth-international-jonathan-gonzalez-making-strides-at-monterrey.

4. Ryan Tolmich, "Jonathan Gonzalez Named to Liga MX Apertura Best XI," December 18, 2017, SBI Soccer, http://sbisoccer.com/2017/12/jonathan-gonzalez-named-to-liga-mx-apertura-best-xi.

5. Tom Marshall, "U.S. Youth International Jonathan Gonzalez Making Strides at Monterrey," ESPN.com, August 22, 2017, http://www.espnfc.com/club/monterrey/220/blog/post/3185741/us-youth-international-jonathan-gonzalez-making-strides-at-monterrey.

6. Carlos Ponce de León, "Jonathan González, La Joya Que EU le Puede Ganar al Tri," *Récord*, September 13, 2017, http://www.record.com.mx/noticias-del-tri/jonathan-gonzalez-la-joya-que-eu-le-puede-ganar-al-tri.

7. Mike Woitalla, "Californian Jonathan Gonzalez Reflects on His Remarkable Rise to Teen Star in Mexico," Soccer America, December 30, 2017, https://www.socceramerica.com/publications/article/76232/californian-jonathan-gonzalez-reflects-on-his-rema.html.

8. Jonathan González (@jgonzalezz25), "Press release," Twitter photos, January 9, 2018, https://twitter.com/jgonzalezz25/status/950819625398362112/photo/1.

9. Mike Woitalla, "Brad Rothenberg: 'Our Federation Lost Jonathan Gonzalez Either by Its Own Arrogance, Apathy or Incompetence,'" Soccer America, January 10, 2018, https://www.socceramerica.com/publications/article/76356/brad-rothenberg-our-federation-lost-jonathan-gon.html.

10. Ibid.

11. Les Carpenter, "How FC Dallas and Their Homegrown Model Could Revolutionize US Soccer," *The Guardian*, November 19, 2015, https://www.theguardian.com/football/2015/nov/19/fc-dallas-mls-homegrown-players-academy.

12. Les Carpenter, "American Soccer's Diversity Problem," *The Guardian*, June 1, 2016, https://www.theguardian.com/football/blog/2016/jun/01/us-soccer-diversity-problem-world-football.

13. Tim Froh, "US Soccer's Coaching Gap," *The Guardian*, April 26, 2017, https://www.theguardian.com/football/2017/apr/26/mls-diversity-problem-coaches.

14. John Kass, "Chicago Fire Soccer Team Shuts Down Anti-Gay Chant," *Chicago Tribune*, August 3, 2016, http://chicagotribune.com/news/columnists/kass/ct-chicago-fire-anti-gay-soccer-chant-kass-0804-20160803-column.html.

15. "Five Things to Know about MNT Defender Omar Gonzalez," U.S. Soccer, April 27, 2017, https://www.ussoccer.com/stories/2017/04/17/20/13/20170418-feat-mnt-five-things-to-know-about-usmnt-defender-omar-gonzalez.

16. Brian Sciaretta, "Alejandro Bedoya Believes That the U.S. Will Win," American Soccer Now, May 14, 2014, http://americansoccernow.com/articles/alejandro-bedoya-believes-that-the-u-s-will-win.

17. Leander Schaerlaeckens, "For Love or Country?" Bleacher Report, July 19, 2017, http://bleacherreport.com/articles/2721963-for-love-or-country-us-mexico-war-for-prospects-tests-players-allegiances.

18. Tom Marshall, "Expect More Switches Like Jonathan Gonzalez – FMF's Dennis te Kloese," ESPN.com, January 11, 2018, http://www.espn.com/soccer/mexico/story/3344925/jonathan-gonzalez-switch-to-mexico-wont-be-the-last-fmfs-dennis-te-kloese.

19. "FIFA Approves Change of National Association for Sofia Huerta," U.S. Soccer, September 14, 2017, https://www.ussoccer.com/stories/2017/09/14/19/03/20170914-news-wnt-fifa-approves-change-of-national-association-for-sofia-huerta.

20. Luis Paez-Pumar, "Why Do Some Mexican Soccer Players Switch Allegiance to the United States?" Remezcla, September 2017, http://remezcla.com/sports/mexico-us-soccer-allegiances/.

Chapter 7: The U-20s and the U-23s: First Team Players-in-Waiting

1. "FIFA U-20 World Cup archive," FIFA, last modified 2017, http://www.fifa.com/fifa-tournaments/archive/u20worldcup/index.html.

2. "FIFA U-20 World Cup Korea Republic 2017," FIFA, last modified 2017, http://www.fifa.com/u20worldcup/.

3. Alicia Rodriguez, "2017 CONCACAF U-20 Championship Recap," MLSsoccer.com, February 27, 2017, https://www.mlssoccer.com/post/2017 /02/27/usa-1-mexico-0-2017-concacaf-u-20-championship-recap.

4. Rob Usry, "USA vs. Venezuela, U20 World Cup 2017: Final Score 1–2, 2014 Forever," Stars and Stripes FC, June 4, 2017, https://www.starsandstripesfc .com/2017/6/4/15736428/usa-vs-venezuela-u20-world-cup-2017-final-score -result-recap.

5. "US roster for FIFA Under-20 World Cup," MLSsoccer.com, May 9, 2017, https://www.mlssoccer.com/post/2017/05/09/us-soccer-team-fifa-under-20 -world-cup-roster.

6. Nicholas Rosano, "Report: Sporting KC's Erik Palmer-Brown signs with Manchester City," MLSsoccer.com, September 10, 2017, https://www .mlssoccer.com/post/2017/09/10/report-sporting-kcs-erik-palmer-brown -signs-manchester-city.

7. "Zions Bank Real Academy," Real Salt Lake, last modified 2017, https://www.rsl.com/academy.

8. "DA Club Directory," US Soccer Development Academy, last modified 2017, http://www.ussoccerda.com/all-clubs.

9. Matt Montgomery, "RSL Academy is in Arizona again after Serrano, Legacy partnership," RSL Soapbox, January 12, 2018, https://www.rslsoapbox .com/2018/1/12/16880770/rsl-academy-arizona-serreno-legacy-partnership.

10. Garrett Cleverly, "Justen Glad signs with Real Salt Lake," Grande Sports Academy, April 7, 2014, http://grandesportsacademy.com/justen-glad -signs-with-real-salt-lake-becomes-10th-player-to-turn-professional-in -grande-sports-academy-history/.

11. "Justen Glad | 24 under 24 | #18," MLSsoccer.com, September 26, 2017, https://www.mlssoccer.com/series/24-under-24/2017/18.

12. "Brooks Lennon," MLSsoccer.com, last modified 2017, https://www .mlssoccer.com/players/brooks-lennon.

13. "Press Pass: U-20 Head Coach Ramos Talks USA Roster, U-20 World Cup," U.S. Soccer, May 11, 2017, http://www.ussoccer.com/stories /2017/05 /11/21/56/20170511-news-u20mnt-tab-ramos-conference-call-2017 -u20-world-cup-usa-roster.

14. Liviu Bird, "U.S. U-20s Dumped from World Cup in Quarterfinals with PK Loss to Serbia," *Sports Illustrated*, June 14, 2015, https://www.si .com /planet-futbol/2015/06/14/usa-u-20-national-team-world-cup-quarterfinal -serbia.

15. Leander Schaerlaeckens, "Freddy Adu Is Right on Track," ESPN.com, November 11, 2011, http://www.espn.com/sports/soccer/news /_/id/7101417/freddy-adu-right-track-mls-soccer.

16. "Nowak Names Roster for 2008 Olympic Games," U.S. Soccer, July 17, 2008, http://www.ussoccer.com/stories/2014/03/17/11/43/nowak-names-roster-for-2008-olympic-games.

17. "Neymar to Play for Brazil at Rio Olympics, not Copa America," *USA Today*, April 21, 2016, https://www.usatoday.com/story/sports/olympics /2016/04/20/barcelona-says-neymar-will-play-with-brazil-at-rio-olympics /83305806/.

18. Scott French, "Gil Could Be the Next Big Thing," ESPN.com, June 8, 2010, http://www.espn.com/los-angeles/worldcup/news/story?id=5187954.

19. "USA Olympic Bid Falls Short in 2–1 Playoff Loss to Colombia," U.S. Soccer, March 29, 2016, https://www.ussoccer.com/stories/2016/03/30 /04/03/160329-u23mnt-loses-olympic-qualifying-playoff-to-colombia.

20. "Luis Gil – USMNT," US Soccer Players, last modified 2017, https://ussoccerplayers.com/player/luis-gil-usmnt.

21. "Andreas Herzog Named Head Coach for U.S. U-23 Men's National Team," U.S. Soccer, January 23, 2015, http://www.ussoccer.com/stories /2015/01/23/13/21/150123-u23mnt-herzog-named-coach.

22. Noah Davis, "U.S. U-23s Olympic Qualifying Loss a Failure Seen Too Many Times Before," ESPN.com, March 30, 2016, http://www.espnfc.us /team/united-states/660/blog/post/2840155/us-u23s-olympic-loss-to-colombia -failure-seen-to-many-times.

23. "Olympic Football Tournaments Beijing 2008—Men," FIFA, last modified 2017, http://www.fifa.com/tournaments/archive/mensolympic/beijing 2008/teams/team=1889265/squadlist.html.

24. Adnan Ilyas, "When Did the USMNT Get So . . . Old?" Stars and Stripes FC, September 16, 2017, https://www.starsandstripesfc.com/2017 /9/16/16286146/usa-usmnt-roster-age-old-world-cup.

25. Ibid.

Chapter 8: Americans Abroad: When Young Players Choose Clubs in Other Countries

1. Andrew King, "In Pulisic's Wake," *FourFourTwo*, August 8, 2017, https://www.fourfourtwo.com/us/features/usmnt-prospects-in-europe-list-breakthroughs-timothy-weah-psg.

2. Michael Luo, "The Patience of Christian Pulisic, American Soccer's Great Hope," *The New Yorker*, June 16, 2017, http://www.newyorker.com/news/sporting-scene/the-patience-of-christian-pulisic-american-soccers-great-hope.

3. Michael Caley, "The Great American Soccer Hope Is Here (for Real, This Time)," FiveThirtyEight, June 9, 2017, https://fivethirtyeight.com/features/the-great-american-soccer-hope-is-here-for-real-this-time/.

4. Brooks Peck, "Christian Pulisic Shaves His Head, Scores Stunning Goal against Mexico," *Howler*, June 11, 2017, http://www.whatahowler.com/christian-pulisic-shaves-his-head-scores-stunning-goal-against-mexico/.

5. Kristian Dyer, "Tough Night for USA Star Pulisic," MLSsoccer.com, September 1, 2017, https://www.mlssoccer.com/post/2017/09/01/tough-night-usa-star-pulisic-frustrated-loss-vs-costa-rica.

6. Jeff Carlisle, "Bruce Arena: 'Unpredictable' Referees Not Protecting U.S.'s Christian Pulisic," ESPN.com, September 4, 2017, http://www.espnfc.com/united-states/story/3196270/bruce-arena-rues-unpredictable-referees-not-protecting-uss-christian-pulisic.

7. George Dohrmann, "The Christian Pulisic Blueprint," Bleacher Report, June 7, 2017, http://bleacherreport.com/articles/2713937-the-christian-pulisic-blueprint.

8. Ibid.

9. Stephan Uersfeld, "Christian Pulisic Becomes Youngest Non-German to Score in Bundesliga," ESPN.com, April 17, 2016, http://www.espnfc.com/borussia-dortmund/story/2852892/christian-pulisic-youngest-non-german-to-score-in-bundesliga.

10. "All the Things Christian Pulisic Did Faster Than Anyone," U.S. Soccer, April 11, 2017, https://www.ussoccer.com/stories/2016/12/20/13/35/161220-feat-mnt-five-things-christian-pulisic-did-faster-than-anyone-else.

11. Jeff Carlisle, "Inconsistent U.S. Have Issues All Over Pitch, Help for Christian Pulisic is Key," ESPN.com, September 7, 2017, http://www.espnfc

.com/team/united-states/660/blog/post/3198185/inconsistent-us-have-issues
-all-over-pitch-help-for-pulisic-is-key.

12. "Bruce Arena: Anger over Immigration Hurting US World Cup Qualifying Campaign," *The Guardian*, September 2017, https://www.theguardian
.com/football/2017/sep/05/usa-honduras-world-cup-qualifier-soccer.

13. Terrance F. Ross, "Why German Soccer Wants American Players,"
The Guardian, December 23, 2015, https://www.theguardian.com/football
/2015/dec/23/why-german-soccer-wants-american-players.

14. Avi Creditor, "Who is Weston McKennie?" *Sports Illustrated*, September 19, 2017, https://www.si.com/soccer/2017/09/19/weston-mckennie
-schalke-usa-fc-dallas.

15. "Schalke's Weston McKennie: the Bundesliga's Next American Star,"
Bundesliga, September 29, 2017, http://www.bundesliga.com/en/news
/Bundesliga/schalke-s-weston-mckennie-next-usa-star-after-dortmund-s
-christian-pulisic-460304.jsp.

16. "Weston McKennie Extends Schalke Contract Until 2022,"
Bundesliga, September 28, 2017, https://www.bundesliga.com/en/news
/Bundesliga/schalke-s-weston-mckennie-extends-contract-until-2022
-460335.jsp.

17. "Weston McKennie: 10 Things You Might Not Know about Schalke's
USA Starlet," Bundesliga, November 19, 2017, https://www.bundesliga
.com/en/news/Bundesliga/weston-mckennie-10-things-on-schalke-s-usa-starlet
-pulisic-usmnt-463874.jsp.

18. Taylor Twellman (@TaylorTwellman), ".@_joshsargent_ agreeing
to sign a contract with Werder Bremen on his 18th birthday. Turned down
Bayern, Dortmund!!" Twitter, September 20, 2017, https://twitter.com
/TaylorTwellman/status/910473643485835264.

19. Sam Stejskal, "Where and How Johannsson Might Wind Up in
MLS," MLSsoccer.com, May 4, 2017, https://www.mlssoccer.com/post/2017
/05/04/stejskal-where-and-how-johannsson-might-wind-mls-duka-move.

20. "MLS Allocation Process," MLSsoccer.com, last modified 2017,
https://www.mlssoccer.com/allocation.

21. Stephan Uersfeld, "Aron Johannsson: I Won't Get a Chance at
Werder Bremen," ESPN.com, August 16, 2017, http://www.espnfc.com/story
/3181251/aron-johannsson-i-wont-get-a-chance-at-werder-bremen.

22. "Werder Sign Talented Young Striker Joshua Sargent," Werder Bremen, September 20, 2017, https://www.werder.de/en/news/news/u23 /20172018/news/sargent-signs-21092017/.

23. "Middlesbrough," Premier League, last modified 2017, https://www .premierleague.com/clubs/13/Middlesbrough/stats?se=54.

24. "Stats Centre," Premier League, last modified 2017, https://www .premierleague.com/stats/top/clubs/goals_conceded?se=54.

25. Bob Williams, "Tim Howard: There is No Divine Right for American Goalkeepers to Play in Premier League," *The Telegraph*, July 8, 2016, http://www.telegraph.co.uk/sport/2016/07/08/tim-howard-there-is-no -divine-right-for-american-goalkeepers-to/.

26. Ben Stanley, "The Rise of American Soccer Talent Cameron Carter-Vickers," *VICE*, June 13, 2015, https://sports.vice.com/en_us/article/yp77yw /the-rise-of-american-soccer-talent-cameron-carter-vickers.

27. John Cross, "England Eye Tottenham's Cameron Carter-Vickers," *Mirror*, September 22, 2016, http://www.mirror.co.uk/sport/football/news /england-eye-tottenhams-cameron-carter-8894904.

28. "Carter-Vickers Gets First Senior USA International Call-up," Tottenham Hotspur, November 6, 2016, http://www.tottenhamhotspur.com /news/cameron-carter-vickers-senior-usa-call-up-061116/.

29. Dan Kilpatrick, "Tottenham Boss Mauricio Pochettino Explains Cameron Carter-Vickers Loan," ESPN.com, August 25, 2017, http://www .espnfc.com/english-premier-league/story/3188530/tottenham-boss-mauricio -pochettino-explains-cameron-carter-vickers-loan.

30. Will Parchman, "Emerson Hyndman Is Entering a Fairly Critical 2017–18 Season," TopDrawerSoccer.com, June 7, 2017, http://www .topdrawersoccer.com/the91stminute/2017/06/emerson-hyndman-is-entering -a-fairly-critical-2017-18-season/.

31. Rob Usry, "Danny Williams: It Killed Me Not to Play in Copa America," Stars and Stripes FC, August 1, 2016, https://www.starsandstripesfc .com/2016/8/1/12342178/danny-williams-copa-america-usmnt-reading.

Chapter 9: Home-Field Advantage (and How to Create Soccer-Specific Support in American Football Stadiums)

1. "FIFA World Cup Archive," FIFA, last modified 2017, http://www .fifa.com/fifa-tournaments/archive/worldcup/index.html.

2. Matias Grez and Stef Blendis, "Defender Dante Remembers Brazil's 'Painful' 7–1 World Cup Defeat to Germany," CNN, August 17, 2017, http://www.cnn.com/2017/07/07/football/dante-brazil-germany-world-cup -2014-7-1/index.html.

3. "FIFA Votes Overwhelmingly to Fast-Track 2026 World Cup Bid Process," *The Guardian*, May 11, 2017, https://www.theguardian.com/football /2017/may/11/fifa-2026-world-cup-bid-process-fast-tracked.

4. Bryan Armen Graham, "Morocco to Challenge North American Joint Bid to Host 2026 World Cup," *The Guardian*, August 11, 2017, https://www .theguardian.com/football/2017/aug/11/morocco-2026-world-cup-bid-north -america-challenge-fifa.

5. Steven Goff, "North America's Bid to Host 2026 World Cup Jeopardized by Falling US Popularity," *The Washington Post*, December 17, 2017, https://www.washingtonpost.com/news/soccer-insider/wp/2017/12/17 /north-americas-bid-to-host-2026-world-cup-jeopardized-by-falling-u-s -popularity/.

6. US Soccer Communications, "United Bid Committee Commences Outreach For Potential Host Cities In Bid For 2026 Fifa World Cup™," Press Release, August 15, 2017.

7. "History," Rose Bowl Stadium, last modified 2017, https://www .rosebowlstadium.com/about/history.

8. "1994 FIFA World Cup USA™," FIFA, last modified 2017, http://www.fifa.com/worldcup/matches/round=3459/match=3104/index.html.

9. "One Year Membership." American Outlaws, last modified 2017, https://www.theamericanoutlaws.com/membership.

10. Liam Daniel Pierce, "American Outlaws Tifo Problematically Calls Gold Cup, an Object, a 'She,'" *VICE*, July 8, 2017, https://sports.vice.com /en_us/article/3knaab/american-outlaws-tifo-problematically-calls-gold-cup -an-object-a-she.

11. American Outlaws (@AmericanOutlaws) "Thanks to all the #USMNT + #USWNT that sent in #AO10 well wishes!" Twitter, September 9, 2017, https://twitter.com/americanoutlaws/status/906689902598860800.

12. "Statement from AO Following World Cup Qualifying Elimination," American Outlaws, https://www.theamericanoutlaws.com/articles/statement -from-ao-following-world-cup-qualifying-elimination.

13. Ibid.

14. "AO Election Center," American Outlaws, http://voao.theamericanoutlaws
.com/ao-election-center/

**Chapter 10: How the Rest of the World Will Weigh in on America's
World Cup Aspirations, and How We Might Respond**

1. "World Cup Winner Betting Odds." Oddschecker, https://www
.oddschecker.com/football/world-cup/winner, last modified January 2018.

2. Ibid.

3. Rory Smith, "2 German Triumphs, and a System Built for More,"
The New York Times, July 3, 2017, https://www.nytimes.com/2017/07/03
/sports/soccer/soccer-world-cup-germany-belgium.html.

4. Fabrizio Romano and Marcus Christenson, "Kylian Mbappé Set to
Join PSG," *The Guardian*, August 27, 2017, https://www.theguardian
.com/football/2017/aug/27/paris-saint-germain-agree-deal-kylian-mbappe
-monaco.

5 "Ireland Asked to Be 33rd Team at World Cup, Says Sepp Blatter"
The Guardian, November 30, 2009, https://www.theguardian.com/foot-
ball/2009/nov/30/republic-of-ireland-world-cup-fifa.

6. David Hytner, "World Cup 2010: French Revolt Leaves Richmond
Domenech High and Dry," *The Guardian*, June 20, 2010, https://www
.theguardian.com/football/2010/jun/20/france-raymond-domenech-nicolas
-anelka.

7. Phil West, "Crushing the Bus," *Paste*, June 14, 2014, https://www
.pastemagazine.com/articles/2014/06/why-france-is-done-failing.html.

8. "The 100 Best Footballers in the World 2017," *The Guardian*, December 19, 2017. https://www.theguardian.com/football/ng-interactive/2017/dec
/19/the-100-best-footballers-in-the-world-2017-interactive.

9. Nate Scott, "Cristiano Ronaldo's Sister Compares His Euro Final
Injury to the Crucifixion of Jesus," *USA Today*, July 12, 2016, http://ftw
.usatoday.com/2016/07/cristiano-ronaldos-sister-jesus-christ-crucification.

10. Aaron West, "Brazil Are the First Team to Qualify for the 2018 FIFA
World Cup," Fox Sports, March 29, 2017, http://www.foxsports.com/soccer
/story/brazil-2018-world-cup-qualifying-032917.

11. Andy Hunter, "Liverpool to Demand at Least £130m from Barcelona
for Philippe Coutinho," *The Guardian*, January 2, 2018, https://www

.theguardian.com/football/2018/jan/02/liverpool-to-demand-huge-fee-from -barcelona-for-philippe-coutinho-january-sale.

12. Andy Hunter, "Jürgen Klopp Says Liverpool's Decision to Sell Philippe Coutinho to Barcelona Was 'Easy,'" *The Guardian*, January 12, 2018, https://www.theguardian.com/football/2018/jan/12/jurgenn-klopp-philippe -coutinho-liverpool-barcelona.

13. John Duerden, "Carlos Queiroz Insists That Iran 'Will Not Go to Russia as Tourists," ESPN.com, June 15, 2017, http://www.espnfc.com /team/iran/469/blog/post/3144226/carlos-queiroz-insists-that-iran-will-not- go-to-russia-as-tourists.

14. Avi Creditor, "U.S. Soccer, SUM Look Into Hosting Other Notable Nations Who Missed World Cup," *Sports Illustrated*, November 14, 2017, https://www.si.com/soccer/2017/11/14/us-soccer-sum-italy-netherlands -ghana-chile.

15. Richard Deitsch, "USA vs. Belgium Draws Another Huge American TV World Cup Audience," July 2, 2014, https://www.si.com/planet-futbol /2014/07/02/usa-belgium-world-cup-tv-ratings-viewers.

16. Bill Carter, "Bigger Than Baseball: 25 Million Watch U.S.-Portugal World Cup Match," *The New York Times*, June 23, 2014, https://www. nytimes.com/2014/06/24/business/media/bigger-than-baseball-us-portugal -world-cup-match-outdoes-world-series-in-ratings.html.

17. Jonathan Tannenwald, "2014 World Cup Final Sets Some U.S. TV records, but Not All," Philly.com, July 14, 2014, http://www.philly.com /philly/blogs/sports/union/2014-World-Cup-final-sets-some-US-TV-records -but-not-all.html.

18. Christian Pulisic, "1,834 Days," The Player's Tribune, November 13, 2017, https://www.theplayerstribune.com/christian-pulisic-usmnt-world-cup.

19. Sacha Pisani, "Bruce Arena Invites 'Hotshot' Europeans to Try CONCACAF Qualifying," *The Sporting News*, October 9, 2017, http://www .sportingnews.com/other-sports/news/arena-invites-hotshot-europeans-to -try-concacaf-qualifying-world-cup/3dht4al2gse71i9wtv80iv9bm.

20. Leander Schaerlaeckens, "The 28-Point Plan for Fixing Men's Soccer in America," Bleacher Report, October 19, 2017, http://bleacherreport.com /articles/2739599-the-28-point-plan-for-fixing-mens-soccer-in-america.

INTERVIEW LIST

Danilo Acosta, by phone (Sandy, Utah), August 1, 2017

Kellyn Acosta, by phone (Frisco, Texas), August 15, 2017

Doug Andreassen, by phone (Seattle), July 28, 2017

Paul Arriola, by phone (Washington, DC), August 25, 2017

DaMarcus Beasley, by phone (Houston), August 15, 2017

Justin Brunken, by phone (Lincoln, Nebraska), August 27, 2017

Russell Canouse, by phone (Washington, DC), August 29, 2017

Andrew Carleton, by phone (Atlanta), September 1, 2017

Crystal Cuadra-Cutler, by email (San Jose, California), August 2, 2017

Joe Cummings, by phone (Huntington Beach, California), July 27, 2017

Korey Donahoo, by phone (Lincoln, Nebraska), August 23, 2017

Landon Donovan, by phone (San Diego), August 14, 2017

Matt Doyle, by email (New York City), July 29, 2017

Brian Dunseth, by phone (Salt Lake City), October 18, 2017

Todd Durbin, by phone (New York City), September 5, 2017

Joaquin Escoto, by phone (San Francisco), July 27, 2017

Benny Feilhaber, by phone (Kansas City, Kansas), February 21, 2017

Matt Gaschk, by email (Sandy, Utah), January 3, 2018

Gabe Gabor, by phone (Miami), August 31, 2017

Bob Gansler, by phone (Kansas City, Kansas), February 28, 2017

Luis Gil, by phone (Carson, California), September 1, 2017

Justen Glad, by phone (Sandy, Utah), July 31, 2017

Luchi Gonzalez, in-person, Frisco, Texas, March 14, 2017

Herculez Gómez, by phone (Bristol, Connecticut), August 22, 2017

Derrick Jones, by phone (Chester, Pennsylvania), August 29, 2017

Alexi Lalas, by phone (New York City), September 25, 2017

Brooks Lennon, by phone (Sandy, Utah), July 31, 2017

Jared Micklos, by phone (Chicago), August 28, 2017

Jakob Nordstrom, in-person, Austin, June 9, 2017 and September 3, 2017

Erik Palmer-Brown, by phone (Kansas City, Kansas), June 6, 2017

Óscar Pareja, in-person, Frisco, Texas, March 14, 2017

Mark Pulisic, by phone (Cincinnati), July 28, 2017

Maxi Rodriguez, by email (Los Angeles), August 21, 2017

Wil Trapp, by phone (Columbus), August 31, 2017

Dan Wiersema, in-person, Austin, August 8, 2017

Tommy Wilson, by phone (Wayne, Pennsylvania), August 14, 2017

Donald Wine II, by phone (Washington, DC), July 28, 2017

Graham Zusi, by phone (Kansas City, Kansas), February 21, 2017

ACKNOWLEDGMENTS

First things first: My loving wife Katie was incredibly supportive throughout this book's germination, pregnant during the bulk of its writing, gracious in her giving me the green light to go to Denver for a USMNT qualifier five weeks before her due date, giving birth to a perfect daughter in the midst of the Gold Cup, and having the misfortune to have her fortieth birthday fall on the very day of the final USMNT qualifier in Trinidad & Tobago. (I honestly hadn't counted on being crestfallen on my wife's special day.) Though not a soccer fan herself, she knows how vital soccer and writing are to me, and one of the many reasons I love her is for adeptness in seeing me through all the exultation and frustration that comes with both those passions.

Similarly, the boisterous extended family I married into—the Heimers and the Kanes, starting with my sister-in-law Christy Heimer and my mother-in-law Janet Lingafelter, have been gracious and giving and supportive in everything beyond just my writing, and they have been instrumental in helping me get the book to the finish line. My own family—especially Lisa & Larry West, Emily & Eric West, and Lise Masselotte—have done the same from places I wish were physically closer. (Who wouldn't want to be closer to Seattle and New Orleans, after all?)

I had the great fortune to share the manuscript with two insightful readers who helped it through its evolution to a fully-realized book.

Carlo Longino, my dear, big-hearted, acerbic-tongued friend and fellow barbecue connoisseur, provided the insights I needed at pivotal moments in the book's evolution. As a fellow USMNT fan, he also knew just what to say in helping me (both of us, really) cope with the ups and downs of the Hex. He did all of this while locked in a battle with cancer that many of us desperately wanted him to win; he breathed his last on October 6, 2017 (hours before the US would take the field against Panama), with friends and family singing "You'll Never Walk Alone" to acknowledge his love for Liverpool as well as the truth of his life.

Jeff Rueter, one of my favorite soccer writers anywhere (for his insight, humor, and access to oft-revelatory information) supported me throughout the process. He read first drafts, read rewrites, and gave valuable perspective that helped me shape the final version of the book.

I'm also grateful to Bobby Warshaw, who read the entirety of the manuscript in its almost-finished form, and Jorge Alonso, Caroline Bramon, and Tim Stafford, for reading select chapters during the final days of edits, when I desperately needed eyes that weren't my own on the text.

No book-writing endeavor is complete without a hunker-down retreat weekend, and I'd like to thank Sarah Coker at Vessel Coworking for the space and cold-brew coffee that made that possible.

MLS continues to be my favorite soccer league in the world in large part due to the people who work to make it professional yet refreshingly approachable. The editorial team at MLSsoccer.com, especially Simon Borg, Arielle Castillo, Ben Couch, and Matt Doyle, have made it a welcoming home, and I'm proud of the coverage that my colleagues have produced—many of whom will find themselves quoted here by virtue of doing excellent work that helps tell the story of soccer in the US. This professionalism and camaraderie extends to the teams' front offices; I offer special thanks to Chris Winkler (Atlanta United FC), Diego Garcia (Colorado Rapids), Carlos Mojica (Columbus Crew SC), Sam Legg (DC United), Jason Minnick (FC Dallas), Zac Emmons and Hector Castelltort (Houston Dynamo), Matt Bodiford and Ryan Schwepfinger (Philadephia Union), Matt Gaschk (Real Salt Lake), and the inestimable Rob Thomson (Sporting Kansas City).

Everyone I interviewed for the book was giving of their time and forthcoming with their insights, and I appreciate their willingness to participate in the project of answering the question about when the US men might win the World Cup. I'd be remiss if I didn't thank Thomas Caughlin of US Soccer for his role in ensuring the Development Academy's perspective would be included in the book.

Working with The Overlook Press for this book (and my prior book, *The United States of Soccer*), has literally transformed my life. Thank you to Peter Mayer, who believed in me and asked me the question that launched this book; Shelby Ozer, who was understanding, steady, and eminently helpful in guiding the book to completion; and Dan Crissman, who opened Overlook's door to my agent five years ago and—in what can certainly be described as full circle—found himself editing this book when Overlook called him back.

And, speaking of my agent—thanks to Lauren Abramo of Dystel, Goderich, & Bourret LLC for her initial belief and continued good counsel.

Finally, to all the soccer-loving friends I've made from sea to shining sea, I'm proud to be joined in allegiance with you, as we strive to grow soccer throughout the United States. I welcome our continued conversations in the stands, in front of televisions broadcasting matches, and on social media. In my hometown of Austin, I'd like to recognize the Austin Gooners, the American Outlaws Austin chapter, Josh Babetski and the MLS in Austin Supporters Group, Zach Christodoulides, Kit McConnico, Justin Simmons, Adam Wagner, Chris Bils, Kevin Lyttle, and Lee Nichols. I look forward to future watch parties with you all.

INDEX